Brazilian
Portuguese

phrasebooks
and
Marcia Monje de Castro

Brazilian Portuguese phrasebook
4th edition – January 2008

Published by
Lonely Planet Publications Pty Ltd ABN 36 005 607 983
90 Maribyrnong St, Footscray, Victoria 3011, Australia

Lonely Planet Offices
Australia Locked Bag 1, Footscray, Victoria 3011
USA 150 Linden St, Oakland CA 94607
UK 2nd floor 186 City Road, London, EC1V 2NT UK

Cover illustration
Rio Flavour by Hugh Ford

ISBN 978 1 74059 731 9

text © Lonely Planet Publications Pty Ltd 2008
cover illustration © Lonely Planet Publications Pty Ltd 2008

10 9 8 7 6 5

Printed through Colorcraft Ltd, Hong Kong
Printed in China

acknowledgments

This phrasebook swayed along the production esplanade thanks to the deckchair planning of Jim Jenkin, then publishing manager, and the follow-up work of his successor, Peter D'Onghia. Commissioning editors Karina Coates and Karin Vidstrup Monk did a samba through the initial research, with poise and finesse, deftly recruiting translator Marcia Monje de Castro, who even managed to have a *feijoada* party in the middle of it all. Rachel Williams jumped in to oversee the fourth edition. Editor Ben Handicott explored all things Brazilian, with assistance from fellow editors Piers Kelly, who proofed and wrote a few words here and there, and Francesca Coles, who chipped in with work on the Phrasebuilder chapter as well as proofing. In a swan-song performance, editor Emma Koch lent a hand, humming quite a few bars of the introduction. Managing editor Annelies Mertens kept her finger on the pulse, discovered it was a bossa nova, and kept everything in time.

Layout artist John Shippick looked up from his beach towel and away from the volleyball long enough to make the book look as beautiful as the girl from Ipanema, who was passing by. Nick Stebbing, technically a genius, provided macro assistance and was way too busy to notice. Layout was checked by Adriana Mammarella, Kate McDonald and Sally Darmody. Series designer Yukiyoshi Kamimura, our resident Brazilian, was inspired by his homeland, and created the illustrations which brighten up the pages. He was also an invaluable source of language and cultural information – *obrigado!* The map came via cartographic designer Wayne Murphy and managing cartographer Paul Piaia. Overseeing the whole production was an armada of project managers, starting with Charles Rawlings-Way, who filled in for Huw Fowles for a time, who filled in for Fabrice Rocher for a longer time, before Fabrice returned in time for the final hurrah. *Oba!*

Special thanks go to Yukiyoshi Kamimura for translating the Sustainable Travel section for this new edition.

make the most of this phrasebook ...

Anyone can speak another language! It's all about confidence. Don't worry if you can't remember your school language lessons or if you've never learnt a language before. Even if you learn the very basics (on the inside covers of this book), your travel experience will be the better for it. You have nothing to lose and everything to gain when the locals hear you making an effort.

finding things in this book

For easy navigation, this book is in sections. The Tools chapters are the ones you'll thumb through time and again. The Practical section covers basic travel situations like catching transport and finding a bed. The Social section gives you conversational phrases, pick-up lines, the ability to express opinions – so you can get to know people. Food has a section all of its own: gourmets and vegetarians are covered and local dishes feature. Safe Travel equips you with health and police phrases, just in case. Remember the colours of each section and you'll find everything easily; or use the comprehensive Index. Otherwise, check the two-way traveller's Dictionary for the word you need.

being understood

Throughout this book you'll see coloured phrases on the right-hand side of each page. They're phonetic guides to help you pronounce the language. You don't even need to look at the language itself, but you'll get used to the way we've represented particular sounds. The pronunciation chapter in Tools will explain more, but you can feel confident that if you read the coloured phrase slowly, you'll be understood.

communication tips

Body language, ways of doing things, sense of humour – all have a role to play in every culture. 'Local talk' boxes show you common ways of saying things, or everyday language to drop into conversation. 'Listen for ...' boxes supply the phrases you may hear. They start with the phonetic guide (because you'll hear it before you know what's being said) and then lead in to the language and the English translation.

contents

brazilian portuguese

Caribbean Sea
St Vincent — — Barbados
Grenada —
— Trinidad & Tobago

NORTH
ATLANTIC
OCEAN

Panama

Venezuela

Colombia

Guyana

Suriname

French Guiana (Fr.)

Ecuador

Macapá

Belém

São Luís

Fortaleza

Manaus

Teresina

Rio Grande
do Norte

Peru

BRAZIL

Paraíba

Pernambuco

Rio
Branco

Porto
Velho

Alagoas

Sergipe

Cuiabá

Salvador da
Bahia

Bolivia

Rondônia

Brasília

Goiânia

Belo
Horizonte

Vitória

Chile

Paraguay

Campo
Grande

Rio de Janeiro
São Paulo

SOUTH
PACIFIC
OCEAN

Curitiba

Florianópolis

SOUTH
ATLANTIC
OCEAN

Argentina

Porto Alegre

Uruguay

■ **national language**

For more details see the **introduction**.

Portuguese is spoken by around 190 million people worldwide, 89% of whom live in Brazil. Brazil, the largest country in South America, is the only Portuguese-speaking nation on the continent. Although the country is large, there's very little regional variation, so you'll have no trouble making yourself understood from top to bottom.

The Portuguese arrived in Brazil at the beginning of the 16th century. Speakers from the different regions in Portugal all brought their own dialectal variations. However, as Portuguese colonists came into contact with the Tupi tribes that lived along the Atlantic coast, the Tupi language, along with Portuguese, became the main languages of Brazil. This was mostly due to the Jesuits, who translated prayers and hymns into Tupi and in doing so recorded and promoted the indigenous language. This situation did not last and the use of Tupi was banned in 1759 when the Jesuits were expelled from Brazil and Portuguese was instated as the country's main language.

Portuguese spoken in Brazil was influenced by Tupi and the Bantu and Yoruba languages of African slaves who were brought to Brazil through till the middle of the 19th century. Over a similar period, European Portuguese also underwent linguistic change through

at a glance ...

language name:
Portuguese

name in language:
português porr·too·ges

language family:
Romance

key country: Brazil

approximate number of speakers: 169 million in Brazil, 190 million Portuguese speakers worldwide

close relatives:
Catalan, Galician, French, Italian, Occitan, Romanian, Spanish

donations to English:
cashew, ipecac, macaw, petunia, piranha, toucan

introduction

7

contact with French. Due to this divergence, Brazilian Portuguese today differs from European Portuguese in approximately the same way that British English differs from American English. European and Brazilian Portuguese have different spelling, different pronunciation and to some extent, different vocabulary. For example, in Portugal, the word for 'train' is *comboio* and in Brazil you'd say *trem*.

This book will ensure not only that you have the right words at your disposal, but that you pronounce them as a true *brasileiro* (if you're a man) or *brasileira* (if you're a woman). Need more encouragement? Remember, the contact you make using Brazilian Portuguese will make your travels unique. Local knowledge, new relationships and a sense of satisfaction are on the tip of your tongue, so don't just stand there, say something!

abbreviations used in this book

m	masculine	sg	singular	pol	polite
f	feminine	pl	plural	inf	informal

The pronunciation guide used in this book is based on the pronunciation of Brazilian Portuguese common in urban areas. There are small variations in pronunciation throughout the country, but they cause little difficulty when communicating.

vowel sounds

Vowel sounds are quite similar to those found in English, so you should be able to get talking with confidence. There are some differences of course: the *ay* sound, for example, is much shorter than the English version of it. But with every conversation you have, the sounds will become more familiar and you'll discover ways to make those same sounds yourself.

symbol	english equivalent	brazilian portuguese example
a	run	*camera*
aa	father	*padre*
ai	aisle	*pai*
aw	saw	*nó*
ay	day	*lei*
e	bet	*cedo*
ee	bee	*fino*
o	go	*gato*
oo	moon	*azul*
ow	how	*saudades*
oy	boy	*noite*

A characteristic feature of Brazilian Portuguese is the use of nasal vowels. Nasal vowels are pronounced as if you're trying to force the sound out of your nose rather than your mouth. It's easier than it sounds. English also has nasal vowels to some extent – when you say 'sing' in English, the 'i' is nasalised by the 'ng'. In our pronunciation guide, we've used ng after nasal vowels to indicate that it's nasal. The following is a list of the vowels that you'll normally see with ng in our phonetic guides.

symbol	english equivalent	brazilian portuguese example
ang	-	amanh**ã**
ayng	-	p**ãe**s
eng	-	t**em**
eeng	-	m**ui**to
ong	-	b**om**
oong	-	seg**un**do
owng	-	fog**ão**
oyng	-	naç**ões**

consonant sounds

The consonant sounds in Brazilian Portuguese are very similar to those of English, and even the rolled 'r' (rr), which doesn't exist in standard English varieties, will be familiar to most people (it's similar to the 'r' in Spanish). Two sounds (ly and ny) which might appear a little strange at first do actually occur in English (eg, 'million' and 'canyon'), but never at the beginning of a syllable as they do in Brazilian Portuguese.

symbol	english equivalent	brazilian portuguese example
b	big	*beber*
d	dig	*dar/dedo*
f	fun	*faca*
g	go	*guia*
h	hat	*resto/serra*
k	kick	*cama*
l	loud	*lixo*
ly	million	*muralhas*
m	man	*macaco*
n	no	*nada*
ny	canyon	*linha*
p	pig	*padre*
r	run	*para*
rr	as the 'r' in run, but stronger and rolled	*ir*
s	so	*grosso*
sh	ship	*chave*
t	tin	*tacho*
v	very	*vago*
w	win	*muito*
z	zoo	*exame*
zh	pleasure	*gentes*

word stress

Stress generally occurs on the second-to-last syllable of a word, though there are exceptions. When a word ends in a written -*r* or is pronounced with a nasalised vowel, the stress falls on the last syllable. Another exception: if a written vowel has an accent marked on it, the stress falls on the syllable containing that vowel.

In our transliteration system, we have indicated the stressed syllable with italics.

writing

Brazilian Portuguese is written with the latin alphabet, which is given below. For spelling purposes, pronunciation of letters is also provided:

alphabet			
a	a	n	e·ne
b	be	o	aw
c	se	p	pe
d	de	q	ke
e	e	r	e·he
f	e·fe	s	e·se
g	ge	t	te
h	a·gaa	u	oo
i	ee	v	ve
j	jo·ta	w	daa·bee·oo
k	kaa	x	hees
l	e·le	y	eep·see·lon
m	e·me	z	ze

Some letters have accent marks which denote stress, or variations in the sound usually represented. The accent marks used include those used on vowels: the acute (´), grave (`) and circumflex (^), indicating stress; and the tilde (~), indicating nasalisation. You'll also notice the tail (cedilla) sometimes used at the bottom of the letter 'c' – 'ç' is pronounced as s.

This chapter is arranged alphabetically and is designed to help you make your own sentences. If you can't find the exact phrase you need in this book, remember, a couple of well-chosen words, a little grammar and a gesture or two and you'll generally get the message across.

a/an

The Brazilian Portuguese words *um* and *uma* correspond to the English article 'a/an'. Whether you use the article *um* or *uma* depends upon the gender of the thing, person or concept talked about. If what you're referring to is masculine you use *um*, If it's feminine you use *uma*.

I'd like a pastry and a beer.

Quero um pastel	ke·ro oom paas·tel
e uma cerveja.	e oo·maa serr·ve·zhaa
(lit: I-like a pastry and a beer)	

Also see **gender**.

adjectives see describing things

any see some

articles see a/an and the

be

Brazilian Portuguese has two words which can be translated as 'be' in English: *ser* and *estar*. Learning to use them perfectly will take some time and effort, but the basic difference in their usage is not too difficult to grasp. They're both irregular verbs (just as 'be' is in English) so you need to remember by heart the various forms they take.

The verb *ser* refers to states that have a degree of permanency or durability about them.

I	am	Australian	eu	sou	australiano m
you sg	are	kind	você	é	gentil m&f
he/she	is	an artist	ele/ela	é	artista m&f
you pl	are	crazy	vocês	são	loucos m
we	are	students	nós	somos	estudantes
they	are	crazy	eles/elas	são	loucos/loucas m/f

The verb *estar* generally refers to events which are temporary in nature.

I	am	on holiday	eu	estou	de férias
you sg	are	drunk	você	está	bêbado m
he/she	is	sick	ele/ela	está	doente m&f
you pl	are	lost	vocês	estão	perdidos m
we	are	travelling	nós	estamos	viajando
they	are	busy	eles/elas	estão	ocupados/ocupadas m/f

comparing things

To compare one thing to another, use the words *mais* (more) and *menos* (less) in the following ways:

mais … do que …   mais … do ke …
more … than …

menos … do que …   me·nos … do ke …
less … than …

This shirt is nicer than that one.
   Esta camisa é mais   es·*taa* kaa·*mee*·zaa e mais
   bonita do que esta.   bo·*nee*·taa do ke es·*taa*
   (lit: this shirt is more nice of
     that this)

To refer to something as the most or least (eg, biggest) use
mais (more) and *menor* (less) in the following ways:

o/a … mais … m/f   o/aa … mais …
the … most …

o/a … menor … m/f   o/aa … me·*nor* …
the … least …

I'd like the cheapest room.
   Quero o quarto mais   *ke*·ro o *kwaar*·to mais
   barato.   baa·*raa*·to
   (lit: I-like the room most cheap)

demonstratives see this & that

describing things

Adjectives are generally placed after the noun. They vary in
form depending on the gender and number of the noun that
they describe:

the pretty young woman
   a jovem bonita   aa *zho*·veng bo·*nee*·taa
   (lit: a young-woman beautiful)

the pretty young women
   as jovens bonitas   as *zho*·vengs bo·*nee*·taas
   (lit: the young-girls beautiful)

the handsome young man
   o rapaz bonito   o haa·*paas* bo·*nee*·to
   (lit: a young-man handsome)

the handsome young men
   os rapazess bonitos   os haa·*paa*·zes bo·*nee*·tos
   (lit: the young-men handsome)

Here are the various endings that adjectives take to agree with the nouns that they describe:

	singular	plural
masculine	-o	-os
feminine	-a	-as

feminine see gender

gender

All nouns are either masculine or feminine. They determine the endings used on adjectives that describe them as well as which forms of the Portuguese equivalents of the articles 'a/an' and 'the' are used. The gender that a given noun takes is often arbitrary. For example, there's no reason why the noun *sol* 'sun' is masculine while *praia* 'beach' is feminine. The dictionary will tell you what gender a noun is, but here are some guidelines for taking a guess at the gender of a noun (there are exceptions though):

often masculine	often feminine
nouns referring to male persons (or male animals)	nouns referring to female persons (or female animals)
nouns ending in -o	nouns ending in -a
nouns ending in -ema, -oma and -ama	nouns ending with -dade

Also see **a/an, the** and **describing things**.

have

Possession can be indicated using the verb *ter* 'to have' which is an irregular verb.

I have a flight at 6pm.

Tenho um vôo às seis   *te·nyo oom vo·o aas says*
da noite.   *da noy·te*
(lit: I-have a flight at-the six
    of-the night)

I	have	a ticket	eu	tenho	uma pasagem
you sg	have	the bill	você	tem	a conta
he/she	has	water	ele/ela	tem	água
we	have	the key	nós	temos	a chave
you pl	have	a letter	vocês	têm	uma carta
they	have	the menu	eles/elas	têm	o cardápio

masculine see gender

more than one

You can make a noun plural by adding *-s*:

book	*livro* m	books	*livros* m pl
bed	*cama* f	beds	*camas* f pl

If the noun ends in *-s*, *-z* or *-r*, and the final syllable is stressed, then the plural is formed by adding *-es*:

singular	plural	singular	plural
portuguese	*português*	portuguese	*portuguêses*
youth	*rapaz* m	youths	*rapazes* m pl
flower	*flor* f	flowers	*flores* f pl

Remember when using plural nouns to change the articles and adjectives used with these nouns to their corresponding plural forms too.

There are some exceptions and additional rules for making nouns plural – they can't all be covered here, so consult a grammar of Portuguese if you'd like to know more.

Also see **a/an**, **describing things**, **some**, and **the**.

my & your

Like English, Brazilian Portuguese uses pronouns to indicate possession. In the table below are the equivalents for the English possessive pronouns. To express possession you place them before the noun they describe and make them agree in number (plural or singular) and gender (masculine or feminine) with the noun.

	singular		plural	
	masculine	feminine	masculine	feminine
	map	letter	maps	letters
my	meu mapa	minha carta	meus mapas	minhas cartas
your sg&pl	seu mapa	sua carta	seus mapas	suas cartas
his/her/its	seu mapa	sua carta	seus mapas	suas cartas
our	nosso mapa	nossa carta	nossos mapas	nossas cartas
their	seu mapa	sua carta	seus mapas	suas cartas

Here's how you'd use possessive pronouns to say that something is yours.

It's my ticket.
  É a minha pasagem.   e a *mee*·nya pa·*saa*·zheng
  (lit: it-is the my ticket)

TOOLS

A simple statement of possession (eg, 'It's mine') is formed by using *É* ('it-is') with the possessive pronoun (to agree with the thing possessed).

It's mine.
  É meu.   e *me*·oo
  (lit: it-is mine)

negative

To make a sentence negative, just add the word *não* (no), before the main verb:

I don't want to walk any more.
  Não quero andar mais.   nowng *ke*·ro ang·*daar* mais
  (lit: no I-want to-walk more)

The double negative isn't only acceptable, but correct:

I can't see anything.
  Não vejo nada.   nowng *ve*·zho *naa*·daa
  (lit: no I-see nothing)

negative words		
never	*nunca*	*noong*·kaa
no/not	*não*	nowng
nobody	*ninguém*	neeng·*geng*
none sg	*nenhum/ nenhuma* m/f	neng·ee·*oom/* neng·ee·oo·maa
nor	*nem*	neng

nouns see gender

number see more than one

planning ahead

The future is usually expressed by using the present tense of the verb *ir*, (go), plus another verb. It's equivalent to 'going to ...' in English:

I'm going to come back next week.
> *Vou voltar na semana*   vo vol·*taarr* na se·*ma*·naa
> *que vem.*   ke veng
> (lit: I-go to-come-back
> in-the week which comes)

I	vou	we	vamos
you sg	vai	you pl	vão
he/she/it	vai	they	vão

Just like in English, you'd also be understood when expressing your plans, if you use the present tense with some indication of time referring to the future:

I'm going to Rio tomorrow.
> *Vou para o Rio*   vo *paa*·ra o *hee*·o
> *amanhã.*   aa·*ma*·nyang
> (lit: I-go to the Rio tomorrow)

plural see **more than one**

pointing something out

The easiest way to point something out in Portuguese is to start your phrase with *É* ... (lit: It-is ...).

That's a beautiful building.
> *É um edifício bonito.*   e oom e·dee·*fee*·syo bo·*nee*·to
> (lit: it-is a building beautiful)

Also see **this & that**.

possession see **have**, **my & your** and **somebody's**

There are a number of ways to indicate possession in Brazilian Portuguese. The easiest way is by using the verb *ter* (see **have**). You could also use possessive pronouns (see **my & your**) or, simplest of all, use the preposition *de* (of) followed by the possessor (see **somebody's**).

To find out who's the owner of something, you can use the simple phrases *De quem é isto …?* (of whom it-is this …?) for a single thing, or *De quem são estes/estas …?* m/f (of whom are-they these …?) for plural things:

Whose seat is this?

De quem é este assento?   de keng e *es·*te aa-*seng·*to
(lit: of whom it-is this seat)

pronouns

Subject pronouns corresponding to 'I', 'you', 'he', 'she', 'it', 'we' and 'they' are often omitted, as verb endings make it clear who the subject is. Use them if you want to emphasise the subject.

singular			plural		
I	*eu*	e·oo	**we**	*nós*	nos
you	*você*	vo·se	**you**	*vocês*	vo·ses
he /it m	*ele*	e·le	**they** m or m&f	*eles*	e·les
she/it f	*ela*	e·laa	**they** f	*elas*	e·laas

Note that unlike in other romance languages (and even the Portuguese spoken in Portugal), Brazilian Portuguese does not commonly distinguish between formal and informal forms of 'you'.

question words

who	*quem*	keng
Who are you?	*Quem é você?*	keng e *vo*·se
what	*(o) que*	(o) ke
What's wrong?	*O que é que há?*	o ke e ke a
which/what	*qual/quais* **sg/pl**	kwow/kais
What's the best restaurant in the city?	*Qual é o melhor restaurante da cidade?*	kwow e o me·*lyorr* hes·tow·*rang*·te daa see·*daa*·de
where	*onde*	*ong*·de
Where is the Australian Embassy?	*Onde fica a embaixada Australiana?*	*ong*·de fee·kaa aa eng·bai·*shaa*·daa ows·traa·lee·*a*·na
when	*quando*	*kwang*·do
When is the flight?	*Quando sai o vôo?*	*kwang*·do sai o *vo*·o
how/by what means	*como é que*	*ko*·mo e ke
How do I find the bus station?	*Como é que vou para a rodoviária?*	*ko*·mo e ke vow *paa*·raa aa ho·do·vee·*aa*·ryaa
how much/ how many?	*quanto/a* **m/f** *quantos/quantas* **m/f pl**	*kwang*·to/*kwang*·taa *kwang*·tos/ *kwang*·taas
How much is it?	*Quanto custa?*	*kwang*·to koos·taa
why	*por que*	porr ke
Why are we stopping here?	*Por que estamos parando aqui?*	porr ke es·*ta*·mos paa·*raang*·do aa·*kee*

some

The plural forms of the words for 'a/an' (*um* and *uma*) are used to express the English 'some'. If what you're referring to is masculine plural, use *uns*, and if it's feminine plural, use *umas*.

I'd like some headache pills.
> *Quero uns comprimidos*   ke·ro oongs kong·pree·*mee*·dos
> *para dor de cabeça.*   paa·raa dorr de kaa·*be*·saa
> (lit: I-like some pills for
> pain of head)

I've had a few to drink.
> *Tomei umas e outras.*   to·*may* oo·maas e *o*·traas
> (lit: I-drank some and
> others)

Also see **a/an** and **gender**.

somebody's

The simplest way of indicating possession is by using the preposition *de* (from), followed by the person who's the owner of the thing. You can only do this with proper nouns (for people or places).

It's Carla's backpack.
> *É a mochila de Carla.*   e aa mo·*shee*·laa de *karr*·laa
> (lit: it-is the backpack
> of Carla)

See also **possession**.

the

There are four words that correspond to the English article 'the'. The form you use is determined by the gender and number of the noun the article is used with:

masculine	o sg	o trem o treng	the train
	os pl	os trens os trengs	the trains
feminine	a sg	a mochila a mo·shee·la	the backpack
	as pl	as mochilas a mo·shee·la	the backpacks

Also see **gender** and **more than one**.

this & that

To refer to or point at a person or object, use one of the following forms (known as demonstratives) before the noun, depending on whether the person or object you're referring to is close or further away, masculine or feminine, and singular or plural:

	singular		plural	
	masculine	**feminine**	**masculine**	**feminine**
close	*este*	*esta*	*estes*	*estas*
away	*aquele*	*aquela*	*aqueles*	*aquelas*

Is this seat free?

Este lugar está vago?   es·te loo·*gaarr* es·*taa vaa*·go
(lit: this seat it-is free)

This view is wonderful.
Esta vista é   es·taa *vees*·taa e
maravilhosa.   maa·raa·vee·*lyo*·zaa
(lit: this view it-is wonderful)

These forms can also be used on their own without an accompanying noun – meaning 'this (one)', 'that (one)', 'these' and 'those'.

Does this market open every day?
Este mercado abre todos   es·te merr·*kaa*·do *aa*·bre *to*·dos
os dias?   os *dee*·aas
(lit: this market open all
the days)

Those are Brazilian.
Aqueles são brasileiros.   a·*ke*·les sowng braa·zee·*lay*·ros
(lit: those they-are
Brazilians)

Also see **pointing something out**.

verbs

Brazilian Portuguese has three types of verbs: those ending in -*ar* (eg, *morar*, 'to live'), those ending in -*er* (eg, *comer*, 'to eat') and those ending in -*ir* (eg, *partir*, 'to leave'). Despite this, the present tense verb endings for each person ('I', 'you', 'we' etc) are very similar for all three so you can recognise them easily:

	-ar	-er	-ir
I	*-o*		
you/he/she/it	*-a*	*-e*	
we	*-amos*	*-emos*	*-imos*
you/they	*-am*	*-em*	

As in any language, some verbs are irregular in Brazilian Portuguese. The most important ones are *ser*, *estar* and *ter* (see **be** and **have**).

word order

Generally, the word order of a sentence is the same as in English (subject-verb-object).

I'd like a room.

Eu quero um quarto.　　　　　*e·oo ke·ro oom kwaarr·to*
(lit: I I-like a room)

yes/no questions

When asking a question, simply make a statement, but raise your intonation inquisitively towards the end of the sentence, as you would in English.

Do you speak English?

Você fala inglês?　　　　　*vo·se faa·laa eeng·gles*
(lit: you speak-you English)

If what you're doing is really making a statement but you're requesting confirmation or agreement, you can put the tag *não é* (lit: not it-is) on the end.

John lives in Rio, doesn't he?

João mora no Rio,　　　　　*zho·owng mo·raa no hee·o*
não é?　　　　　　　　　　*nowng e*
(lit: John lives-he in Rio
not it-is)

In rapid everyday speech the tag *não é* sounds more like ne.

language difficulties
dificuldades com a lingua

Do you speak (English)?
Você fala (inglês)?
vo·*se faa*·laa (eeng·*gles*)

Does anyone speak (English)?
Alguém aqui fala (inglês)?
ow·*geng* aa·*kee faa*·laa (eeng·*gles*)

Do you understand?
Você entende?
vo·*se* eng·*teng*·de

Yes, I understand.
Sim, entendo.
seeng eng·*teng*·do

No, I don't understand.
Não, não entendo.
nowng nowng eng·*teng*·do

I speak (English).
Eu falo (inglês).
e·oo *faa*·lo (eeng·*gles*)

I don't speak (Portuguese).
Eu não falo (português).
e·oo *faa*·lo (porr·too·*ges*)

I speak a little.
Eu falo um pouquinho.
e·oo *faa*·lo oom po·*kee*·nyo

I (don't) understand.
Eu (não) entendo.
e·oo (nowng) eng·*teng*·do

What does 'bem-vindo' mean?
O que quer dizer 'bem-vindo'?
o ke kerr dee·*zerr* beng *veeng*·do

How do you ...?	*Como se ...?*	*ko*·mo se ...
pronounce this	*pronuncia isto*	pro·noong·*see*·aa *ees*·to
write 'ajuda'	*escreve 'ajuda'*	es·*kre*·ve aa·*zhoo*·daa

Could you please …?	Você poderia … por favor?	vo·se po·de·ree·aa … porr faa·vorr
repeat that	repetir isto	he·pe·teerr ees·to
speak more slowly	falar mais devagar	faa·laarr mais de·vaa·gaarr
write it down	escrever num papel	es·kre·verr noom paa·pel

false friends

Beware of false friends – words which can look and sound like English words but have a different meaning altogether.

atualmente ak·twow·meng·te nowadays
  not 'actually' which is *na verdade*, na verr·da·de

longe long·zhe far away
  not 'long' which is *comprido* m, kong·pree·do or *comprida* f, kong·pree·daa

magazine ma·ga·zeen department store
  not 'magazine' which is *revista*, he·vees·ta

novela no·ve·la soap opera
  not 'novel' which is *romance*, ho·mang·se

pretender pre·teng·de intend
  not 'pretend' which is *fingir*, feeng·geer

puxar poo·shaarr pull
  not 'push' which is *empurrar*, eng·poo·raarr

sorte sorr·te luck
  not 'sort' which is *typo*, tee·po

cardinal numbers

0	zero	ze·ro		6	seis	says
1	um	oom		7	sete	se·te
2	dois	doys		8	oito	oy·to
3	três	tres		9	nove	naw·ve
4	quatro	kwaa·tro		10	dez	dez
5	cinco	seeng·ko				

11	onze	ong·ze
12	doze	do·ze
13	treze	tre·ze
14	quatorze	kaa·torr·ze
15	quinze	keeng·ze
16	dezesseis	de·ze·says
17	dezesete	de·ze·se·te
18	dezoito	de·zoy·to
19	dezenove	de·ze·naw·ve
20	vinte	veeng·te
21	vinte e um	veeng·te e oom
22	vinte e dois	veeng·te e doys
30	trinta	treeng·taa
40	quarenta	kwaa·reng·taa
50	cinquenta	seen·kweng·taa
60	sessenta	se·seng·taa
70	setenta	se·teng·taa
80	oitenta	oy·teng·taa
90	noventa	no·veng·taa
100	cem	seng
200	duzentos	doo·zeng·tos
1,000	mil	mee·oo
1,000,000	um milhão	oom mee·lyowng

ordinal numbers

1st	*primeiro/primeira* m/f	pree·*may*·ro/pree·*may*·raa
2nd	*segundo/segunda* m/f	se·*goong*·do/se·*goong*·daa
3rd	*terceiro/terceira* m/f	terr·*say*·ro/terr·*say*·raa
4th	*quarto/quarta* m/f	kwaarr·to/kwaarr·taa
5th	*quinto/quinta* m/f	keeng·to/keeng·taa

fractions

frações

a quarter	*um quarto*	oom *kwaarr*·to
a third	*um terço*	oom *terr*·so
a half	*metade*	me·*taa*·de
three-quarters	*três quartos*	tres *kwaarr*·tos
all (of it)	*inteiro/inteira* m/f	eeng·*tay*·ro/eeng·*tay*·raa
all (of them)	*tudo/tuda* m/f	*too*·do/*too*·daa
none	*nenhum*	ne·*yoom*

useful amounts

quantias & quantidades úteis

How much?	*Quanto?*	*kwang*·to
How many?	*Quantos/Quantas?* m/f	*kwang*·tos/*kwan*·taas
Please give	*Por favor*	porr faa·*vorr*
me ...	*me dê ...*	me de ...
a few	*alguns*	ow·*goons*
(just) a little	*(só) um*	(saw) oom
	pouquinho	po·*kee*·nyo
a lot	*muito*	*mweeng*·to
less	*menos*	me·nos
many	*muitos/*	*mweeng*·tos/
	muitas m/f	*mweeng*·taas
more	*mais*	mais
some	*um pouco*	oom *po*·ko

telling the time

The 24-hour clock is usually used when telling the time in Brazilian Portuguese. Alternatively, you can add *da manhã* (in the morning), *da tarde* (in the afternoon), or *da noite* (in the evening) to specify the exact time.

Time is given using a plural form of the verb 'be', *ser* (*são*), except in the case of 1 o'clock, when the singular form (*é*) is used.

What time is it?	*Que horas são?*	ke *aw·*raas sowng
It's (one) o'clock.	*É (um) hora.*	e (oom) *aw·*raa
It's (ten) o'clock.	*São (dez) horas.*	sowng (des) *aw·*raas
Five past (ten).	*(Dez) e cinco.*	(des) e *seeng·*ko
Quarter past (ten).	*(Dez) e quinze.*	(des) e *keeng·*ze
Half past (ten).	*(Dez) e meia.*	(des) e *may·*aa

After the half hour, state the number of minutes to the next hour until that hour arrives.

Quarter to (ten).	*Quinze para as (dez).*	*keeng·*ze *paa·*raa aas (des)
Twenty to (ten).	*Vinte para as (dez).*	*veeng·*te *paa·*raa aas (des)
in the morning	*da manhã*	daa ma·*nyang*
in the afternoon	*da tarde*	daa *taarr·*de
in the evening	*da noite*	daa *noy·*te
At what time …?	*A que horas …?*	aa ke *aw·*raas …
At (ten).	*Às (dez).*	aas (des)
At (7.57pm).	*Às (sete e cinquenta e sete da noite).*	aas (*se·*te e seeng·*kweng·*taa e *se·*te daa *noy·*te)

days of the week

Monday	segunda-feira	se·goong·daa·fay·raa
Tuesday	terça-feira	terr·saa·fay·raa
Wednesday	quarta-feira	kwaarr·taa·fay·raa
Thursday	quinta-feira	keeng·taa·fay·raa
Friday	sexta-feira	ses·taa·fay·raa
Saturday	sábado	saa·baa·doo
Sunday	domingo	do·meeng·go

the calendar

o calendário

months

January	janeiro	zha·nay·ro
February	fevereiro	fe·ve·ray·ro
March	março	marr·so
April	abril	aa·bree·oo
May	maio	maa·yo
June	junho	zhoo·nyo
July	julho	zhoo·lyo
August	agosto	aa·gos·to
September	setembro	se·teng·bro
October	outubro	o·too·bro
November	novembro	no·veng·bro
December	dezembro	de·zeng·bro

dates

What date is it today?

Qual é a data de hoje?   kwow e aa daa·taa de o·zhe

It's (18 October).

Hoje é dia (dezoito de   o·zhe e dee·aa (de·zoy·to de
outubro).   o·too·bro)

seasons

summer	*verão* m	ve·*rowng*
autumn	*outono* m	o·*to*·no
winter	*inverno* m	een·*verr*·no
spring	*primavera* f	pree·maa·*ve*·raa
... season	*época* f de ...	e·po·kaa de ...
dry	*seca*	*se*·kaa
monsoon	*monção*	mong·*sowng*
wet	*chuvas*	*shoo*·vaas

present

presente

now	*agora*	aa·*go*·raa
this ...		
afternoon	*esta tarde*	es·taa *taarr*·de
morning	*esta manhã*	es·taa ma·*nyang*
month	*este mês*	es·te mes
week	*esta semana*	es·taa se·*ma*·naa
year	*este ano*	es·te *a*·no
today	*hoje*	o·zhe
tonight	*hoje à noite*	o·zhe aa *noy*·te

past

passado

(three days) ago	*(três dias) atrás*	(tres *dee*·aas) aa·*traas*
day before	*antes de*	*ang*·tes de
yesterday	*ontem*	*ong*·teng
yesterday	*ontem*	*ong*·teng
last ...		
month	*mês passado*	mes paa·*saa*·do
night	*noite passada*	*noy*·te paa·*saa*·daa
week	*semana*	se·*ma*·naa
	passada	paa·*saa*·daa
year	*ano passado*	*a*·no paa·*saa*·do

since (May)	desde (Maio)	des·de (maa·yo)
yesterday ...	ontem ...	ong·teng ...
afternoon	à tarde	aa taarr·de
evening	à noite	aa noy·te
morning	de manhã	de ma·nyang

future

futuro

day after tomorrow	depois de amanhã	de·poys de aa·ma·nyang
in (six days)	daqui a (seis dias)	daa·kee aa (says dee·aas)
tomorrow	amanhã	aa·ma·nyang
next ...	... que vem	... ke veng
month	mês	mes
week	semana	se·ma·naa
year	ano	a·no
tomorrow ...	amanhã ...	aa·ma·nyang ...
afternoon	à tarde	aa taarr·de
evening	à noite	aa noy·te
morning	de manhã	de ma·nyang
until (June)	até (junho)	aa·te (zhoo·nyo)

during the day

durante o dia

afternoon	tarde f	taar·de
day	dia m	dee·aa
evening	noite f	noy·te
midday	meio dia m	may·oo dee·a
midnight	meia noite f	may·aa noy·te
morning	manhã f	ma·nyang
night	noite f	noy·te
sunrise	nascer m do sol	naa·serr do sol
sunset	pôr m do sol	porr do sol

How much is it?
Quanto custa?   kwang·to koos·taa

Can you write down the price?
Você pode escrever o preço?   vo·se po·de es·kre·verr o pre·so

That's too expensive.
Está muito caro.   es·taa mweeng·to kaa·ro

I don't want to pay the full price.
Não quero pagar o   nowng ke·ro paa·gaarr o
preço todo.   pre·so to·do

Do you accept ...?	Vocês aceitam ...?	vo·ses aa·say·tang ...
credit cards	cartão de	kaarr·towng de
	crédito	kre·dee·to
debit cards	saque	sa·kee
	eletrônico	e·le·tro·nee·ko
travellers	traveller	tra·ve·ler
cheques	cheque	she·kee

I'd like to ...	Gostaria de ...	gos·taa·ree·aa de ...
cash a cheque	descontar um	des·kon·taarr oom
	cheque	she·kee
change a	trocar	tro·kaarr
travellers	traveller	traa·ve·ler
cheque	cheques	she·kes
change money	trocar	tro·kaar
	dinheiro	dee·nyay·ro
get a cash	fazer um saque	fa·zerr oom saa·ke
advance	adiantado	aa·dee·an·taa·do
withdraw	retirar	he·tee·raarr
money	dinheiro	dee·nyay·ro

Can I use my credit card to withdraw money?
Posso usar o meu *po·so oo·zaarr o me·oo*
cartão de crédito para *kaar·towng de kre·dee·to paa·raa*
retirar dinheiro? *he·tee·raarr dee·nyay·ro*

Where's …?	*Onde tem …?*	*ong·de teng …*
an automatic teller machine	*um caixa automático*	*oom kai·shaa ow·to·maa·tee·ko*
a foreign exchange office	*uma loja de câmbio*	*oo·maa lo·zhaa de kam·bee·o*

What's the …?	*Qual …?*	*kwow …*
exchange rate	*o câmbio do dia*	*o kang·byo do dee·aa*
charge for that	*a taxa cobrada*	*aa taa·shaa ko·braa·daa*

I'd like …, please.	*Gostaria de …*	*gos·taa·ree·aa …*
a refund	*ser reembolsado*	*serr he·eng·bol·saa·do*
my change	*ter o meu troco*	*terr o me·oo tro·ko*
to return this	*devolver isto*	*de·vol·verr ees·to*

Could I have a …, please?	*Pode me dar …, por favor?*	*po·de me daarr … porr faa·vorr*
bag	*um saco*	*oom saa·ko*
receipt	*o recibo*	*o he·see·bo*

getting around

andando por aí

Which ... goes to (Niterói)?	*Qual o ... que vai para (Niterói)?*	kwow o ... ke vai paa·raa (nee·te·*roy*)
boat	*barco*	*baarr*·ko
bus	*ônibus*	o·nee·boos
plane	*avião*	aa·vee·*owng*
train	*trem*	treng
When's the ... (bus)?	*Quando sai o ... (ônibus)?*	kwang·do sai o ... (o·nee·boos)
first	*primeiro*	pree·*may*·ro
last	*último*	ool·tee·mo
next	*próximo*	pro·see·mo

What time does it leave?
A que horas sai? — aa ke *aw*·raas sai

What time does it get to (Paraty)?
À que horas chega em (Paraty)? — àa ke *aw*·raas *she*·gaa eng (paa·*raa*·tee)

How long will it be delayed?
Quanto tempo vai atrasar? — kwang·to teng·po vai aa·*traa*·zaarr

Is this seat free?
Este lugar está vago? — es·te loo·*gaarr* es·*taa* vaa·go

That's my seat.
Este é o meu lugar. — es·te e o *me*·oo loo·*gaarr*

Please tell me when we get to (Búzios).
Por favor me avise quando chegarmos à (Búzios). — porr faa·*vor* me aa·*vee*·ze kwang·do she·*gaarr*·mos aa (*boo*·zee·os)

Please stop here.
Por favor pare aqui. por faa-*vorr* paa-re aa-*kee*

How long do we stop here?
Quanto tempo ficaremos *kwang*-to *teng*-po fee-ka-*re*-mos
parados aqui? paa-*raa*-dos aa-*kee*

tickets

passagem

Where do I buy a ticket?
Onde que eu compro a *ong*-de ke e-oo *kong*-pro aa
passagem? paa-*sa*-zheng

Do I need to book?
Preciso reservar? pre-*see*-zo he-zer-*vaarr*

A ... ticket (to Petrópolis).	*Uma passagem de ... (para Petrópolis).*	oo-maa paa-*sa*-zheng de ... (*paa*-raa pe-*tro*-po-lees)
1st-class	*primeira classe*	pree-*may*-raa *klaa*-se
2nd-class	*segunda classe*	se-*goom*-daa *klaa*-se
child's	*criança*	kree-*ang*-sa
one-way	*ida*	ee-daa
return	*ida e volta*	ee-daa e *vol*-taa
student's	*estudante*	es-too-*dang*-te

I'd like a/an ... seat.	*Gostaria de um lugar ...*	gos-taa-*ree*-aa de oom loo-*gaarr* ...
aisle	*no corredor*	no ko-he-*dorr*
(non-)smoking	*na área de (não) fumantes*	na *aa*-re-aa de (nowng) foo-*mang*-tes
window	*na janela*	naa zhaa-*ne*-laa

Is there (a) ...?	*Tem ...?*	teng ...
air- conditioning	*ar condicionado*	aarr kong-dee-syo-*naa*-do
blanket	*cobertor*	ko-berr-*torr*
toilet	*banheiro*	ba-*nyay*-ro

I'd like to ... my ticket, please.	Gostaria de ... minha passagem, por favor.	gos·taa·*ree*·aa de ... mee·nya paa·*saa*·zheng porr faa·*vor*
cancel	cancelar	kang·se·*laarr*
change	trocar	tro·*kaarr*
confirm	confirmar	kong·feerr·*maarr*

How long does the trip take?
Quanto tempo de viagem?
kwang·to teng·po de vee·*aa*·zheng

Is it a direct route?
É uma rota direta?
e oo·maa ho·taa dee·*re*·taa

listen for ...

aa·traa·*zaa*·do	atrasado	delayed
aa·*zheng*·te de vee·*aa*·zhengs	agente de viagens	travel agent
bee·lye·te·*ree*·aa	bilheteria	ticket window
es·te/aa·*ke*·le	este/aquele	this/that one
kang·se·*laa*·do	cancelado	cancelled
o·*raa*·ryo	horário	timetable
plaa·taa·*forr*·maa	plataforma	platform
shay·o	cheio	full

luggage

bagagem

Where can I find ...?	Onde posso encontrar ...?	ong·de po·so eng·kon·*traarr* ...
a luggage locker	um guarda volumes	oom *gwaarr*·daa vo·*loo*·mes
a trolley	um carrinho	oom kaa·*hee*·nyo
the baggage counter	o balcão de bagagem	o baal·*kowng* de baa·*gaa*·zheng
the left-luggage office	o balcão de guarda volumes	o baal·*kowng* de *gwaarr*·daa vo·*loo*·mes

My luggage	Minha	mee·nya
has been ...	bagagem foi ...	baa·gaa·zheng foy ...
damaged	danificada	da·nee·fee·kaa·daa
lost	perdida	perr·dee·daa
stolen	roubada	ho·baa·daa

That's (not) mine.
Isto (não) é meu.
ees·to (nowng) e me·oo

Can I have some coins/tokens?
*Pode me dar umas
moedas/fichas?*
po·de me daarr oo·maas
mo·e·daas/fee·shaas

plane

avião

Where does flight (RG 615) arrive/depart?
*De onde sai/chega o vôo
(RG 615)?*
de ong·de sai/she·gaa o vo·o
(e·he ge say·sen·tos e keen·ze)

Where's ...?	Onde fica ...?	ong·de fee·kaa ...
arrivals	portão de chegada	porr·towng de she·gaa·daa
departures	portão de partida	porr·towng de paarr·tee·daa
gate (20)	portão (vinte)	porr·towng (veeng·te)
the airport shuttle	o ônibus do aeroporto	o o·nee·boos do aa·e·ro·porr·to

For phrases about getting through customs, see **border crossing**, page 49.

PRACTICAL

boat

barco

What's the sea like today?
Como está o mar hoje?   ko·mo es·*taa* o maarr o·zhe

Are there life jackets?
Tem colete salva-vidas?   teng ko·*le*·te sow·vaa·*vee*·daas

What island/beach is this?
Que ilha/praia é esta?   ke ee·*lyaa*/*prai*·aa e es·taa

I feel seasick.
Estou enjoado/   es·to eng·zho·*aa*·do/
enjoada. m/f   eng·zho·*aa*·daa

cabin	*cabine* f	kaa·*bee*·ne
car deck	*deck* m *de carro*	de·kee de *kaa*·ho
captain	*capitão* m	kaa·pee·*towng*
deck	*deck* m	de·kee
ferry	*barca* f	*baarr*·kaa
hammock	*rede* f	he·de
lifeboat	*barco* m	*baarr*·ko
	salva-vidas	sow·vaa·*vee*·daas
life jacket	*colete* m	ko·*le*·te
	salva-vidas	sow·vaa·*vee*·daas
yacht	*iate* m	ee·*aa*·te

listen for ...

baa·*gaa*·zheng aa·kong·pa·*nyaa*·daa	*bagagem acompanhada*	carry-on baggage
borr·zheeng pas	*boarding pass*	boarding pass
e·se·so de baa·*gaa*·zheng	*excesso de bagagem*	excess baggage
fee·shaa	*ficha*	token
paa·saa·*porr*·te	*passaporte*	passport
trang·zee·to	*trânsito*	transit

bus & coach

How often do buses come?
*Qual a frequência dos
ônibus?*
kwow aa fre·*kweng*·see·aa dos
o·nee·boos

Is this the bus to (Campinas)?
*Este ônibus vai para
(Campinas)?*
es·te o·nee·boos vai *paa*·raa
(kang·*pee*·naas)

Does it stop at (Ilheús)?
Ele para em (Ilheús)?
e·le *paa*·raa eng (ee·*lye*·oos)

What's the next stop?
*Qual é a próxima
parada?*
kwow e aa *pro*·see·maa
paa·*raa*·daa

I'd like to get off at (Ipanema).
*Gostaria de saltar
em (Ipanema).*
gos·taa·*ree*·aa de sow·*taarr*
eng (ee·paa·*ne*·maa)

city/local bus	*ônibus* m *local*	o·nee·boos lo·*kow*
intercity bus	*ônibus* m *inter urbano*	o·nee·boos eeng·terr oorr·*ba*·no

train

What station is this?
   Que estação é esta?   ke es·taa·*sowng* e *es*·taa

What's the next station?
   Qual é a próxima   kwow e aa *pro*·see·maa
   estação?   es·taa·*sowng*

Does it stop at (Ouro Preto)?
   Ele pára em (Ouro Preto)?   e·le *paa*·raa eng (o·ro *pre*·to)

Do I need to change?
   Preciso trocar de trem?   pre·*see*·so tro·*kaarr* de treng

Is it direct/express?
   É direto/rápido?   e dee·*re*·to/*haa*·pee·do

Which carriage is …?	*Qual o vagão …?*	kwow o vaa·*gowng* …
1st class	*de primeira classe*	de pree·*may*·raa *klaa*·se
for (Sabará)	*para (Sabará)*	*paa*·raa (saa·baa·*raa*)

taxi

I'd like a taxi …	*Gostaria de marcar um táxi …*	gos·taa·*ree*·aa de maarr·*kaarr* oom *taak*·see …
at (9am)	*para as (nove da manhã)*	*paa*·raa aas (*naw*·ve daa ma·*nyang*)
now	*agora*	aa·*go*·raa
tomorrow	*amanhã*	aa·ma·*nyang*

Where's the taxi rank?
   Onde fica a fila de   ong·de *fee*·kaa aa *fee*·laa de
   táxi?   *taak*·see

Is this taxi free?
   Este táxi está livre?   *es*·te *taak*·see es·*taa* *lee*·vre

Please put the meter on.
Por favor ligue o taxímetro.
porr fa·*vorr lee*·ge o taak·*see*·me·tro

How much is it to …?
Quanto custa até …?
kwang·to *koos*·taa aa·*te* …

Please take me to (this address).
Me leve para este endereço por favor.
me *le*·ve *paa*·raa *es*·te eng·de·*re*·so porr faa·*vorr*

Please …	Por favor …	porr faa·*vorr* …
slow down	*vai mais devagar*	vai *mais* de·vaa·*gaarr*
stop here	*pare aqui*	*paa*·re aa·*kee*
wait here	*espere aqui*	es·*pe*·re aa·*kee*

car & motorbike

hire

I'd like to hire a/an …	Gostaria de alugar …	gos·taa·*ree*·aa de aa·loo·*gaarr* …
4WD	*um carro quatro por quatro*	oom *kaa*·ho *kwaa*·tro porr *kwaa*·tro
automatic	*um automático*	oom ow·to·*maa*·tee·ko
car	*um carro*	oom *kaa*·ho
manual	*um manual*	oom ma·noo·*ow*
motorbike	*uma motocicleta*	*oo*·ma mo·to·see·*kle*·taa

with …	com …	kong …
a driver	*motorista*	mo·to·*rees*·taa
air-conditioning	*ar condicionado*	aarr kong·dee·syo·*naa*·do

PRACTICAL

How much for daily/weekly hire?
Quanto custa para alugar por dia/ semana?
kwang·to koos·taa paa·raa aa·loo·*gaarr* porr dee·aa/ se·*ma*·naa

Does that include insurance/mileage?
Inclui seguro e kilometragem?
eeng·*kloo*·ee se·*goo*·ro e kee·lo·me·*traa*·zheng

Do you have a guide to the road rules in English?
Você teria um guia de ruas em inglês?
vo·*se* te·*ree*·aa oom gee·aa de *hoo*·aas eng eeng·*gles*

Do you have a road map?
Você teria um mapa de ruas?
vo·*se* te·*ree*·aa oom *maa*·paa de *hoo*·aas

on the road

Is this the road to (Salvador)?
Esta é a estrada para (Salvador)?
es·*taa* e aa es·*traa*·daa paa·raa (sow·*vaa*·dorr)

Where's a petrol station?
Onde tem um posto de gasolina?
ong·de teng oom *pos*·to de gaa·zo·*lee*·naa

Please fill it up.
Enche o tanque, por favor.
eng·she o *tang*·ke porr faa·*vorr*

I'd like (30) litres.
Coloque (trinta) litros.
ko·*lo*·ke (*treen*·ta) *lee*·tros

diesel	*diesel* m	*dee*·sel
LPG	*gás* m	gas
unleaded	*gasolina* f *comum*	gaa·zo·*lee*·naa ko·*moong*

Can you check the …?	Pode checar …?	po·de she·kaarr …
oil	o óleo	o o·lyo
tyre pressure	os pneus	os pee·ne·oos
water	a água	aa aa·gwaa

What's the speed limit?

Qual o limite de velocidade?	kwow o lee·mee·te de ve·lo·see·daa·de

(How long) Can I park here?

(Quanto tempo) Posso estacionar aqui?	(kwang·to teng·po) po·so es·taa·syo·naarr aa·kee

Do I have to pay?

Tem que pagar?	teng ke paa·gaarr

signs

Entrada	eng·traa·daa	Entrance
Estrada dê Preferência	es·traa·daa de pre·fe·reng·syaa	Give Way
Mão Única	mowng oo·nee·kaa	One-way
Pare	paa·re	Stop
Pedágio	pe·daa·zhyo	Toll
Proibido Entrar	pro·ee·bee·do eng·traarr	No Entry
Rua Sem Saída	hoo·aa seng saa·ee·daa	No Through Road
Saída	saa·ee·daa	Exit (freeway)

problems

The car has broken down (at Manaus).

O carro quebrou (em Manaus).	o kaa·ho ke·bro (eng maa·nows)

The motorbike won't start.

A motocicleta náo está pegando.	a mo·to·se·kle·taa nowng es·ta pe·gang·do

I need a mechanic.

Preciso de um mecânico.	pre·see·so de oom me·ka·nee·ko

I've had an accident.
Sofri um acidente.
so·*free* oom aa·see·*deng*·te

I have a flat tyre.
Meu pneu furou.
me·oo pee·*ne*·oo foo·*ro*

I've lost my car keys.
Perdi a chave do carro.
perr·*dee* a *shaa*·ve do *kaa*·ho

I've locked the keys inside.
Tranquei a chave dentro do carro.
trang·*kay* aa *sha*·ve *deng*·tro do *kaa*·ho

I've run out of petrol.
Estou sem gasolina.
es·*to* seng gaa·zo·*lee*·naa

Can you fix It (today)?
Você pode consertar (hoje)?
vo·*se po*·de kong·serr·*taarr* (o·zhe)

How long will it take?
Quanto tempo vai levar?
kwang·to *teng*·po vai le·*vaarr*

petrol
gasolina f
gaa·zo·*lee*·naa

windscreen
parabrisa m
paa·raa·*bree*·zaa

battery
bateria f
baa·te·*ree*·aa

engine
motor m
mo·*torr*

headlight
farol m
faa·*rol*

tyre
pneu f
pee·*ne*·oo

bicycle

I'd like ...	Queria ...	ke·*ree*·aa ...
my bicycle repaired	consertar a minha bicicleta	kong·serr·*taarr* a *mee*·nyaa bee·see·*kle*·taa
to buy a bicycle	comprar uma bicicleta	kong·*praarr* oo·maa bee·see·*kle*·taa
to hire a bicycle	alugar uma bicicleta	aa·loo·*gaarr* oo·maa bee·see·*kle*·taa

I'd like a ... bike.	Queria uma bicicleta ...	ke·*ree*·aa oo·maa bee·see·*kle*·taa ...
mountain	de montanha	de mong·*ta*·nya
racing	de corrida	de ko·*hee*·daa
second-hand	de segunda mão	de se·*goong*·daa mowng

How much is it per ...?	Quanto custa por ...?	*kwang*·to *koos*·taa porr ...
day	dia	*dee*·aa
hour	hora	*aw*·raa

Do I need a helmet?
Preciso usar capacete?
pre·*see*·so oo·*zaarr* kaa·paa·*se*·te

Is there a bicycle-path map?
Existe algum mapa de rotas para bicicleta?
e·*zees*·te ow·*goom* maa·paa de ho·taas *paa*·raa bee·see·*kle*·taa

I have a puncture.
Furou o pneu.
foo·*ro* o pee·*ne*·oo

I'm ...	Estou ...	es·to ...
in transit	em trânsito	eng *trang*·zee·to
on business	à negócios	aa ne·*go*·syos
on holiday	à turismo	aa too·*rees*·mo

I'm here for ...	Vou ficar por ...	vo fee·*kaarr* porr ...
(10) days	(dez) dias	(dez) *dee*·aas
(two) months	(dois) meses	(doys) *me*·ses
(three) weeks	(três) semanas	(tres) se·*ma*·naas

listen for ...

eng *groo*·po	em grupo	**group**
kong aa faa·*mee*·lya	com a família	**family**
paa·saa·*porr*·te	passaporte	**passport**
so·*zee*·nyo	sozinho	**alone**
vees·to	visto	**visa**

I'm going to (Recife).

Estou indo para (Recife).   es·to eeng·do paa·raa (he·*see*·fe)

I'm staying at the (Ipanema Hotel).

Estou no (Hotel Ipanema).   es·to no (o·*tel* ee·pa·*nee*·maa)

The children are on this passport.

As crianças estão neste passaporte.   aas kree·*ang*·saas es·*towng* *nes*·te paa·saa·*porr*·te

I have nothing to declare.
   Não tenho nada a   nowng *te*·nyo *naa*·daa aa
   declarar.   de·klaa·*raarr*

I have something to declare.
   Tenho algo a declarar.   *te*·nyo *ow*·go aa de·klaa·*rarr*

Do I have to declare this?
   Preciso declarar isto?   pre·*see*·so de·klaa·*raarr ees*·to

That's (not) mine.
   Isto (não) é meu.   *ees*·to (nowng) e *me*·oo

I didn't know I had to declare it.
   Não sabia que tinha   nowng saa·*bee*·aa ke *tee*·nyaa
   que declarar isto.   ke de·klaa·*raarr ees*·to

signs

Alfândega	aal·*fang*·de·gaa	**Customs**
Controle de	kong·*tro*·le de	**Passport**
Passaporte	paa·sa·*porr*·te	**Control**
Free-shop	free·shop	**Duty-free**
Imigração	ee·mee·graa·*sowng*	**Immigration**
Quarentena	kwaa·reng·*te*·naa	**Quarantine**

directions
direções

Where's ...?   *Onde fica ...?*   *ong·de fee·kaa ...*
   a bank   *o banco*   *o bang·ko*
   a market   *o mercado*   *o merr·kaa·do*
   the tourist   *a secretaria*   *aa se·kre·taa·ree·aa*
     office   *de turismo*   *de too·rees·mo*

Can you show me (on the map)?
Você poderia me   *vo·se po·de·ree·aa me*
mostrar (no mapa)?   *mos·traarr (no maa·paa)*

What's the address?
Qual é o endereço?   *kwow e o eng·de·re·so*

How far is it?
Qual a distância   *kwow aa dees·tang·syaa*
daqui?   *daa·kee*

How do I get there?
Como é que eu chego lá?   *ko·mo e ke e·oo she·go laa*

It's ...   *Fica ...*   *fee·kaa ...*
   behind ...   *atrás ...*   *aa·traaz ...*
   close   *perto*   *perr·to*
   here   *aqui*   *a·kee*
   in front of ..,   *na frente de ...*   *naa freng·te de ...*
   near ...   *perto ...*   *perr·to ...*
   next to ...   *ao lado de ...*   *ow laa·do de ...*
   on the corner   *na esquina*   *na es·kee·naa*
   opposite ...   *do lado oposto ...*   *do laa·do o·pos·to ...*
   straight ahead   *em frente*   *eng freng·te*
   there   *lá*   *laa*

north   *norte*   *norr·te*
south   *sul*   *sool*
east   *leste*   *les·te*
west   *oeste*   *o·es·te*

directions

by bus	de ônibus	de o·nee·boos
by taxi	de táxi	de taak·see
by train	de trem	de treng
on foot	a pé	aa pe

Turn …	Vire …	vee·re …
at the corner	à esquina	aa es·kee·naa
at the	no sinal de	no see·now de
traffic lights	trânsito	trang·zee·to
left	à esquerda	aa es·kerr·daa
right	à direita	aa dee·ray·taa

What … is this?	Que …?	ke …
avenue	avenida	aa·ve·nee·daa
	é esta	e es·taa
lane	travessa é esta	traa·ve·saa e es·taa
street	rua é esta	hoo·aa e es·taa
village	vilarejo	vee·laa·re·zho
	é este	e es·te

traffic lights
sinal m *de
trânsito*
see·now de
trang·zee·to

shop
loja f
*lo·*zhaa

pedestrian
crossing
travessia f *de
pedestre*
traa·ve·see·aa de
pe·des·tre

bus
ônibus m
o·nee·boos

intersection
interseção f
eeng·terr·se·sowng

corner
esquina f
es·kee·naa

taxi
táxi m
taak·see

finding accommodation

Where's a …?	Onde tem …?	ong·de teng …
bed and breakfast	uma pensão	oo·maa peng·sowng
camping ground	um local para acampamento	oom lo·kow paa·raa aa·kang·paa·meng·to
guesthouse	uma hospedaria	oo·maa os·pe·daa·ree·a
hotel	um hotel	oom o·tel
room	um quarto	oom kwaarr·to
youth hostel	um albergue da juventude	oom ow·berr·ge daa zhoo·veng·too·de

Can you recommend somewhere …?	Você pode recomendar algum lugar …?	vo·se po·de he·ko·meng·daarr ow·goom loo·gaarr …
cheap	barato	baa·raa·to
good	bom	bong
luxurious	de luxo	de loo·sho
nearby	perto daqui	perr·to daa·kee
romantic	romântico	ho·mang·tee·ko

What's the address?
Qual é o endereço?   kwow e o en·de·re·so

For responses, see **directions**, page 51.

booking ahead & checking in

Do you have a ... room?	Tem um quarto de ...?	teng oom kwaarr·to de ...
double	casal	kaa·zow
single	solteiro	sol·tay·ro
twin	duplo	doo·plo

How much is it per ...?	Quanto custa por ...?	kwang·to koos·taa porr ...
night	noite	noy·te
person	pessoa	pe·so·aa
week	semana	se·ma·naa

I'd like to book a room, please.
Eu gostaria de fazer   e·oo gos·taa·ree·aa de faa·zerr
uma reserva, por favor.   oo·maa he·zer·vaa porr faa·vorr

I have a reservation.
Eu tenho uma reserva.   e·oo te·nyo oo·maa he·zerr·vaa

My name's ...
Meu nome é ...   me·oo no·me e ...

For (three) nights/weeks.
Para (três) noites/   paa·raa (tres) noy·tes/
semanas.   se·ma·naas

From (July 2) to (July 6).
De (dois de julho) até   de (doys de zhoo·lyo) aa·te
(seis de julho).   (says de zhoo·lyo)

Can I see it?
Posso ver?   po·so verr

I'll take it.
Eu fico com ele.   e·oo fee·ko kong e·lee

signs

Banheiro	ba·nyay·ro	Bathroom/ Toilet
Não Tem Vaga	nowng teng vaa·gaa	No Vacancy
Tem Vaga	teng vaa·gaa	Vacancy

Do I need to pay upfront?

Tem que pagar	teng ke paa-*gaarr*
adiantado?	aa-dee-ang-*taa*-do

Can I pay …?	*Posso pagar*	po-so paa-*gaarr*
	com …?	kong …
by credit	*cartão de*	kaarr-*towng* de
card	*crédito*	*kre*-dee-to
by travellers	*travellers cheque*	tra-ve-lers *she*-kee
cheque		
in (US)	*dólar*	*do*-laarr
dollars	*(americano)*	(aa-me-ree-*ka*-no)

For other methods of payment, see **money**, page 35.

listen for …		
paa-raa *kwang*-taas	*Para quantas*	**How many**
noy-tes	*noites?*	**nights?**
he-se-pee-*sowng*	*recepção*	**reception**
paa-saa-*porr*-te	*passaporte*	**passport**
shaa-ve	*chave*	**key**
shay-o	*cheio*	**full**

requests & queries

When/Where is breakfast served?

Onde/Quando é servido	ong-de/*kwang*-do e serr-*vee*-do
o café da manhã?	o kaa-*fe* daa ma-*nyang*

Please wake me at (seven).

Por favor me acorde	porr faa-*vor* me aa-*kor*-de
às (sete).	aas (*se*-te)

Can I use the …?	*Posso usar …?*	po-so oo-*zaarr* …
kitchen	*a cozinha*	aa ko-*zee*-nyaa
laundry	*a lavanderia*	aa laa-vang-de-*ree*-aa
telephone	*o telefone*	o te-le-*fo*-ne

Do you have a/an …?	Tem …?	teng …
elevator	elevador	e·le·vaa·dorr
laundry service	serviço de lavanderia	serr·vee·so de laa·vang·de·ree·aa
message board	quadro de recados	kwaa·dro de he·kaa·dos
safe	cofre	ko·fre
swimming pool	piscina	pee·see·na
Do you … here?	Vocês …?	vo·ses …
arrange tours	organizam passeios	orr·ga·nee·zang paa·say·os
change money	trocam dinheiro	tro·kang dee·nyay·ro
Could I have …, please?	Pode me dar …, por favor?	po·de me daarr … porr faa·vorr
a mosquito net	um mosquiteiro	oom mos·kee·tay·ro
a receipt	um recibo	oom he·see·bo
an extra blanket	um outro cobertor	oom o·tro ko·berr·torr
my key	minha chave	mee·nyaa shaa·ve

local talk

dive	porcaria f	porr·kaa·ree·aa
rat-infested	infestado de rato	eeng·fes·taa·do de haa·to
top spot	ótimo lugar m	o·tee·mo loo·gaarr

Is there a message for me?
Tem recado para mim?   teng he·kaa·do paa·raa meeng

Can I leave a message for someone?
Posso deixar um   po·so day·shaarr oom
recado para alguém?   he·kaa·do paa·raa ow·geng

I'm locked out of my room.
Fiquei preso/presa fora   fee·kay pre·so/pre·saa fo·raa
do quarto. m/f   do kwaarr·to

complaints

It's too …	É muito …	e mweeng·to …
bright	claro	klaa·ro
cold	frio	free·o
dark	escuro	es·koo·ro
expensive	caro	kaa·ro
noisy	barulhento	baa·roo·lyeng·to
small	pequeno	pe·ke·no

This (pillow) isn't clean.
Este (travesseiro) está sujo.

es·te (traa·ve·say·ro) es·taa soo·zho

air-conditioning
ar condicionado m
aarr kong·dee·syo·naa·do

key
chave f
shaa·ve

fan
ventilador m
veng·tee·laa·dorr

bed
cama f
ka·maa

toilet
taza f del baño
ta·sa del ba·nyo

bathroom
banheiro m
ba·nyay·ro

TV
televisão m
te·le·vee·sowng

accommodation

57

The ... doesn't	O ... não está	o ... *nowng* es·*taa*
work.	funcionando.	foong·syo·*nang*·do
air-	*ar*	aarr
conditioning	*condicionado*	kong·dee·syo·*naa*·do
fan	*ventilador*	veng·tee·laa·*dorr*
toilet	*banheiro*	ba·*nyay*·ro

checking out

fazendo o check out

What time is checkout?
A que horas é o check out? aa ke *aw*·raas e o shek owt

Can I have a late checkout?
Posso fazer o check out po·so faa·*zerr* o shek owt
mais tarde? mais *taar*·de

Can you call a taxi for me (for 11 o'clock)?
Pode chamar um po·de shaa·*maarr* oom
taxi para mim *taak*·see *paa*·ra meeng
(para às onze horas)? (*paa*·raa aas *ong*·ze *aw*·raas)

I'm leaving now.
Estou indo embora   es·*to* eeng·do eng·*bo*·raa
agora.   aa·*go*·raa

Can I leave my bags here?
Posso deixar minhas   *po*·so day·*shaarr* mee·nyaas
malas aqui?   *maa*·laas aa·*kee*

There's a mistake in the bill.
Houve um erro na conta.   *o*·ve oom *e*·ho naa *kong*·taa

I'll be back ...	*Estarei de volta ...*	es·taa·*ray* de *vol*·taa ...
in (three) days	*em (três) dias*	eng (tres) *dee*·aas
on (Tuesday)	*na (terça-feira)*	naa (*terr*·saa·*fay*·raa)

Could I have	*Pode devolver ...,*	*po*·de de·vol·*verr* ...
my ..., please?	*por favor?*	por faa·*vorr*
deposit	*o meu*	o *me*·oo
	depósito	de·*po*·zee·to
passport	*o meu*	o *me*·oo
	passaporte	paa·saa·*porr*·te
valuables	*os meus*	os *me*·oos
	objetos de	o·bee·*zhe*·tos de
	valor	vaa·*lorr*

I had a great stay, thank you.
Foi ótima a estadia,   foy *o*·tee·ma aa es·taa·*dee*·aa
obrigado/obrigada. m/f   o·bree·*gaa*·do/o·bree·*gaa*·daa

I'll recommend it to my friends.
Vou recomendar aos   vo he·ko·meng·*daarr* ows
meus amigos.   *me*·oos aa·*mee*·gos

camping

Do you have …? *Tem …?* teng …
  a laundry   *uma*   oo·maa
     lavanderia   laa·vang·de·ree·aa
  a site   *um lugar*   oom loo·gaarr
  electricity   *eletricidade*   e·le·tree·see·daa·de
  shower facilities   *chuveiro*   shoo·vay·ro
  tents for hire   *barracas*   baa·haa·kaas
     para alugar   paa·raa aa·loo·gaarr

How much is it *Quanto custa* kwang·to koos·taa
per …? *por …?* porr …
  person   *pessoa*   pe·so·aa
  tent   *barraca*   baa·haa·kaa
  vehicle   *veículo*   ve·ee·koo·lo

Can I …? *Posso …?* po·so …
  camp here   *acampar*   aa·kang·paarr
     aqui   aa·kee
  park next   *estacionar*   es·taa·see·o·naarr
  to my tent   *ao lado da*   ow laa·do daa
     minha   mee·nyaa
     barraca?   baa·haa·kaa

Who do I ask to stay here?
  A quem eu peço para   aa keng e·oo pe·so paa·raa
  ficar aqui?   fee·kaarr aa·kee

Is the water drinkable?
  A água é potável?   a aa·gwaa e po·taa·vel

Is it coin-operated?
  Isto funciona com   ees·to foong·syo·naa kong
  moedas?   mo·e·daas

Could I borrow (a mallet)?
  Posso pegar (um isqueiro)   po·so pe·gaarr (oom ees·kay·ro)
  emprestado?   eng·pres·taa·do

renting

I'm here about the … for rent.

Estou aqui por causa do …	es·*to* aa·*kee* porr *kow*·zaa do …
para alugar.	*paa*·raa aa·loo·*gaarr*

Do you have a/an … for rent?

Você tem … para	vo·*se* teng … *paa*·raa
alugar?	aa·loo·*gaarr*

apartment	*apartamento* m	aa·paarr·taa·*meng*·to
cabin	*cabine* f	kaa·*bee*·ne
house	*casa* f	*kaa*·zaa
room	*quarto* m	*kwaarr*·to
(partly)	*(parcialmente)*	(paarr·see·ow·*meng*·te)
furnished	*mobiliado/*	mo·bee·*lyaa*·do/
	mobiliada m/f	mo·bee·*lyaa*·daa
unfurnished	*sem mobília*	seng mo·*bee*·lyaa

tongue torture

Tongue twisters are very popular in Brazil, and they're not a bad way to get your mouth around a new language. Try these for a bit of r practice:

O rato roeu a roupa do rei de Roma.
o *haa*·to ro·*e*·oo aa *ho*·paa do re de *ro*·maa
(The rat chewed the clothes of the king of Rome.)

Três pratos de trigo para três tigres tristes.
tres *praa*·tos de *tree*·go *paa*·raa tres *tee*·gres *trees*·tes
(Three plates of wheat for three sad tigers.)

accommodation

staying with locals

Can I stay at your place?
Posso ficar na sua   po·so fee·*kaarr* naa *soo*·aa
casa?   *kaa*·zaa

Is there anything I can do to help?
Posso ajudar em   po·so aa·zhoo·*daarr* eng
alguma coisa?   ow·*goo*·maa *koy*·zaa

I have my own …	*Tenho o meu*	te·nyo o me·oo
	próprio …	pro·pree·o …
mattress	*colchão*	kol·*showng*
sleeping bag	*saco de*	*saa*·ko de
	dormir	dorr·*meerr*

Can I …?	*Posso …?*	po·so …
bring anything	*trazer*	traa·*zerr*
for the meal	*alguma*	ow·*goo*·maa
	coisa para a	*koy*·zaa *paa*·raa aa
	refeição	he·fay·*sowng*
do the dishes	*lavar a louça*	laa·*varr* aa *lo*·saa
set/clear	*arrumar/*	aa·hoo·*maarr/*
the table	*limpar a mesa*	leeng·paarr aa *me*·zaa
take out the	*jogar o lixo*	zho·*gaarr* o *lee*·sho
rubbish	*fora*	*foo*·raa

Thanks for your hospitality.
Obrigado/Obrigada   o·bree·*gaa*·do/o·bree·*gaa*·daa
pela hospitalidade. m/f   pe·laa os·pee·taa·lee·*daa*·de

For dining-related expressions, see **eating out,** page 141.

looking for ...

procurando por ...

Where's ...?	Onde fica ...?	ong·de fee·kaa ...
a bookshop	a livraria	aa lee·vraa·ree·aa
a department store	a loja de departamentos	aa lo·zhaa de de·paarr·taa·meng·tos
a supermarket	o supermercado	o soo·perr·merr·kaa·do

Where can I buy (a padlock)?
> Onde posso comprar (um cadeado)?
> ong·de po·so kong·praarr (oom kaa·de·aa·do)

For more shops, see the **dictionary** and for phrases on asking and giving directions, see **directions**, page 51.

making a purchase

fazendo compras

I'd like to buy (an adaptor plug).
> Gostaria de comprar (um adaptador).
> gos·taa·ree·aa de kong·praarr (oom aa·daa·pee·taa·dorr)

How much is it?
> Quanto custa?
> kwang·to koos·taa

Can you write down the price?
> Você pode escrever o preço?
> vo·se po·de es·kre·verr o pre·so

Do you have any others?
> Você tem outros?
> vo·se teng o·tros

Can I look at it?
> Posso ver?
> po·so verr

I'm just looking.
> Estou só olhando.
> es·to so o·lyang·do

shopping

Do you accept ...?	Vocês aceitam ...?	vo·ses aa·say·tang ...
credit cards	cartão de crédito	kaarr·towng de kre·dee·to
debit cards	saque eletrônico	sa·kee e·le·tro·nee·ko
travellers cheques	traveller cheque	tra·ve·ler she·kee

Could I have a ..., please?	Pode me dar um ..., por favor?	po·de me daarr oom ... porr faa·vorr
bag	saco	saa·ko
receipt	recibo	he·see·bo

Could I have it wrapped?
Pode embrulhar?
po·de eng·broo·lyaarr

Does it have a guarantee?
Tem garantia?
teng gaa·rang·tee·aa

Can I have it sent overseas?
Vocês podem enviar parao exterior?
vo·ses po·deng eng·vee·aarr paa·raa o es·te·ree·orr

Can you order it for me?
Pode fazer o pedido para mim?
po·de faa·zerr o pe·dee·do paa·raa meeng

Can I pick it up later?
Posso pegar mais tarde?
po·so pe·gaarr mais taarr·de

It's faulty.
Está com defeito.
es·taa kong de·fay·to

I'd like ..., please.	Gostaria de ...	gos·taa·ree·aa de ...
a refund	ser reembolsado	serr he·eng·bol·saa·do
my change	ter o meu troco	terr o me·oo tro·ko
to return this	devolver isto	de·vol·verr ees·to

bargaining

That's too expensive.
Está muito caro.   es·*taa* mweeng·to *kaa*·ro

Can you lower the price?
Pode baixar o preço?   po·de bai·*shaarr* o *pre*·so

I don't want to pay the full price.
Não quero pagar o   nowng *ke*·ro paa·*gaarr* o
preço todo.   *pre*·so to·do

Do you have something cheaper?
Tem uma coisa mais   teng ōo·maa *koy*·zaa mais
barata?   baa·*raa*·taa

I'll give you (five reals).
Dou (cinco reais).   do (*seeng*·ko he·*ais*)

local talk		
bargain	*pechincha* f	pe·*sheeng*·shaa
rip-off	*roubo* m	*ho*·bo
sale	*liquidação* f	lee·kee·*daa* sowng
specials	*preço* m	*pre*·so
	especial	es·pe·see·*ow*

clothes

Can I try it on?
Posso experimentar?   po·so es·pe·ree·meng·*taarr*

My size is (14).
Meu número é (quatorze).   me·oo *noo*·me·ro e (kaa·*torr*·ze)

It doesn't fit.
Não cabe.   nowng *kaa*·be

For clothing items, see the **dictionary**.

repairs

Can I have my (backpack) repaired here?
Vocês consertam a (mochila)?
vo·*ses* kong·*serr*·tang aa (mo·*shee*·laa)

When will my ... be ready?	*Quando ...?*	*kwang*·do ...
camera	*fica pronta a câmera*	*fee*·kaa *prong*·taa aa *ka*·me·raa
(sun)glasses	*ficam prontos os óculos (de sol)*	*fee*·kang *prong*·tos os *o*·koo·los (de sol)
shoes	*fica pronto o sapato*	*fee*·kaa *prong*·to o saa·*paa*·to

darn holes		
buttons	*botões* m pl	bo·*toyngs*
needle	*agulha* f	aa·*goo*·lyaa
scissors	*tesoura* f	te·*zo*·raa
thread	*linha* f	*lee*·nya

hairdressing

I'd like (a) ...	*Gostaria de ...*	gos·taa·*ree*·aa de ...
blow wave	*secar*	se·*kaarr*
colour	*pintar*	peeng·*taarr*
haircut	*cortar*	korr·*taarr*
my beard trimmed	*aparar a barba*	aa·paa·*raarr* aa *baarr*·baa
shave	*fazer a barba*	faa·*zerr* aa *baarr*·baa
trim	*aparar*	aa·paa·*raarr*

Don't cut it too short.
Não corta muito.   nowng *korr*·taa *mweeng*·to

Shave it all off!
Raspa tudo!   *haas*·paa *too*·do

Please use a new blade.
Por favor use uma   por fa·*vorr* oo·ze oo·maa
gilete nova.   zhee·*le*·te *no*·vaa

I should never have let you near me!
Não deveria nunca   nowng de·ve·*ree*·aa *noong*·kaa
ter deixado você   terr day·*shaa*·do vo·*se*
chegar perto de mim!   she·*gaarr perr*·to de meeng

For colours, see the **dictionary**.

books & reading

livros e leitura

Do you have ...?   *Tem ...?*   teng ...
  a book by   *algum livro*   ow·*goom lee*·vro
  (Jorge   *do (Jorge*   do (*zhorzh*
  Amado)   *Amado)*   aa·*maa*·do)
  an entertain-   *um guia de*   oom *gee*·aa de
  ment guide   *entretenimento*   eng·tre·te·nee·*meng*·to

> **listen for ...**
>
> mais ow·*goo*·maa *koy*·zaa
> *Mais alguma coisa?*   **Anything else?**
>
> nowng nowng *te*·mos
> *Não, não temos.*   **No, we don't have any.**
>
> *po*·so aa·zhoo·*daarr*
> *Posso ajudar?*   **Can I help you?**

shopping

I'd like a ...	Gostaria de comprar um ...	gos·taa·*ree*·aa de kong·*praarr* oom ...
dictionary	dicionário	dee·see·o·*naa*·ryo
newspaper	jornal	zhorr·*now*
(in English)	(em inglês)	(eng eeng·*gles*)
notepad	bloco de notas	*blo*·ko de *no*·taas

Is there an English-language ...?	Tem uma ... de língua inglesa?	teng oo·maa ... de *leeng*·gwaa eeng·*gle*·saa
bookshop	livraria	lee·vraa·*ree*·aa
section	seção	se·*sowng*

Can you recommend a book for me?
Você poderia me recomendar algum livro?
vo·*se* po·de·*ree*·aa me he·ko·meng·*daarr* ow·*goom* lee·vro

Do you have Lonely Planet guidebooks?
Vocês tem os guias de viagem do Lonely Planet?
vo·*ses* teng os *gee*·aas de vee·*aa*·zheng do *lo*·ne·lee *pla*·ne·tee

music

música

I'd like a ...	Gostaria de comprar ...	gos·taa·*ree*·aa de kong·*praarr* ...
blank tape	uma fita virgem	oo·maa *fee*·taa veerr·zheng
CD	um CD	oom se·*de*

I'm looking for something by (Caetano Veloso).
Estou procurando por alguma coisa (do Caetano Veloso).
es·*to* pro·koo·*rang*·do porr ow·*goo*·maa *koy*·zaa (do kaa·e·*ta*·no ve·*lo*·zo)

What's his/her best recording?
Qual é o melhor disco dele/dela? m/f
kwow e o me·*lyorr* dees·ko de·le/de·laa

Can I listen to this?
Posso escutar?
po·so es·koo·*taarr*

PRACTICAL

Souvenir hunters will find music, local crafts and musical instruments worthy mementos of their trip. Artisan fairs (*feira de artesanato*) are common weekend events in larger cities and offer a good range of souvenirs.

regional souvenirs

Is there a souvenir typical of this region?

Tem algum lenbrança	teng al·*goom* leng·*braan*·sa
específico desta	es·pe·see·*fee*·ko *des*·ta
região ?	re·*zhowng*

artesanato indígena – Indian handicrafts, including wooden and woven items
artigos de couro – leather goods
bikini fio dental – 'dental floss' bikinI – the original string bikini. The name says it all.
jóia – jewellery
pedras preciosas – gemstones
rede – cotton hammocks, usually dyed in bright colours

musical instruments

The instruments that feature in traditional Brazilian music make great souvenirs.

berimbau – a stringed instrument commonly used In *capoeira* performances. It consists of a bow with metal string attached to a dried gourd which acts as a resonating chamber. A rod and a ring or coin is struck against the string to produce sound.

pandeiro – originally from East Africa, the tambourine is considered an essential part of Brazilian rhythm and is common throughout the country

reco-reco – a grooved piece of bamboo or iron also used in *capoeira*. A rod is scraped against the grooves to produce the rasping sound.

photography

I need ... film for this camera.	Preciso de filme ... para esta câmera.	pre·see·zo de feel·me ... paa·raa es·taa ka·me·raa
APS	sistema APS	sees·te·maa aa pe e·se
B&W	Preto e Branco	pre·to e brang·ko
colour	colorido	ko·lo·ree·do
slide	de slide	de ees·lai·de
(200) speed	(duzentos) velocidade	(doo·zeng·tos) ve·lo·see·daa·de

Can you ...?	Você pode ...?	vo·se po·de ...
develop this film	revelar este filme	he·ve·laarr es·te feel·me
load my film	colocar o filme	ko·lo·kaarr o feel·me

I need a passport photo taken.
Preciso tirar foto para passporte.   pre·see·zo tee·raarr fo·to paa·raa paa·saa·porr·te

When will it be ready?
Quando fica pronto?   kwang·do fee·kaa prong·to

How much is it?
Quanto custa?   kwang·to koos·taa

I'm not happy with these photos.
Não gostei destas fotos.   nowng gos·tay des·taas fo·tos

communications

comunicações

post office

correios e telégrafos

I want to send a ...	*Quero enviar ...*	*ke·ro eng·vee·aarr ...*
fax	*um fax*	oom faks
letter	*uma carta*	*oo·maa kaarr·taa*
parcel	*uma encomenda*	oo·maa eng·ko·meng·daa
postcard	*um cartão postal*	oom kaarr·*towng* pos·*tow*

I want to buy ...	*Quero comprar ...*	*ke·ro kong·praarr ...*
an aerogram	*um aerograma*	oom aa·e·ro·*gra*·maa
an envelope	*um envelope*	oom eng·ve·*lo*·pe
stamps	*selos*	*se*·los

airmail	*via aéreo/ aérea* m/f	*vee*·aa aa·*e*·re·o/ aa·*e*·re·aa
customs declaration	*declaração* f *da alfândega*	de·klaa·raa·*sowng* daa aal·*fang*·de·gaa
domestic	*doméstico*	do·*mes*·tee·ko
express	*rápido/ rápida* m/f	*haa*·pee·do/ *haa*·pee·daa
fragile	*frágil*	*fraa*·zheel
international	*internacional*	eeng·terr·naa·syo·*now*
mail	*correspondência* f	ko·hes·pong·*deng*·syaa
mailbox	*caixa* f *postal*	*kai*·sha pos·*tow*
postcode	*CEP* m	*se*·pee
registered	*registrado/ registrada* m/f	he·zhees·*traa*·do/ he·zhees·*traa*·daa
surface mail	*via terrestre*	*vee*·aa te·*hes*·tre

Please send it by air/surface mail to (Australia).

Por favor envie via
aérea/terrestre para a
(Austrália).

porr faa·*vorr* eng·*vee*·e *vee*·aa
aa·e·re·aa/te·*hes*·tre *paa*·raa aa
(ows·*traa*·lya)

It contains (souvenirs).

Contém (souvenirs).

kong·*teng* (soo·ve·*neers*)

Where's the poste restante section?

Onde fica a seção de
Poste Restante?

ong·de *fee*·kaa a se·*sowng* de
pos·te hes·*tang*·te

Is there any mail for me?

Tem alguma
correspondência
para mim?

teng ow·*goo*·maa
ko·hes·pong·*deng*·syaa
paa·raa meeng

phone

What's your phone number?

Qual é o número do teu
telefone?

kwow e o *noo*·me·ro do te·oo
te·le·*fo*·ne

Where's the nearest public phone?

Onde fica o telefône
público mais perto?

ong·de *fee*·kaa o te·le·*fo*·ne
poo·blee·ko mais *perr*·to

Do you have a phonebook I can look at?

Posso dar uma
olhada no catálogo
telefônico?

po·so daarr oo·maa
o·*lyaa*·daa no kaa·*taa*·lo·go
te·le·*fo*·nee·ko

How much does ... cost?	*Quanto custa ...?*	kwang·to koos·taa ...
a (three)-minute call	*uma* *ligação de* *(três) minutos*	oo·maa lee·gaa·*sowng* de (tres) mee·*noo*·tos
each extra minute	*cada minuto* *extra*	*kaa*·daa mee·*noo*·to es·traa

I want to ...	Quero ...	*ke·ro ...*
buy a phone card	comprar um cartão telefônico	kong·*praarr* oom kaar·*towng* te·le·fo·nee·ko
call (Singapore)	telefonar (para Cingapura)	te·le·fo·*naarr* (*paa*·raa seen·gaa·*poo*·raa)
make a local call	fazer uma chamada local	faa·*zerr* oo·maa shaa·*maa*·daa *lo*·kow
reverse the charges	fazer uma chamada a cobrar	faa·*zerr* oo·maa shaa·*maa*·daa aa ko·*braarr*
speak for (three) minutes	falar por (três) minutos	faa·*laarr* por (tres) mee·noo·tos

The number is ...
O número é ...　　　　　　o *noo*·me·ro e ...

What's the area code for (Recife)?
Qual é o código de　　　kwow e o *ko*·dee·go de
discagem para (Recife)?　dees·*ka*·zheng *paa*·raa (he·*see*·fe)

What's the country code for (New Zealand)?
Qual é o código de　　　kwow e o *ko*·dee·go de
discagem para　　　　　dees·*ka*·zheng *paa*·raa
(Nova Zelândia)?　　　　(*no*·vaa ze·*lang*·dee·aa)

It's engaged.
Está ocupado.　　　　　es·*taa* o·koo·*paa*·do

I've been cut off.
A ligação caiu.　　　　　aa lee·gaa·*sowng* kaa·*ee*·oo

The connection's bad.
A conexão está ruim.　　aa ko·nek·*sowng* es·*taa* hoo·*eeng*

Hello.	*Alô.*	aa·lo
Can I speak to ...?	*Posso falar com ...?*	po·so faa·*laarr* kong ...
It's ...	*Aqui é ...*	a·*kee* e ...
Is ... there?	*O/A ... está?* m/f	o/aa ... es·*taa*

listen for ...

e·le/e·laa nowng es·*taa* *Ele/Ela não está.*		He/She is not here.
es·*pe*·raa oom mee·noo·*tee*·nyo *Espera um minutinho.*		One moment.
keng es·*taa* faa·*lang*·do *Quem está falando?*		Who's calling?
kong keng vo·*se* kerr faa·*laarr* *Com quem você quer falar?*		Who do you want to speak to?
kwow o se·oo *noo*·me·ro paa·raa kong·*taa*·to *Qual o seu número para contato?*		What's your contact number?
vo·*se* dees·*ko* o *noo*·me·ro e·*haa*·do *Você discou o número errado.*		Wrong number.

Can I leave a message?
Posso deixar um recado?   po·so day·*shaarr* oom he·*kaa*·do

Please tell him/her I called.
Por favor diga a   por faa·*vorr* dee·gaa a
ele/ela que eu liguei.   e·le/e·laa ke e·oo lee·*gay*

I'll call back later.
Eu vou ligar mais tarde.   e·oo vo lee·*gaarr* mais *taarr*·de

My number is ...
Meu telefone é ...   me·oo te·le·*fo*·ne e ...

PRACTICAL

74

mobile/cell phone

telephone celular

I'd like a ...	Eu gostaria de ...	e·oo gos·taa·ree·aa de ...
charger for	comprar uma	kong·praarr oo·maa
my phone	bateria para o	baa·te·ree·aa paa·raa o
	meu telephone	me·oo te·le·fo·ne
mobile/cell	alugar um	aa·loo·gaarr oom
phone for hire	cellular	se·loo·laarr
prepaid mobile/	comprar um	kong·praarr oom
cell phone	cellular	se·loo·laarr
	pré-pago	pre·paa·go
SIM card for	comprar um	kong·praarr oom
your network	cartão SIM	kaarr·towng seeng
	para sua rede	paa·raa soo·aa he·de

What are the rates?
Qual é o valor cobrado?   kwow e o vaa·lorr ko·braa·do

(30c) per (30) seconds.
(Trinta centavos) por   (treeng·taa seng·taa·vos) porr
(trinta) segundos.   (treeng·taa) se·goong·dos

---

internetese

The word *Internetês* (Internetese) has been coined to describe the confusing mixture of English and Portuguese terms in Brazilian cyberspace. New words such as *surfar* (surf) and *scâner* (scanner) have been adapted from English but sometimes there are Portuguese alternatives for common internet terms:

bate-papo m	internet chat
ciberespaço m	cyberspace
endereço m *de email*	email address
hiperligação m	hyperlink
internauta f	net nerd
página f *inicial*	homepage
utilizador m&f	user

communications

the internet

Where's the local Internet cafe?
Onde tem um internet   *ong·de teng oom eeng·terr·ne·tee*
café na redondeza?   *kaa·fe naa he·dong·de·zaa*

I'd like to ...	*Gostaria de ...*	*gos·taa·ree·aa de ...*
check my email	*checar meu e-mail*	*she·kaarr me·oo e·mail*
get Internet access	*ter acesso à internet*	*terr aa·se·so aa eeng·terr·ne·tee*
use a printer	*usar a impressora*	*oo·zaarr aa eeng·pre·so·raa*
use a scanner	*usar o escaner*	*oo·zaarr o ees·ka·nerr*

Do you have ...?	*Vocês tem ...?*	*vo·ses teng ...*
a Zip drive	*um zip drive*	*oom zeep drai·vee*
Macs	*Apple Mac*	*e·pel mak*
PCs	*PC*	*pe·se*

How much per ...?	*Quanto custa por ...?*	*kwang·to koos·taa por ...*
hour	*hora*	*aw·raa*
(five) minutes	*(cinco) minutes*	*(seeng·ko) mee·noo·tos*
page	*página*	*paa·zhee·naa*

How do I log on?
Como é que eu entro?   *ko·mo e ke e·oo eng·tro*

Please change it to the English-language setting.
Troca para inglês,   *tro·kaa paa·raa eeng·gles*
por favor.   *porr faa·vorr*

It's crashed.
Deu crash.   *de·o krash*

Where can I …?	Onde posso …?	ong·de po·so …
I'd like to …	Gostaria de …	gos·taa·ree·aa de …
cash a cheque	descontar um cheque	des·kong·taarr oom she·kee
change a travellers cheque	trocar traveller cheques	tro·kaarr traa·ve·ler she·kes
change money	trocar dinheiro	tro·kaar dee·nyay·ro
get a cash advance	fazer um saque adiantado	fa·zerr oom saa·ke aa·dee·ang·taa·do
withdraw money	retirar dinheiro	he·tee·raarr dee·nyay·ro
Where's …?	Onde tem …?	ong·de teng …
a foreign exchange office	uma loja de câmbio	oo·maa lo·zhaa de kang·byo
an automatic teller machine	um caixa automático	oom kai·shaa ow·to·maa·tee·ko

What time does the bank open?
A que horas abre o banco?	aa ke aw·raas aa·bre o bang·ko

Can I use my credit card to withdraw money?
Posso usar o meu cartão de crédito para retirar dinheiro?	po·so oo·zaarr o me·oo kaar·towng de kre·dee·to paa·raa he·tee·raarr dee·nyay·ro

What's the ...? *Qual ...?* kwow ...
  exchange rate   *o câmbio do*   o *kang*·byo do
                                  dia   *dee*·aa
  charge for   *a taxa*   aa *taa*·shaa
    that   *cobrada*   ko·*braa*·daa

Has my money arrived yet?
O meu dinheiro já   o *me*·oo dee·*nyay*·ro zhaa
chegou?   she·*go*

How long will it take to arrive?
Quanto tempo vai levar   *kwang*·to *teng*·po *vaa*·ee le·*vaarr*
para chegar?   *paa*·raa she·*gaarr*

The automatic teller machine took my card.
O caixa eletrônico   o *kai*·shaa e·le·*tro*·nee·ko
engoliu meu cartão.   eng·go·*lee*·oo *mee*·oo kaar·*towng*

I've forgotten my PIN.
Esqueci a minha   es·ke·*see* aa *mee*·nyaa
senha.   *se*·nyaa

---

listen for ...

aa·*see*·ne aa·*kee*
  Assine aqui.   **Sign here.**

nowng po·*de*·mos faa·*zerr ee*·so
  Não podemos fazer isso.   **We can't do that.**

te·mos oom pro·*ble*·maa
  Temos um problema.   **There's a problem.**

ee·deng·tee·*daa*·de   *identidade*   **identification**
paa·saa·*porr*·te   *passaporte*   **passport**

PRACTICAL

sightseeing

passeando

I'd like a/an ...	Gostaria de um ...	gos·taa·*ree*·aa de oom ...
audio set	aparelho de audio	aa·paa·*re*·lyo de ow·dee·o
catalogue	catálogo	kaa·*taa*·lo·go
guide (person)	guia	*gee*·aa
guidebook in English	guia em Inglês	*gee*·aa eng eeng·*gles*
(local) map	mapa (local)	*maa*·paa (lo·*kow*)

Do you have information on ... sights?	Vocês tem informações sobre passeios ...?	vo·*ses* teng eeng·forr·maa·*soyngs* so·bre paa·*se*·os ...
cultural	culturais	kool·too·*rais*
historical	históricos	ees·*to*·ree·kos
religious	religiosos	he·lee·zhee·o·zos

I'd like to see ...
Gostaria de ver ...   gos·ta·*ree*·a de ver ...

What's that?
O que é isso?   o ke e *ee*·so

Who made it?
Quem fez isso?   keng fes *ee*·so

How old is it?
Quantos anos tem?   *kwang*·tos *a*·nos teng

Could you take a photograph of me?
Você poderia tirar   vo·*se* po·de·*ree*·aa tee·*raarr*
minha foto, por favor?   *mee*·nyaa *fo*·to porr faa·*vor*

sightseeing

79

Can I take a photograph?
Posso tirar uma foto?   po·so tee·*raarr* oo·ma *fo*·to

Can I take a photograph of you?
Posso tirar uma foto   po·so tee·*raarr* oo·ma *fo*·to
de você(s)? sg/pl   de vo·*se(s)*

I'll send you the photograph.
Eu te envio a foto.   *e*·oo te eng·*vee*·o a fo·to

getting in

What time does it open/close?
A que horas abre/fecha?   a ke *aw*·raas *aa*·bre/fe·shaa

What's the admission charge?
Qual o preço da entrada?   kwow o *pre*·so daa eng·*traa*·daa

Is there a	*Tem desconto*	teng des·*kong*·to
discount for …?	*para …?*	*paa*·raa …
children	*crianças*	kree·*ang*·saas
families	*famílias*	faa·*mee*·lyaas
groups	*grupos*	*groo*·pos
older people	*pessoas*	pe·*so*·aas
	idosas	ee·*do*·zaas
pensioners	*pensionistas*	peng·see·o·*nees*·taas
students	*estudantes*	es·too·*dang*·tes

galleries & museums

When's the gallery open?
Quando abre a galeria?   kwang·do *aa*·bre aa gaa·le·*ree*·aa

What kind of art are you interested in?
Você se interessa por   vo·*se* se eeng·te·*re*·saa porr
que tipo de arte?   ke *tee*·po de *aarr*·te

What's in the collection?
O que tem na coleção?   o ke teng naa ko·le·*sowng*

What do you think of (Renaissance art)?
O que você acha (arte   o ke vo·*se aa*·shaa (*aarr*·te
Renascença)?   he·naas·*seng*·saa)

It's a (Volpi) exhibition.
É uma (Volpi) exposição.   e *oo*·maa (*vol*·pee) es·po·zee·*sowng*

I'm interested in …
Estou interessado/   es·*to* eeng·te·re·*saa*·do/
interessada em … m/f   eeng·te·re·*saa*·daa eng …

I like the works of …
Eu gosto do   *e*·oo *gos*·to do
trabalho do/da ,,. m/f   traa·*baa*·lyo do/daa …

It reminds me of …
Lembra o/a … m/f   *leng*·braa o/aa …

… **art**	*arte … f*	*aarr*·te …
graphic	*gráfica*	*graa*·fee·kaa
impressionist	*impressionista*	eeng·pre·syo·*nees*·taa
indigenous	*indígena*	eeng·*dee*·zhe·naa
modern	*moderna*	mo·*derr*·naa
performance	*performance*	perr·*forr*·mang·se
popular	*popular*	*aarr*·te po·poo·*laarr*

tours

Can you recommend a ...?	Vocês podem recomendar um ...?	vo·ses po·deng he·ko·meng·daarr oom ...
When's the next ...?	Quando sai o próximo ...?	kwang·do sai o pro·see·mo ...
boat-trip	barco	baar·ko
day trip	passeio do dia	paa·se·yo do dee·aa
tour	tour	toor
Is ... included?	Inclui ...?	eeng·kloo·ee ...
accommodation	ospedagem	os·pe·daa·zheng
food	comida	ko·mee·daa
transport	transporte	trans·porr·te

The guide will pay.
O guia vai pagar.
o gee·aa vai paa·gaarr

The guide has paid.
O guia pagou.
o gee·aa paa·go

How long is the tour?
Quanto tempo dura o passeio?
kwang·to teng·po doo·raa o paa·say·o

What time should we be back?
A que horas estaremos de volta?
a ke aw·raas es·taa·re·mos de vol·taa

I'm with them.
Estou com eles.
es·to kong e·les

I've lost my group.
Perdi o meu grupo.
perr·dee o me·oo groo·po

I'm attending a ...	Estou participando de ...	es·to paar·tee·see·*pang*·do de ...
conference	uma conferência	oo·maa kong·fe·*reng*·syaa
course	um curso	oom *koor*·so
meeting	uma reunião	oo·maa he·oo·nee·*owng*
trade fair	uma feira de negócios	oo·maa *fay*·raa de ne·*go*·see·os

I'm with ...	Estou com ...	es·*to* kong ...
my colleagues	meus/minhas colegas de trabalho m/f	me·oos/mee·nyaas ko·*le*·gaas de traa·*baa*·lyo
(the UN)	(a ONU)	(aa *o*·noo)
(two) others	outros (dois)	*o*·tros (doys)

I'm alone.
Estou sozinho. es·*to* so·*zee*·nyo

I have an appointment with ...
Tenho uma hora marcada com ... teng·nyo oo·maa aw·raa maarr·*kaa*·daa kong ...

I'm staying at ..., room ...
Estou no ..., quarto ... es·*to* no ... *kwaarr*·to ...

I'm here for ...	Ficarei aqui por ...	fee·kaa·*ray* aa·*kee* porr ...
(two) days	(dois) dias	(doys) *dee*·aas
(two) weeks	(duas) semanas	(*doo*·aas) se·*ma*·naas

Here's my ...	Aqui está ...	a·kee es·taa ...
What's your ...?	Qual o seu ...?	kwow o se·oo ...
address	endereço	eng·de·re·so
business card	cartão de visitas	kaar·towng de vee·zee·taas
email address	endereço de e-mail	eng·de·re·so de e·mail
fax number	número de fax	noo·me·ro de faks
mobile number	número do celular	noo·me·ro do se·loo·laarr
pager number	número do pager	noo·me·ro do pa·zher
work number	telefone do trabalho	te·le·fo·ne do traa·baa·lyo
Where's the ...?	Onde é ...?	ong·de e ...
business centre	o centro de negócios	o seng·tro de ne·go·syos
conference	a conferência	aa kong·fe·reng·syaa
meeting	a reunião	a he·oo·nee·owng
I'd like to ...	Gostaria de ...	gos·taa·ree·aa de ...
check my email	checar meu e-mail	she·kaarr me·oo e·mail
send a fax	enviar um fax	eng·vee·aarr oom faks

That went very well.
Correu tudo muito bem. ko·he·oo too·do mweeng·to beng

Thank you for your time.
Obrigado/Obrigada pela atenção. m/f o·bree·gaa·do/o·bree·gaa·daa pe·laa aa·teng·sowng

Shall we go for a ...?	Vocês gostariam de ...?	vo·ses gos·taa·ree·ang de ...
drink	beber alguma coisa	be·berr ow·goo·maa koy·zaa
meal	jantar	zhang·taarr

| It's on me. | Eu convido. | e·oo kong·vee·do |

I have a disability.
Eu tenho uma   e·oo te·nyo oo·ma
deficiência física.   de·fee·see·eng·syaa fee·zee·kaa

I'm deaf.
Sou surdo.   so soorr·do

I have a hearing aid.
Uso aparelho para   oo·zo aa·paa·re·lyo paa·raa
surdez.   soor·des

I need assistance.
Preciso de ajuda.   pre·see·zo de a·zhoo·daa

What services do you have for people with a disability?
Quais os serviços que   kwais os serr·vee·sos ke
vocês oferecem para   vo·ses o·fe·re·seng paa·raa
pessoas com   pe·so·aas kong
deficiência física?   de·fee·see·eng·syaa fee·zee·kaa

Are there disabled toilets?
Tem banheiro para   teng ba·nyay·ro paa·raa
deficientes físicos?   de·fee·see·eng·tes fee·zee·kos

Are there rails in the bathroom?
Tem corrimão no   teng ko·hee·mowng no
banheiro?   ba·nyay·ro

Are there disabled parking spaces?
Tem vaga para   teng vaa·gaa paa·raa
deficientes físicos?   de·fee·see·eng·tes fee·zee·kos

Is there wheelchair access?
Tem acesso para cadeira de rodas?
teng aa·*se*·so *paa*·raa kaa·*day*·raa de ho·daas

How wide is the entrance?
Qual a largura da entrada?
kwow aa laarr·*goo*·raa daa eng·*traa*·daa

Is there a lift?
Tem elavador?
teng e·le·vaa·*dor*

How many steps are there?
Quantos degraus tem?
kwang·tos de·*grows* teng

Are guide dogs permitted?
É permitida a entrada de cães-guia?
e perr·mee·*tee*·daa aa eng·*traa*·daa de ka·*eengs*·gee·aa

Could you call me a disabled taxi?
Você poderia me chamar um taxi para deficientes físicos?
vo·*se* po·de·*ree*·aa me shaa·*maarr* oom *taak*·see *paa*·raa de·fee·see·*eng*·tes *fee*·zee·kos

Could you help me cross the street safely?
Você poderia me atravessar com segurança?
vo·*se* po·de·*ree*·aa me aa·traa·ve·*saarr* kong se·goo·*rang*·saa

Is there somewhere I can sit down?
Tem algum lugar onde eu posso sentar?
teng ow·*goom* loo·*gaarr* ong·de e·oo po·so seng·*taarr*

disabled person	*pessoa com deficiência física*	pe·*so*·aa kong de·fee·see·*eng*·syaa *fee*·zee·kaa
guide dog	*cães-guia* m	ka·*eengs*·gee·aa
older person	*pessoa idosa*	pe·*so*·aa ee·*do*·zaa
ramp	*rampa* f	*hang*·paa
walking frame	*andador* m	ang·daa·*dorr*
walking stick	*bengala* f	beng·*gaa*·laa
wheelchair	*cadeira* f *de rodas*	kaa·*day*·raa de ho·daas

travelling with children

viajando com crianças

Is there a ...?	Aqui tem ...?	aa·kee teng ...
baby change room	uma sala para trocar bebê	oo·maa saa·laa paa·raa tro·kaarr be·be
child discount	desconto para criança	des·kong·to paa·raa kree·ang·saa
child-minding service	serviço de babá	serr·vee·so de baa·baa
child-sized portion	porção para criança	porr·sowng paa·raa kree·ang·saa
children's menu	cardápio para criança	kaar·daa·pyo paa·raa kree·an·saa
creche	creche	kre·she
family ticket	passagem para familia	paa·saa·zheng paa·raa faa·mee·lyaa

Where's the nearest ...?	Qual ... mais perto?	kwow ... mais perr·to
drinking fountain	o bebedouro	o be·be·do·ro
park	o parque	o paarr·ke
playground	o playground	o play·grownd
swimming pool	a piscina	aa pee·see·naa
tap	a torneira	aa torr·nay·raa
theme park	o parque de diversões	o paarr·ke de dee·ver·soyngs
toyshop	a loja de brinquedos	aa lo·zhaa de breeng·ke·dos

I need a/an …	Preciso de …	pre·see·zo de …
baby seat	um assento de criança	oom aa·seng·to de kree·ang·saa
(English-speaking) babysitter	uma babá (que fale ingles)	oo·maa baa·baa (ke faa·le eeng·gles)
booster seat	assento de elevação	aa·seng·to de e·le·vaa·sowng
highchair	uma cadeira de criança	oo·maa kaa·day·raa de kree·ang·saa
plastic sheet	um lençol plástico	oom leng·sol plaas·tee·ko
plastic bag	um saco plástico	oom saa·ko plaas·tee·ko
potty	um troninho	oom tro·nee·nyo
pram/pusher	carrinho de bebê	kaa·hee·nyo de be·be
sick bag	saco de vomito	saa·ko de vo·mee·to

Do you sell …?	Vocês vendem …?	vo·ses veng·deng …
baby pain killers	analgésico para bebê	aa·naal·zhe·zee·ko paa·raa be·be
baby wipes	toalha molhada de bebê	to·aa·lyaa mo·lyaa·daa de be·be
disposable nappies	fraldas descartáveis	frow·daas des·kaarr·taa·vays
tissues	lencinhos de papel	leng·see·nyos de paa·pel

Do you hire prams?
Vocês alugam carrinho de bebê?
vo·ses aa·loo·gang kaa·hee·nyo de be·be

Are there any good places to take children around here?
Tem algum lugar agradável para levar as crianças por aqui perto?
teng ow·goom loo·gaarr aa·graa·daa·vel paa·raa le·vaarr aas kree·ang·saas porr aa·kee perr·to

Is there space for a pram?
Tem espaço para o　　　　teng es·*paa*·so *paa*·raa o
carrinho de bebê?　　　　kaa·*hee*·nyo de be·*be*

Are children allowed?
É permitida a　　　　　e perr·mee·*tee*·daa aa
entrada de crianças?　　eng·*traa*·daa de kree·*ang*·saas

Where can I change a nappy?
Onde posso trocar　　　ong·de po·so tro·*kaarr*
a fralda?　　　　　　aa *frow*·daa

Do you mind if I breast-feed here?
Você se importa se　　　vo·se se eeng·*porr*·taa se
eu amamentar aqui?　　e·oo aa·maa·meng·*taarr* aa·*kee*

Could I have some paper and pencils, please?
Pode me dar papel e　　po·de me daarr paa·*pel* e
lapis, por favor?　　　*laa*·pees porr faa·*vorr*

Is this suitable for (five-)year-old children?
Isto é adequado para　　*ees*·to e *aa*·de·*kwaa*·do *paa*·raa
crianças de (cinco)　　　kree·*ang*·saas de (*seeng*·ko)
anos de idade?　　　　*a*·nos de ee·*daa*·de

Do you know a dentist/doctor who is good with children?
Voce conhece algum　　vo·*se* ko·*nye*·se ow·*goom*
médico/dentista bom　　me·dee·ko/deng·*tees*·taa bong
para crianças?　　　　paa·raa kree·*ang*·saas

For children's sicknesses, see **health**, page 177.

---

brazilian family tree

Ancient Celtic myths refer to the mist-shrouded island of Hy Brazil – a stormless haven somewhere in the Atlantic. The island appeared on charts in the 14th century and was to remain on British maps as late as the 1870s. Some scholars have suggested that Portuguese explorers were familiar with the Celtic stories and named the South American country after Hy Brazil. A more accepted theory is that Brazil is derived from the name of a dye-producing East Indian tree. When a similar tree was discovered in the new land it became Brazil's first successful export and lent the country its present name.

talking with children

Do you like ...?	Você gosta ...?	vo·se gos·taa ...
school	da escola	daa es·ko·laa
sport	de esporte	de es·porr·te
your teacher	do seu professor m	do se·oo pro·fe·sorr
	da sua professora f	da soo·aa pro·fe·so·raa

When's your birthday?
Quando é o seu   kwang·do e o se·oo
aniversário?   aa·nee·ver·saa·ryo

Do you go to school?
Você vai para escola?   vo·se vai paa·raa es·ko·laa

What grade are you in?
Em que ano você está?   eng ke a·no vo·se es·taa

What do you do after school?
O que você faz depois da   o ke vo·se faaz de·poys daa
escola?   es·ko·laa

Do you learn English?
Você aprende ingles?   vo·se aa·preng·de eeng·gles

I come from very far away.
Eu venho de muito   e·oo veng·nyo de mweeng·to
longe.   long·zhe

Are you lost?
Você está perdido/   vo·se es·taa perr·dee·do/
perdida? m/f   perr·dee·daa

basics

conhecimentos básicos

Yes.	*Sim.*	seeng
No.	*Não.*	nowng
Please.	*Por favor.*	por faa-*vorr*
Thank you (very much).	*(Muito) Obrigado/ Obrigada.* m/f	*(mweeng*-to) o-bree-*gaa*-do/ o-bree-*gaa*-daa
You're welcome.	*De nada.*	de *naa*-daa
Excuse me.	*Com licença.*	kong lee-*seng*-saa
Sorry.	*Desculpa.*	des-*kool*-paa

greetings & goodbyes

saudações & despedidas

A greeting kiss on the cheek Is quite common between women, and also between members of the opposite sex, even on first encounters. The number of kisses ranges from one to three, depending on the region. Shaking hands is the normal greeting between men, though a hug between friends is not uncommon.

Hello.	*Olá.*	o-*laa*
Hi.	*Oi.*	oy

Good ...		
afternoon	*Boa tarde.*	bo-aa *taarr*-de
day	*Bom dia.*	bong *dee*-aa
evening	*Boa noite.*	bo-aa *noy*-te
morning	*Bom dia.*	bong *dee*-aa

How are you?
  Como vai?   ko·mo vai

Fine, and you?
  Bem, e você?   beng e vo·se

What's your name?
  Qual é o seu nome?   kwow e o se·oo no·me

My name is …
  Meu nome é …   me·oo no·me e …

I'd like to introduce you to …
  Eu gostaria de te   e·oo gos·taa·ree·aa de te
  apresentar ao/à … m/f   aa·pre·zeng·taarr aa·o/aa …

I'm pleased to meet you.
  Prazer em conhecê-lo/la. m/f   praa·zerr eng ko·nye·se·lo/laa

This is my …	*Este é meu … m*	*es·te e me·oo …*
	Esta é minha … f	*es·taa e mee·nyaa …*
colleague	*colega m&f*	ko·le·gaa
daughter	*filha*	fee·lyaa
friend	*amigo/*	aa·mee·go/
	amiga m/f	aa·mee·gaa
husband	*marido*	maa·ree·do
partner	*companheiro/*	kong·pa·nyay·ro/
(intimate)	*companheira m/f*	kong·pa·nyay·raa
son	*filho*	fee·lyo
wife	*esposa*	es·po·zaa

For family members, see **family,** page 97.

| **See you later.** | *Até mais tarde.* | aa·te mais taarr·de |
| **Goodbye.** | *Tchau.* | tee·show |

---

many thanks

You'll notice that there are two words for 'thank you' in Brazilian Potuguese, *obrigado* and *obrigada*. Their use is determined by the gender of the person doing the thanking. A male uses *obrigado* and a female uses *obrigada*.

addressing people

It's always best to address older people using *Senhor* or *Senhora*. You'll notice that first names are used with titles, often more so than family names.

Mr/Sir	*Senhor*	se·*nyorr*
Mrs/Ms	*Senhora*	se·*nyo*·raa
Miss	*Senhorita*	se·nyo·*ree*·taa
Doctor	*Doutor/Doutora* m/f	do·*torr*/do·to·raa
Professor	*Professor/*	pro·fe·*sorr*/
	Professora m/f	pro·fe·so·raa
young man/woman	*moço/moça* m/f	mo·so/mo·sa
mate	*cara* m	*kaa*·raa

making conversation

How's everything?
  Tudo bem? — *too*·do beng

Do you live here?
  Você mora aqui? — vo·*se mo*·raa aa·*kee*

It's so hot/cold !
  Que calor/frio ! — ke kaa·*lorr*/*free*·o

It's so quiet here.
  Aqui é tão tranquilo. — a·*kee* e towng trang·*kwee*·lo

What a beautiful view.
  Que vista linda. — ke *vees*·taa *leeng*·daa

This is great!
  Isso é demais! — *ee*·so e de·*mais*

Where are you going?
  Onde você está indo? — *ong*·de vo·*se* es·*taa eeng*·do

What are you doing?
  O que você está fazendo? — o ke vo·*se* es·*taa* faa·*zeng*·do

meeting people

Do you like it here?
Você gosta daqui? · vo·*se* gos·taa daa·*kee*

I love it here.
Eu adoro. · e·oo aa·*do*·ro

What's this called?
Como se chama isto? · *ko*·mo se *sha*·maa ees·to

Can I take a photo (of you)?
Posso tirar uma foto · *po*·so tee·*raarr* oo·maa *fo*·to
(de você)? · (de vo·*se*)

That's (beautiful), isn't it!
Isto é (lindo) você · ees·to e (*leeng*·do) vo·*se*
não acha? · nowng *aa*·shaa

Just joking.
Estou brincando. · es·*to* breeng·*kang*·do

Are you here on holiday?
Você está aqui em férias? · vo·*se* es·*taa* a·*kee* eng *fe*·ree·aas

gringo

Chances are high that when travelling in Brazil, you'll hear or be addressed as *gringo* (or *gringa* for women). In Brazilian Portuguese, the term refers to almost anyone who is not Brazilian (including people from other countries in Latin America). It's generally not an insult (although if it's modified by *burro/burra* m/f, 'stupid', then it probably is!), so there's usually no need to take offence.

I'm here ... · Estou aqui ... · es·*to* a·*kee* ...
  for a holiday · em férias · eng *fe*·ree·aas
  on business · à negócios · aa ne·*go*·syos
  to study · à estudos · aa es·*too*·dos

How long are you here for?
Quanto tempo você vai · *kwang*·to *teng*·po vo·*se* vai
ficar aqui? · fee·*kaarr* aa·*kee*

I'm here for (four) weeks/days.
Ficarei aqui (quatro) · fee·kaa·*ray* aa·*kee* (*kwaa*·tro)
semanas/dias. · se·*ma*·naas/*dee*·aas

What a beautiful day!
  Que lindo dia!   ke *leeng*-do *dee*-aa

Want to talk about the weather? See **outdoors**, page 138.

local talk		
Hey!	*Ei!*	ay
Great!	*Ótimo!*	o-tee-mo
Sure.	*É claro.*	e *klaa*-ro
Maybe.	*Talvez.*	taal-*vez*
No way!	*De jeito nenhum!*	de *zhay*-to ne-*yoom*
Just a minute.	*Só um minuto.*	so oom mee-*noo*-to
It's OK.	*Está bom.*	es-*taa* bong
Good luck!	*Boa sorte!*	*bo*-aa *sorr*-te
No problem.	*Não tem problema.*	nowng teng pro-*ble*-maa

nationalities

nacionalidades

Where are you from?
  De onde você é?   de *ong*-de vo-*se* e

I'm from ...	*Eu sou ...*	e-oo so ...
Australia	*da Austrália*	daa ows-*traa*-lyaa
Canada	*do Canadá*	do kaa-naa-*daa*
Singapore	*de Cingapura*	de seeng-gaa-*poo*-raa

age

idade

How old ...?	*Quantos anos ...?*	*kwang*-tos *a*-nos ...
are you	*você tem*	vo-*se* teng
is he/she	*ele/ela tem* m/f	*e*-le/*e*-laa teng

meeting people

95

I'm ... years old.
Tenho ... anos.   te·nyo ... a·nos

He/She is ... years old.
Ele/Ela tem ... anos. m/f   e·le/e·laa teng ... a·nos

Too old!
Muito velho/velha! m/f   mweeng·to ve·lyo/ve·lya

I'm younger than I look.
Sou mais novo/nova do   so mais no·vo/no·vaa do
que aparento. m/f   ke aa·paa·reng·to

For your age, see **numbers & amounts**, page 29.

occupations & studies

ocupação & educação

What's your occupation?
Você trabalha em que?   vo·se traa·baa·lyaa eng ke

I'm a ...	*Eu sou ...*	e·oo so ...
chef	*chefe* m&f *de cozinha*	she·fe de ko·zee·nyaa
computer programmer	*programador/ programadora de computação* m/f	pro·gra·maa·dorr/ pro·gra·maa·do·raa de kong·poo·ta·sowng
exporter	*exportador/ exportadora* m/f	es·porr·taa·dorr/ es·porr·taa·do·raa
journalist	*jornalista* m&f	zhor·naa·lees·taa
teacher	*professor/ professora* m/f	pro·fe·sorr/ pro·fe·so·raa

I work in ...	*Trabalho na área de ...*	traa·baa·lyo naa aa·re·aa de ...
administration	*administração*	aad·mee·nees· traa·sowng
health	*saúde*	saa·oo·de
sales & marketing	*vendas e marketing*	veng·daas e maarr·ke·teeng

I'm ...	Eu ...	e·oo ...
self-employed	sou autônomo/	so ow·to·no·mo/
	autônoma m/f	ow·to·no·maa
unemployed	estou	es·to
	desempregado/	de·zeng·pre·gaa·do/
	desempregada m/f	de·zeng·pre·gaa·daa

What are you studying?

O que você está	o ke vo·se es·taa
estudando?	es·too·dang·do

I'm studying ...	Estou estudando ...	es·to es·too·dang·do ...
humanities	ciências	see·eng·syaas
	humanas	oo·ma·naas
Portuguese	português	porr·too·ges
science	ciências	see·eng·syaas

For other occupations and areas of study, see the **dictionary**.

family

Do you have a ...?	Você tem ...?	vo·se teng ...
I (don't) have a ...	Eu (não) tenho ...	e·oo (nowng) te·nyo ...
brother	irmão	eerr·mowng
daughter	filha	fee·lyaa
family	família	fa·mee·lyaa
father	pai	pai
grandfather	avô	aa·vo
grandmother	avó	aa·vaw
granddaughter	neta	ne·taa
grandson	neto	ne·to
husband	marido	maa·ree·do
mother	mãe	maing
partner	companheiro/	kong·pa·nyay·ro/
(intimate)	companheira m/f	kong·pa·nyay·raa
sister	irmã	eer·mang
son	filho	fee·lyo
wife	esposa	es·po·zaa

Are you married?
Você é casado/casada? m/f   vo·*se* e kaa·*zaa*·do/ kaa·*zaa*·daa

I live with someone.
Moro com uma pessoa.   *mo*·ro kong *oo*·maa pe·*so*·aa

	Eu sou ...	*e*·oo so ...
I'm ...		
married	*casado/*	kaa·*zaa*·do/
	casada m/f	kaa·*zaa*·daa
separated	*separado/*	se·paa·*raa*·daa
	separada m/f	se·paa·*raa*·do/
single	*solteiro/*	sol·*tay*·ro/
	solteira m/f	sol·*tay*·raa

farewells

Tomorrow is my last day here.
Amanhã é o meu   a·ma·*nyang* e o *me*·oo
ultimo dia aqui.   *ool*·tee·mo *dee*·aa aa·*kee*

	Aqui está meu ...	a·*kee* es·*taa* me·oo ...
Here's my ...		
What's your ...?	*Qual o seu ...?*	kwow o *se*·oo ...
address	*endereço*	eng·de·*re*·so
email address	*endereço de*	eng·de·*re*·so de
	e-mail	e-*mail*
phone number	*número de*	*noo*·me·ro de
	telephone	te·le·*fo*·ne

If you come to (Scotland), you can stay with me.
Se você for à (Escócia)   se vo·*se* forr aa (es·*ko*·syaa)
pode ficar na minha   *po*·de fee·*kaarr* naa *mee*·nyaa
casa.   *kaa*·zaa

Keep in touch!
Mantenha contato!   mang·*te*·nyaa kong·*taa*·to

It's been great meeting you.
Foi ótimo te conhecer.   foy o·*tee*·mo te ko·nye·*serr*

interests

interesses

common interests

interesses comuns

What do you do in your spare time?
O que você gosta de fazer nas horas livres? — o ke vo·*se gos*·taa de faa·*zerr* naas *aw*·raas *lee*·vres

Do you like ...?	*Você gosta de ...?*	vo·*se gos*·taa de ...
I (don't) like ...	*Eu (não) gosto de ...*	*e*·oo (nowng) *gos*·to de ...
arts and crafts	*artesanato* m	aarr·te·zaa·*naa*·to
Brazilian music	*música* f *brasileira*	*moo*·zee·kaa braa·zee·*lay*·raa
capoeira	*capoeira* f	kaa·po·*ay*·raa
carnival	*carnaval* m	kaarr·naa·*vow*
cooking	*cozinhar*	ko·zee·*nyaarr*
dancing	*dançar*	dang·*saarr*
drawing	*desenhar*	de·ze·*nyaarr*
films	*cinema* f	see·*ne*·maa
gardening	*jardinagem* f	zhaarr·dee·*naa*·zheng
hiking	*fazer caminhadas*	faa·*zerr* kaa·mee·*nyaa*·daas
live shows	*show* m *ao vivo*	show ow *vee*·vo
music	*música* f	*moo*·zee·kaa
painting	*pintar*	peeng·*taarr*
photography	*fotografia* f	fo·to·graa·*fee*·aa
reading	*ler*	lerr
shopping	*fazer compras*	faa·*zerr* kong·praas
socialising	*socializar*	so·see·aa·lee·*zaarr*
sport	*esporte* m	es·*porr*·te
travelling	*viajar*	vee·aa·*zhaarr*

For sporting activities, see **sport**, page 125.

interests

99

music

Do you …?	Você …?	vo·se …
dance	dança	dang·saa
go to concerts	vai à shows	vai aa shows
listen to music	escuta música	es·koo·taa moo·zee·kaa
play an instrument	toca algum instrumento	to·kaa ow·goom eengs·troo·meng·to
sing	canta	kang·taa
What … do you like?	De que … você gosta?	de ke … vo·se gos·taa
bands	bandas de música	bang·daas de moo·zee·kaa
music	música	moo·zee·kaa
singers	cantores	kang·to·res

kung fu dancing

Capoeira originated as an African martial art developed by slaves to fight their masters. It was disguised with the introduction of musical accompaniment to make it seem like dance. In its modern form, it combines elements of dance and fighting and is known for its fluid and circular movements.

classical music	música f clássica	moo·zee·kaa klaa·see·kaa
blues	blues m	blooz
electronic music	música f eletrônica	moo·zee·kaa e·le·tro·nee·kaa
jazz	jazz m	zhez
pop	pop m	po·pee
rock	rock m	ho·kee
traditional music	música f tradicional	moo·zee·kaa traa·dee·syo·now
world music	world music m	wol·dee mee·oo·zeek

Planning to go to a concert? See **tickets**, page 38 and **going out**, page 109.

cinema & theatre

I feel like going to a ...	Estou com vontade de ir ...	es·to kong vong·taa·de de eerr ...
Did you like the ...?	Você gostou ...?	vo·se gos·to ...
ballet	do balé	do baa·le
film	do filme	do feel·me
play	da peça	daa pe·saa
I thought it was ...	Eu achei ...	e·oo aa·shay ...
excellent	excelente	es·se·leng·te
long	longo	long·go
OK	bom	bong

What's showing at the cinema/theatre tonight?
O que está passando no cinema/teatro hoje à noite?

o ke es·taa paa·sang·do no see·ne·maa/te·aa·tro o·zhee aa noy·te

Is it in English?
É em ingles?

e eng eeng·gles

Does it have (English) subtitles?
Tem sub-título (em inglês?)

teng soo·bee·tee·too·lo (eng eeng·gles)

I want to sell this ticket.
Quero vender este ingresso.

ke·ro veng·derr es·te eeng·gre·so

Is this seat taken?
Este lugar está vago?

es·te loo·gaarr es·taa vaa·go

Have you seen ...?
Você viu ...?

vo·se vee·oo ...

Who's in it?
É com quem?

e kong keng

It stars ...
É com ...

e kong ...

interests

101

I (don't)	Eu (não)	e·oo (nowng)
like ...	gosto de ...	gos·to de ...
action movies	filmes de ação	feel·mes de aa·sowng
animated films	filmes de animação	feel·mes de aa·nee·maa·sowng
Brazilian cinema	cinema (brasileiro)	see·ne·maa (braa·zee·lay·ro)
comedies	comédias	ko·me·dyaas
documentaries	documentários	do·koo·meng·taa·ree·os
drama	drama	dra·maa
film noir	filme noir	feel·me noir
horror movies	filme de terror	feel·me de te·horr
sci-fi	ficção científica	feek·sowng see·eng·tee·fee·kaa
thrillers	suspense	soos·peng·se
war movies	filme de guerra	feel·me de ge·haa

feelings & opinions

sentimentos & opiniões

feelings

sentimentos

Some feelings (like those in the first list) are described using 'be', *estar*, while others (see the second list) use 'be with', *estar com*.

Are you ...?	Você está ...?	vo·*se* es·*taa* ...
I'm (not) ...	(Não) Estou ...	(nowng) es·*to* ...
annoyed	*irritado/*	ee·hee·*taa*·do/
	irritada m/f	ee·hee·*taa*·daa
happy	*feliz*	fe·*lees*
sad	*triste*	*trees*·te
surprised	*surpreso/*	soorr·*pre*·zo/
	supresa m/f	soorr·*pre*·zaa
tired	*cansado/*	kang·*saa*·do/
	cansada m/f	kang·*saa*·daa
worried	*preocupado/*	pre·o·koo·*paa*·do/
	preocupada m/f	pre·o·koo·*paa*·daa

Are you ...?	Você está com ...?	vo·*se* es·*taa* kong ...
I'm (not) ...	(Não) Estou com ...	(nowng) es·*to* kong...
cold	*frio*	*free*·o
embarrassed	*vergonha*	verr·*go*·nyaa
hot	*calor*	kaa·*lorr*
hungry	*fome*	*fo*·me
in a hurry	*pressa*	*pre*·saa
thirsty	*sede*	*se*·de

If feeling unwell, see **health**, page 177.

feelings & opinions

103

intense feelings		
a little	*um pouco*	oom *po·*ko
I'm a little sad.	*Estou um pouco triste.*	es·*to* oom po·ko *trees*·te
very	*muito/ muita* m/f	*mweeng·*to/ mweeng·taa
I feel very lucky.	*Estou com muita sorte.*	es·*to* kong mweeng·taa *sorr*·te
extremely	*super*	soo·perr
I'm extremely happy.	*Estou super feliz.*	es·*to* soo·perr fe·*lees*

opinions

opiniões

Did you like it?
Você gostou?   vo·*se* gos·*to*

What do you think of it?
O que você achou?   o ke vo·*se* aa·*sho·*oo

I thought it was …	*Achei …*	aa·*shay* …
It's …	*É …*	e …
awful	*péssimo/ péssima* m/f	*pe·*see·mo/ *pe·*see·ma
beautiful	*lindo/ linda* m/f	*leeng·*do/ *leeng·*daa
boring	*chato*	*shaa·*to
great	*ótimo/ótima* m/f	*o·*tee·mo/*o·*tee·ma
interesting	*interessante*	eeng·te·re·*sang·*te
OK	*bom*	bong
too expensive	*muito caro/cara* m/f	*mweeng·*to *kaa·*ro/*kaa·*raa

SOCIAL

104

politics & social issues

Who do you vote for?
Em quem você vota? eng keng vo·se *vo*·taa

I support the ...	*Eu voto para o*	e·oo *vo*·to paa·raa o
party.	*partido ...*	paarr·*tee*·do ...
I'm a member	*Eu sou membro*	e·oo so *meng*·bro
of the ... party.	*do partido ...*	do paarr·*tee*·do ...
communist	*comunista*	ko·moo·*nees*·taa
conservative	*conservador*	kong·serr·vaa·*dorr*
democratic	*democrata*	de·mo·*kraa*·taa
green	*verde*	*verr*·de
liberal	*liberal*	lee·be·*row*
social	*democrata-*	de·mo·*kraa*·taa·
democratic	*social*	so·see·*ow*
socialist	*socialista*	so·see·aa·*lees*·taa
workers	*dos*	dos
	trabalhadores	traa·baa·lyaa·*do*·res

Did you hear about ...?
Você ouviu falar ...? vo·*se* o·*vee*·oo faa·*laarr* ...

Do you agree with it?
Você concorda com isto? vo·*se* kong·*korr*·daa kong *ees*·to

I (don't) agree with ...
Eu (não) concordo e·oo (nowng) kong·*korr*·do
com ... kong ...

How do people feel about ...?
O que as pessoas o ke aas pe·*so*·aas
acham ...? *aa*·shang ...

How can we protest against ...?
Como podemos ko·mo po·*de*·mos
protestar contra ...? pro·tes·*taarr* kong·traa ...

How can we support ...?
Como podemos ko·mo po·*de*·mos
apoiar ...? aa·po·*yaarr* ...

abortion	aborto m	aa·*borr*·to
animal rights	*direitos* m *dos animais*	dee·*ray*·tos dos aa·nee·*mais*
crime	*crime* m	*kree*·me
discrimination	*descriminação* f	des·kree·mee·na·*sowng*
drugs	*drogas* f pl	*dro*·gaas
the economy	*a economia* f	aa e·ko·no·*mee*·aa
education	*educação* f	e·doo·kaa·*sowng*
the environment	*o meio ambiente* m	o *may*·o ang·bee·*eng*·te
equal opportunity	*direitos* m pl *iguais*	dee·*ray*·tos ee·*gwais*
euthanasia	*euthanasia* f	e·oo·taa·*naa*·zyaa
globalisation	*globalização* f	glo·baa·lee·zaa·*sowng*
human rights	*direitos* m pl *humanos*	dee·*ray*·tos oo·*ma*·nos
immigration	*imigração* f	ee·mee·graa·*sowng*
income distribution·	*distribuição* f *de renda*	dees·tree·boo·ee·*sowng* de *heng*·daa
inequality	*desigualdade* f	de·zee·gwow·*daa*·de
inflation	*inflação* f	eeng·flaa·*sowng*
party politics	*política* f *partidária*	po·*lee*·tee·kaa paarr·tee·*daa*·ree·aa
privatisation	*privatização* f	pree·vaa·tee·zaa·*sowng*
racism	*racismo* m	haa·*sees*·mo
sexism	*machismo* m	maa·*shees*·mo
slums	*favelas* f pl	faa·*ve*·laas
social disparity	*disparidade* f *social*	dees·paa·ree·*daa*·de so·see·*ow*
social welfare	*justiça* f *social*	zhoos·*tee*·sa so·see·*ow*
unemployment	*desemprego* m	de·*zeng*·pre·go
work safety	*segurança* f *no trabalho*	se·goo·*rang*·saa no traa·*baa*·lyo
workers rights	*direitos* m *dos trabalhadores*	dee·*ray*·tos dos traa·baa·lyaa·*do*·res

the environment

Is there a … problem here?
Aqui tem problema de …?   a·*kee* teng pro·*ble*·maa de …

What should be done about …?
O que deveria ser feito   o ke de·ve·*ree*·aa serr *fay*·to
sobre …?   *so*·bre …

conservation	*conservação* f	kong·ser·va·*sowng*
deforestatlon	*desflorestamento* m	des·flo·res·taa·*meng*·to
drought	*seca* f	se·kaa
ecosystem	*eco-sistema* f	e·ko·sees·*te*·maa
endangered	*espécles* f pl	es·*pe*·syes
specles	*ameaçadas de*	aa·me·a·*saa*·daas de
	extinção	es·teeng·*sowng*
genetically	*alimentos* m pl	aa·lee·*meng*·tos
modified food	*geneticamente*	ge·ne·tee·kaa·*meng*·te
	modificados	mo·dee·fee·*kaa*·dos
hunting	*caça* f	*kaa*·saa
hydroelectricity	*energia* f	e·nerr·*zhee*·aa
	hidroelétrica	ee·dro·e·*le*·tree·kaa
irrigation	*irrigação* f	ee·hee·gaa·*sowng*
nuclear energy	*energia* f	e·nerr·*zhee*·aa
	nuclear	noo·kle·*aarr*
nuclear testing	*teste* m *nuclear*	*tes*·te noo·kle·*aarr*
ozone layer	*camada* f *de*	kaa·*maa*·daa de
	ozônio	o·zo·nee·o
pesticides	*pesticidas* f pl	pes·tee·*see*·daas
pollution	*poluição* f	po·loo·ee·*sowng*
recycling	*programa* f *de*	pro·*gra*·maa de
programme	*reciclagem*	he·see·*klaa*·zheng
toxic waste	*resíduos* m pl *tóxicos*	he·*zee*·dwos *tok*·see·kos
water supply	*abastecimento* m	aa·baas·te·see·*meng*·to
	de água	de *aa*·gwaa

Is this a protected …?	Está é …	es·taa e …
forest	uma floresta protegida	oo·maa flo·res·taa pro·te·zhee·daa
species	uma espécie protegida	oo·maa es·pe·sye pro·te·zhee·daa

indigenous languages

During the early days of colonisation, many Portuguese missionaries and colonists learnt how to speak *Tupinambá*, an indigenous language spoken along the Brazilian coast. Use of the language became so widespread within the colony that it became known as *Língua Brasilica* (Brazilian language) and later *Língua Geral* (general language). *Tupinambá* has since become extinct although *Nheengatu*, a derivation of the *Língua Geral*, is still spoken in the Negro River basin. It wasn't until the mid-eighteenth century that the Portuguese language truly began to predominate and hundreds of local languages were slowly wiped out by colonial expansion. Historians have estimated that, prior to the arrival of the Portuguese, there were probably 400 or 500 languages spoken within the present boundaries of Brazil. Today less than 200 remain. Most of these are facing extinction, although the *Guaraní* language, spoken by over 30,000 people, is showing little evidence of decline.

Indigenous languages, particularly *Tupinambá*, have had a significant influence on Brazilian Portuguese. The words *jabuti* (turtle), *jacaré* (alligator), *capim* (grass), *cipó* (vine) and *piranha* (piranha) all originate from *Tupinambá*. Other Brazilian Portuguese words derived from indigenous languages include *abacaxi* (pineapple), *mandioca* (manioc flour), *caju* (cashew) and *tatu* (armadillo).

SOCIAL

where to go

para onde ir

What's there to do in the evenings?
O que se tem para fazer à noite?
o ke se teng *paa*·raa faa·*zerr* aa *noy*·te

What's on ...?	*O que está acontecendo ...?*	o ke es·*taa* aa·kong·te·*seng*·do ...
locally	*aqui perto*	aa·*kee* perr·to
this weekend	*neste final de semana*	nes·te fee·*now* de se·*ma*·naa
today	*hoje*	o·zhe
tonight	*à noite*	aa *noy*·te
Where can I find ...?	*Onde posso encontrar ...?*	ong·de po·so eng·kong·*traar* ...
clubs	*um lugar para dançar*	oom loo·*gaarr* paa·raa dang·*saarr*
gay venues	*lugares gays*	loo·*gaa*·res gays
places to eat	*lugares para comer*	loo·*gaa*·res paa·raa ko·*merr*
pubs	*um bar*	oom baarr
Is there a local ... guide?	*Existe algum guia de ... dessa área?*	e·*zees*·te ow·*goom gee*·aa de ... *de*·saa *aa*·re·aa
entertainment	*entretenimento*	eng·tre·te·nee·*meng*·to
film	*cinema*	see·*ne*·maa
gay	*de lugares gays*	de loo·*gaa*·res gays
music	*música*	*moo*·zee·kaa

I feel like going to a ...	Estou com vontade de ir ...	es·to kong vong·taa·de de eerr ...
ballet	ao balé	ow baa·le
bar	a um bar	aa oom baarr
cafe	a um café	aa oom kaa·fe
concert	a um show	aa oom show
film	ao cinema	ow see·ne·maa
karaoke bar	a um karaoke	aa oom kaa·raa·o·ke
nightclub	a uma boate	aa oo·maa bo·aa·te
party	a uma festa	aa oo·maa fes·taa
performance	a uma performance	aa oo·maa perr·forr·mang·se
play	a uma obra	aa oo·maa o·braa
pub	a um bar	aa oom baarr
restaurant	a um restaurante	aa oom hes·tow·rang·te

For more on bars and drinks, see **eating out,** page 149.

invitations

What are you doing ...?	O que você está fazendo ...?	o ke vo·se es·taa faa·zeng·do ...
now	agora	aa·go·raa
this weekend	neste final de semana	nes·te fee·now de se·ma·naa
tonight	hoje à noite	o·zhe aa noy·te

Would you like to go (for a) ...?	Você gostaria de ir ...?	vo·se gos·taa·ree·aa de irr ...
chat somewhere	bater um papo em algum lugar	baa·terr oom paa·po eng ow·goom loo·gaarr
coffee	tomar um café	to·maarr oom kaa·fe
drink	beber alguma coisa	be·berr ow·goo·maa koy·zaa
meal	jantar	zhang·taarr
walk	caminhar	kaa·mee·nyaarr

I feel like going ... dancing	Eu gostaria de dançar ...	e·oo gos·taa·ree·aa de dang·saarr ...
samba	samba	sang·ba
forró	forró	fo·ho
gafieira	gafieira	gaa·fee·ay·raa
lambada	lambada	lang·baa·daa

My round.
Minha vez.
mee·nyaa vez

Do you know a good restaurant?
Você conhece um bom restaurante?
vo·se ko·nye·se oom bom hes·tow·rang·te

Do you want to come to the concert with me?
Você quer vir ao show comigo?
vo·se kerr veerr ow show ko·mee·go

We're having a party.
Estamos dando uma festa.
es·ta·mos dang·do oo·maa fes·taa

You should come.
Você deveria vir.
vo·se de·ve·ree·aa veer

responding to invitations

Sure!
Claro!
klaa·ro

Yes, I'd love to.
Sim, adoraria.
seeng aa·do·raa·ree·aa

That's very kind of you.
É muito gentil de sua parte.
e mweeng·to zheng·teel de soo·aa paarr·te

Where shall we go?
Onde podemos ir?
ong·de po·de·mos eerr

No, I'm afraid I can't.
Não, infelizmente não posso.
nowng eeng·fe·lees·meng·te nowng po·so

going out

Sorry, I can't sing/dance.
    Desculpe, mas eu   des·*kool*·pe mas *e*·oo
    não sei cantar/   nowng say kang·*taarr*/
    dançar.   dang·*saarr*

What about tomorrow?
    Que tal amanhã?   ke tow aa·ma·*nyang*

arranging to meet

What time will we meet?
    A que horas nos   aa ke *aw*·raas nos
    encontramos?   eng·kong·*tra*·mos

Where will we meet?
    Onde vamos nos   *ong*·de *va*·mos nos
    encontrar?   eng·kong·*traarr*

Let's meet	*Vamos nos*	*va*·mos nos
at …	*encontrar …*	eng·kong·*traarr* …
(eight) o'clock	*às (oito) horas*	aas (*oy*·to) *aw*·raas
the (entrance)	*na (entrada)*	naa (eng·*traa*·daa)

I'll pick you up.
    Eu te pego.   *e*·oo te *pe*·go

Are you ready?
    Você está pronto/   vo·*se* es·*taa prong*·to/
    pronta? m/f   *prong*·taa

I'm ready.
    Estou pronto/pronta. m/f   es·*to prong*·to/*prong*·taa

I'll be coming later.
    Eu vou mais tarde.   *e*·oo vo mais *taarr*·de

Where will you be?
Onde você vai estar?   ong·de vo·*se* vai es·*taarr*

If I'm not there by (nine), don't wait for me.
Se eu não chegar   se e·oo nowng she·*gaarr*
até às (nove), não me   aa·*te* aas (*no*·ve) nowng me
espere mais.   es·*pe*·re mais

OK!
Tá bom!   taa bong

I'll see you then.
Te vejo depois.   te ve·zho de·*poys*

See you later/tomorrow.
Até mais tarde/   aa·*te* mais *taarr*·de/
amanhã.   aa·ma·*nyang*

I'm looking forward to it.
Vou aguardar   vo aa·gwaar·*daarr*
ansiosamente.   ang·see·o·zaa·*meng*·te

Sorry I'm late.
Desculpe o atraso.   des·*kool*·pe o aa·*traa*·zo

Never mind.
Não tem problema.   nowng teng pro·*ble*·ma

---

samba jamming

From the religious dances of *Candomblé* to the martial arts movements of *capoeira*, dancing finds its way into almost all aspects of the Brazilian lifestyle. No dance has achieved the same popularity as *samba*, a composite of diverse indigenous, African and European dancing styles.

The origins of *samba* lie in a fusion between the indigenous *lundu* dance and the *batuque*, a circular dance practiced by African slaves. By the late-nineteenth century, these styles adopted European characteristics to become *mesemba* and eventually modern *samba*. The percussive music of *samba* is equally rich in its origins and influences.

Spontaneous *samba* jam sessions called *batucadas* erupt in the streets on occasions of national celebration.

going out

113

drugs

I don't take drugs.
  Eu não uso drogas.   e·oo nowng *oo·*zo *dro·*gaas

I take ... occasionally.
  Eu tomo ... de vez em   e·oo *to·*mo ... de vez eng
  quando.   *kwang·*do

Do you want to have a smoke?
  Você quer fumar um   vo·*se* kerr foo·*maarr* oom
  unzinho?   oom·zee·nyo

Do you have a light?
  Você tem isqueiro?   vo·*se* teng ees·*kay·*ro

I'm high.
  Estou doidão/   es·*to* doy·*downg/*
  doidona. m/f   doy·*do·*naa

asking someone out

convidando alguém para sair

Would you like to do something (tomorrow)?
Você quer fazer alguma   vo·se kerr faa·zerr ow·goo·maa
coisa (amanhã)?   koy·zaa (aa·ma·nyang)

Yes, I'd love to.
Sim, adoraria.   seeng aa·do·raa·ree·aa

No, I can't.
Não, não posso.   nowng nowng po·so

Where would you like to go (tonight)?
Onde você quer ir   ong·de vo·se kerr eer
(hoje à noite)?   (o·zhe aa noy·te)

pick-up lines

cantadas

Would you like a drink?
Você quer beber alguma   vo·se kerr be·berr ow·goo·maa
coisa?   koy·zaa

You look like someone I know.
Você parece com alguém   vo·se paa·re·se kong ow·geng
que eu conheço.   ke e·oo ko·nye·so

You're a fantastic dancer.
Você dança super bem.   vo·se dang·saa soo·perr beng

You're so beautiful!
Você é lindo/linda! m/f   vo·se e leeng·do/leeng·daa

Can I …?	Posso …?	po·so …
dance with you	dançar com você	dang·saarr kong vo·se
sit here	sentar aqui	seng·taarr aa·kee
take you	levar você em	le·vaarr vo·se eng
home	casa	kaa·zaa

local talk

He/She is a ...	Ele/Ela é ...	e·le/e·laa e ...
bastard	um canalha m	oom kaa·*naa*·lyaa
bitch	uma cadela f	oo·maa kaa·*de*·laa

He/She is ...	Ele/Ela é ...	e·le/e·laa e ...
great	demais	de·*mais*
hot	tesão	te·*sowng*
very nice	super legal	soo·perr le·*gow*

What a babe!
Que gato/gata! m/f   ke *gaa*·to/*gaa*·taa

He/She gets around.
Ele/Ela dá suas   e·le/e·laa daa soo·aas
voltas. m/f   *vawl*·taas

rejections

I'm here with   *Estou com minha/*   es·to kong mee·nyaa
my ...   *meu ...* m/f   me·oo ...
    boyfriend   *namorado* m   naa·mo·*raa*·do
    girlfriend   *namorada* f   naa·mo·*raa*·daa

Excuse me, I have to go now.
Me dá licença, eu   me daa lee·*seng*·saa e·oo
tenho que ir embora.   te·nyo ke eerr eng·*bo*·raa

I'd rather not.
Prefiro que não.   pre·*fee*·ro ke nowng

No, thank you.
Não, obrigado/   nowng o·bree·*gaa*·do/
obrigada. m/f   o·bree·*gaa*·daa

getting closer

I like you very much.
Gostei muito de você. — gos·*tay* mweeng·to de vo·*se*

You're great.
Você é muito legal. — vo·*se* e *mweeng*·to le·*gow*

Can I kiss you?
Posso te dar um beijo? — *po*·so te daarr oom *bay*·zho

Do you want to come inside for a while?
*Você quer entrar
um pouco?* — vo·*se* kerr eng·*traarr*
oom *po*·ko

Do you want a massage?
*Você quer uma
massagem?* — vo·*se* kerr *oo*·maa
maa·*saa*·zheng

local talk

I'm not interested.
*Não estou
interessado/
interessada.* m/f — nowng es·*to*
eeng·te·re·*saa*·do/
eeng·te·re·*saa*·daa

Leave me alone!
Me deixe em paz! — me *day*·she eng paas

Piss off!
Sai fora! — sai *fo*·raa

Give me a break!
Dá um tempo! — daa oom *teng*·po

sex

Kiss me.
Me beija. me *bay*·zhaa

I want you.
Eu quero você. e·oo *ke*·ro vo·*se*

I want to make love to you.
Eu quero fazer amor e·oo *ke*·ro faa·*zerr* aa·*morr*
com você. kong vo·*se*

Let's go to bed.
Vamos para a cama. va·mos *paa*·raa aa *ka*·maa

Do you have a (condom)?
Você tem (camisinha)? vo·*se* teng (kaa·mee·*zee*·nyaa)

Let's use a (condom).
Vamos usar (camisinha). va·mos oo·*zaarr* (kaa·mee·*zee*·nyaa)

I won't do it without protection.
Não faço sem proteção. nowng *faa*·so seng pro·te·*sowng*

Touch me here.
Me toca aqui. me *to*·kaa aa·*kee*

Do you like this?
Você gosta disso? vo·*se* gos·taa *dee*·so

I (don't) like that.
Eu (não) gosto disso. e·oo (nowng) *gos*·to *dee*·so

I think we should stop now.
Acho que devemos parar *aa*·sho ke de·*ve*·mos paa·*raarr*
agora. aa·*go*·raa

Oh yeah!	*Uau!*	oo·*ow*
Oh my god!	*Ai meu Deus!*	ai *me*·oo *de*·oos
That's great.	*Que delícia.*	ke de·*lee*·syaa
Easy tiger!	*Calma!*	*kaal*·maa
faster	*mais rápido*	mais *haa*·pee·do
harder	*mais forte*	mais *forr*·te
slower	*mais devagar*	mais de·vaa·*gaarr*
softer	*mais suave*	mais soo·*aa*·ve

SOCIAL

It's my first time.
É a minha primeira vez.   e aa *mee*·nyaa pree-*may*·raa vez

It helps to have a sense of humour.
É bom ter senso de humor.   e bong terr *seng*·so de oo·*morr*

Don't worry, I'll do it myself.
Não se preocupe, eu   nowng se pre·o·*koo*·pe e·oo
mesmo/mesma faço. m/f   mes·mo/mes·maa *faa*·so

That was ...	*Foi ...*	foy ...
amazing	*incrível*	eeng·*kree*·vel
weird	*estranho*	es·*tra*·nyo
wild	*uma loucura*	oo·maa lo·*koo*·raa

Can I ...?	*Posso ...?*	*po*·so ...
call you	*te ligar*	te lee·*gaarr*
meet you	*te encontrar*	te eng·kong·*traarr*
tomorrow	*amanhã*	aa·ma·*nyang*
stay over	*dormir aqui*	dorr·*meerr* aa·*kee*

love

amor

I love you.
Eu te amo.   e·oo te *a*·mo

I think we're good together.
Eu acho que nós somos   e·oo *aa*·sho ke nos *so*·mos
ótimos juntos.   o·tee·mos *zhoong*·tos

Will you ...?	*Você quer ...*	vo·*se* kerr ...
	comigo?	ko·*mee*·go
go out with me	*sair*	saa·*eerr*
live with me	*morar*	mo·*raarr*
marry me	*casar*	kaa·*zaarr*

problems

Are you seeing someone else?
*Você está saindo com
outra pessoa?*
vo·*se* es·*taa* saa·*eeng*·do kong
o·traa pe·*so*·aa

We're just friends.
Somos só amigos.
so·mos so aa·*mee*·gos

You're just using me for sex.
*Você está só me usando
para sexo.*
vo·*se* es·*ta* so me oo·*zang*·do
paa·raa sek·so

I don't think it's working out.
*Acho que não está
dando certo.*
aa·sho ke nowng es·*taa*
dang·do serr·to

We'll work it out.
Vamos tentar resolver.
va·mos teng·*taarr* he·sol·verr

leaving

I have to leave tomorrow.
*Eu tenho que ir
embora amanhã.*
e·oo te·nyo ke eerr
eng·*bo*·raa aa·ma·*nyang*

I'll ...
Eu vou ...
e·oo vo ...

  keep in touch
  *manter
  contato*
  vo mang·*terr*
  kong·*taa*·to

  miss you
  *sentir
  sua falta*
  seng·*teerr*
  soo·aa fow·taa

terms of endearment		
amorzão	aa·morr·*zowng*	big love
coração	ko·raa·*sowng*	heart
meu bem	me·oo beng	my good
meu amor	me·oo aa·*morr*	my love
querido/ *querida* m/f	ke·*ree*·do/ ke·*ree*·daa	dear

religion

religião

What's your religion?
Qual é a sua religião?
kwow e aa *soo*·aa
he·lee·zhee·*owng*

I'm not religious.
Não sou religioso/ religiosa. m/f
nowng so he·lee·zhee·o·zo/ he·lee·zhee·o·zaa

I'm …	Sou …	so …
agnostic	*agnóstico/ agnóstica* m/f	aag·*nos*·tee·ko/ aag·*nos*·tee·kaa
Buddhist	*Budista*	boo·*dees*·taa
Catholic	*Católico/ Católica* m/f	kaa·*to*·lee·ko/ kaa·*to*·lee·kaa
Christian	*Cristão/ Cristã* m/f	krees·*towng*/ krees·*tang*
Hindu	*Hindu*	eeng·*doo*
Jewish	*Judeu/ Judia* m/f	zhoo·de·oo/ zhoo·dee·aa
Muslim	*Muçulmano/ Muçulmana* m/f	moo·sool·*ma*·no/ moo·sool·*ma*·naa
spiritist	*Espírita*	es·*pee*·ree·taa

gender bending

Remember, gender is indicated on nouns and adjectives. A useful and almost guaranteed way to tell the gender: if it ends in -*a*, it's femine, in -*o*, it's masculine.

out of africa

In addition to being home to various world religions, Brazil accommodates a number of unique faiths, often blends of indigenous beliefs, African cults, and mainstream religions that have been introduced to the country. Two of the more common cults that you might come across are *Candomblé* and *Umbanda*.

Candomblé, an African word denoting a dance in honour of the gods, is a general term for the cult in Bahia, and was brought by the Nago, Yoruba, and Jeje peoples. Elsewhere in Brazil the cult is known by different names and it has been adapted to include elements from other belief systems, from christiananity to indigenous faiths: in Rio it's *Macumba*; in Amazonas and Pará it's *Babassuê*; in Pernambuco and Alagoas it's *Xangô*; in Rio Grande do Sul it's either *Pará* or *Batuque*; and the term *Tambor* is used in Maranhão.

Umbanda, or white magic, is a mixture of *Candomblé* and spiritism. It traces its origins from various sources, including Bantu culture.

I (don't)	*Eu (não)*	e·oo (nowng)
believe in ...	*acredito em ...*	aa·kre·*dee*·to eng ...
astrology	*astrologia*	aas·tro·lo·*zhee*·aa
fate	*destino*	des·*tee*·no
God	*Deus*	de·oos
Can I ... here?	*Posso ... aqui?*	po·so ... aa·*kee*
Where can I ...?	*Onde posso ...?*	ong·de po·so ...
attend	*assistir*	aa·sees·*teerr*
mass	*uma missa*	oo·maa *mee*·saa
pray	*rezar*	he·*zaarr*
worship	*venerar*	ve·ne·*haarr*

cultural differences

Is this a local or national custom?
Este é um costume   es·te e oom kos·*too*·me
local ou nacional?   lo·*kow* o·oo naa·see·o·*now*

I don't want to offend you.
Não quero ofendê-lo/   nowng *ke*·ro o·feng·*de*·lo/
ofendê-la. m/f   o·feng·*de*·laa

I'm not used to this.
Não estou   nowng es·*to*
acostumado/   aa·kos·too·*maa*·do/
acostumada com isso. m/f   aa·kos·too·*maa*·daa kong *ee*·so

I'd rather not join in.
Prefiro não fazer parte.
pre·*fee*·ro nowng faa·*zerr* *paarr*·te

I'll try it.
Vou experimentar.
vo es·pe·ree·meng·*taarr*

I didn't mean to do/say anything wrong.
Não tive intenção de fazer/dizer qualquer coisa errada.
nowng *tee*·ve eeng·teng·*sowng* de faa·*zerr*/dee·*zerr* kwow·*kerr* koy·zaa e·*haa*·daa

I'm sorry, it's against my …	*Me desculpe, mas é contra minha …*	me des·*kool*·pe maas e *kong*·traa mee·*nyaa* …
beliefs	*crença*	*kreng*·saa
religion	*religião*	he·lee·zhee·*owng*

This is …	*Isto é …*	*ees*·to e …
different	*diferente*	dee·fe·*reng*·te
fun	*divertido*	dee·verr·*tee*·do
interesting	*interessante*	eeng·te·re·*sang*·te

sporting interests

interesses esportivos

What sport do you …?	Que esporte você …?	ke es·porr·te vo·se …
follow	acompanha	aa·kong·pa·nyaa
play	pratica	praa·tee·kaa

I play …	Eu jogo …	e·oo zho·go …
basketball	basquete	baas·ke·te
tennis	tênis	te·nees
volleyball	vôlei	vo·lay

I do …	Eu faço …	e·oo faa·so …
athletics	atletismo	aat·le·tees·mo
karate	karatê	kaa·raa·te
scuba diving	mergulho	merr·goo·lyo

I follow …	Eu acompanho …	e·oo aa·kong·pa·nyo …
football (soccer)	futebol de campo	foo·te·bol de kang·po
motor racing	corrida de carros	ko·hee·daa de kaa·hos
surfing	surfe	soorr·fe

I …	Eu …	e·oo …
cycle	ando de bicicleta	ang·do de bee·see·kle·taa
run	corro	ko·ho
walk	caminho	ka·mee·nyo

For more sports, see the **dictionary**.

Do you like (cricket)?
Você gosta (de cricket)?   vo·se gos·taa (de *kree*·ke·tee)

Yes, very much.
Sim, gosto muito.   seeng gos·to mweeng·to

Not really.
Não muito.   nowng mweeng·to

I like watching it.
Eu gosto de assistir.   e·oo gos·to de aa·sees·teerr

Who's your   *Qual é o seu …*   kwow e o se·oo …
favourite …?   *favorito?*   faa·vo·ree·to
  sportsperson   *esportista*   es·porr·tees·taa
  team   *time*   tee·me

---

scoring

What's the score?
Quanto está o jogo?   kwang·to es·taa o zho·go

draw/even   *empate*   eng·paa·te
love   *zero*   ze·ro
match-point   *match point*   me·tee po·eeng·tee
nil   *zero*   ze·ro

going to a game

indo a um jogo

Would you like to go to a game?
Você gostaria de ir   vo·se gos·taa·*ree*·aa de eerr
a um jogo?   aa oom zho·go

Who are you supporting?
Para quem você torce?   *paa*·raa keng vo·se torr·se

Who's ...?	Quem está ...?	keng es·*taa* ...
playing	*jogando*	zho·*gang*·do
winning	*ganhando*	ga·*nyang*·do

That was a ... game!	Foi um jogo ...!	foy oom zho·go ...
bad	*ruim*	hoo·*eeng*
boring	*chato*	*shaa*·to
great	*ótimo*	o·tee·mo

playing sport

praticando esporte

Do you want to play?
Você quer jogar?
vo·*se* kerr zho·*gaarr*

Can I join in?
Posso jogar com vocês?
po·so zho·*gaarr* kong vo·ses

That would be great.
Seria ótimo.
se·*ree*·aa o·tee·mo

I can't.
Não posso.
nowng po·so

I have an injury.
*Estou machucado/
machucado.* m/f
es·to maa·shoo·*kaa*·do
maa·shoo·*kaa*·daa

Your/My point.
Teu/Meu ponto.
te·oo/me·oo pong·to

Kick/Pass it to me!
*Chuta/Passa para
mim!*
shoo·taa/paa·saa paa·raa
meeng

You're a good player.
Você é um bom jogador.
vo·*se* e oom bong zho·gaa·*dorr*

Thanks for the game.
*Obrigado/obrigada
pelo jogo.* m/f
o·bree·*gaa*·do/o·bree·*gaa*·daa
pe·lo zho·go

Where's a good place to …?	Onde tem um bom lugar para …?	ong·de teng oom bong loo·gaarr paa·raa …
fish	pescar	pes·kaarr
go horse riding	andar à cavalo	ang·daar aa kaa·vaa·lo
run	correr	ko·herr
ski	esquiar	es·kee·aarr
snorkel	fazer snorkel	faa·zerr ees·norr·kel
surf	surfar	soor·faarr

Where's the nearest …?	Onde fica … mais perto?	ong·de fee·kaa … mais perr·to
golf course	o campo de golfe	o kang·po de gol·fe
gym	a ginástica	aa zhee·naas·tee·kaa
swimming pool	a piscina	aa pee·see·naa
tennis court	a quadra de tênis	aa kwaa·draa de te·nees

What's the charge per …?	Quanto custa por …?	kwang·to koos·taa porr …
day	dia	dee·aa
game	jogo	zho·go
hour	hora	aw·raa
visit	visita	vee·zee·taa

Can I hire a …?	Posso alugar uma …?	po·so aa·loo·gaarr oo·maa …
ball	bola	bo·laa
bicycle	bicicleta	bee·see·kle·taa
court	quadra	kwaa·draa
racquet	raquete	haa·ke·te

Do I have to be a member to attend?

*Tem que ser membro
para entrar?*

teng ke ser *meng*-bro
paa-raa eng-*traarr*

Is there a women-only session?

*Tem uma seção só
para mulheres?*

teng *oo*-maa se-*sowng* so
paa-raa moo-*lye*-res

Where are the changing rooms?

*Onde ficam os
vestiários?*

ong-de *fee*-kang os
ves-tee-*aa*-ree-os

diving

mergulho

Where's a good diving site?

*Onde tem um lugar
bom para mergulho?*

ong-de teng oom loo-*gaarr*
bong *paa*-raa merr-*goo*-lyo

Is the visibility good?

A visibilidade é boa?

aa vee-zee-bee-lee-*daa*-de e *bo*-aa

How deep is the dive?

Qual a profundidade?

kwow aa pro-foong-dee-*daa*-de

I need an air fill.

*Preciso encher o
tanque de ar.*

pre-*see*-zo eng-*sherr* o
tang-ke de aarr

Is it a … dive?	*Este é um mergulho …?*	es-te e oom merr-*goo*-lyo …
boat	*a partir de um barco*	aa paarr-*teerr* de oom *baar*-ko
shore	*litorâneo*	lee-to-*ra*-ne-o

Are there …?	*Tem …?*	teng …
currents	*corrente*	ko-*heng*-te
sharks	*tubarão*	too-ba-*rowng*
whales	*baleia*	baa-*le*-yaa

sport

129

I want to hire (a) …	Quero alugar …	ke·ro aa·loo·gaarr …
buoyancy vest	colete	ko·le·te
diving equipment	equipamento de mergulho	e·kee·paa·meng·to de merr·goo·lyo
flippers	nadadeiras	na·da·dei·ras
mask	máscara	maas·kaa·raa
regulator	regulador	he·goo·laa·dorr
snorkel	snorkel	ees·norr·kel
tank	tanque	tang·ke
weight belt	cinto com peso	seeng·to kong pe·zo
wetsuit	roupa de borracha	ho·paa de bo·haa·shaa

I'd like to …	Gostaria de …	gos·taa·ree·aa de …
explore caves	explorar cavernas	es·plo·raar kaa·verr·naas
explore wrecks	explorar navios naufragados	es·plo·raar naa·vee·os now·fraa·gaa·dos
go night diving	fazer um mergulho noturno	faa·zerr oom merr·goo·lyo no·toor·no
go scuba diving	mergulhar com tanque	merr·goo·lyaarr kong tang·ke
go snorkelling	fazer snorkel	faa·zerr ees·norr·kel
join a diving tour	fazer parte de um grupo de mergulho	faa·zerr paarr·te de oom groo·po de merr·goo·lyo
learn to dive	aprender a mergulhar	aa·preng·derr aa merr·goo·lyaarr

buddy	companheiro m	kong·pa·*nyay*·ro
cave	caverna f	kaa·*verr*·naa
a dive	mergulho m	merr·*goo*·lyo
to dive	mergulhar	merr·goo·*lyaarr*
diving boat	barco m para	*baar*·ko paa·raa
	mergulho	merr·*goo*·lyo
diving course	curso m de	*koor*·so de
	mergulho	merr·*goo*·lyo
night dive	mergulho m	merr·*goo*·lyo
	noturno	no·*toorr*·no
wreck	navio m	naa·*vee*·o
	naufragado	now·fraa·*gaa*·do

See also **watersports**, page 134.

extreme sports

		esportes radicais
I'd like to go ...	Eu queria	e·oo ke·*ree*·aa
	fazer ...	faa·zerr ...
abseiling	rapel	haa·*pel*
caving	exploração de	es·plo·raa·*sowng* de
	cavernas	kaa·*verr*·naas
canyoning	canyoning	kang·nyo·*neeng*
hang-gliding	vôo livre	*vo*·o *lee*·vre
mountain	mountain	maa·oong·tayng
biking	bike	*bai*·kee
paragliding	parapente	paa·raa·*peng*·te
parasailing	parasailing	paa·raa·*say*·leeng
rock-climbing	escalada	es·kaa·*laa*·daa
skydiving	skydiving	ees·kai·*dai*·veeng
white-water	rafting	*haa*·fee·teeng
rafting		

Is the equipment secure?
  Este equipamento é   es·te e·kee·paa·*meng*·to e
  seguro?   se·*goo*·ro

This is insane.
  Isto é loucura.   *ees*·to e lo·*koo*·raa

sport

131

horse riding

How much is a (one) hour ride?
> Quanto é o passeio de
> (uma) hora?
>
> kwang·to e o paa·se·yo de
> (oo·maa) aw·raa

How long is the ride?
> Quanto tempo é
> o passeio?
>
> kwang·to teng·po e
> o paa·se·yo

I'm (not) an experienced rider.
> Eu (não) sou experiente.
>
> e·oo (nowng) so es·pe·ree·eng·te

Can I rent a hat and boots?
> Posso alugar um
> chapéu e botas?
>
> po·so aa·loo·gaarr oom
> shaa·pe·oo e bo·taas

bit	freio m	fre·yo
bridle	rédea f	he·dyaa
canter	galope m	gaa·lo·pe
crop	chicote m	shee·ko·te
gallop	galope m	gaa·lo·pe
groom	tratar	tra·taarr
horse	cavalo m	kaa·vaa·lo
pony	pônei m	po·nay
reins	rédeas f pl	he·dyaas
saddle	sela f	se·laa
stable	estábulo m	es·taa·boo·lo
stirrup	estribo m	es·tree·bo
trot	trote m	tro·te
walk	andar	ang·daar

soccer

Who plays for (Flamengo)?
Quem joga no   keng *zho*·gaa no
(Flamengo)?   (flaa·*meng*·go)

He's a great (player).
Ele é um ótimo   *e*·le e oom *o*·tee·mo
(jogador).   (zho·gaa·*dorr*)

He played brilliantly in the match against (Argentina).
Ele jogou muito bem   *e*·le *zho*·goo *mweeng*·to beng
no jogo contra   no *zho*·go *kong*·traa
(a Argentina).   (aa aarr·zheng·*tee*·naa)

Which team is at the top of the league?
Que time está na frente ke *tee*·me es·*taa* naa *freng*·te
da liga?   daa *lee*·gaa

What a great/terrible team!
Que time ótimo/horrível! ke *tee*·me *o*·tee·mo/o·*hee*·vel

ball	*bola* f	*bo*·laa
coach	*técnico* m	*tek*·nee·ko
corner (kick)	*escanteio* m	es·kang·*te*·yo
fan	*fã* m&f	fang
foul	*falta* f	*fow*·taa
free kick	*bater a falta*	baa·*terr* aa *fow*·taa
goal	*gol* m	gol
goal (place)	*trave* f	*tra*·ve
goalkeeper	*goleiro* m	go·*lay*·ro
offside	*lateral*	laa·te·*row*
penalty	*pênalti* m	*pe*·now·tee
player	*jogador* m	zho·gaa·*dorr*
red card	*cartão* m *vermelho*	kaarr·*towng* verr·*me*·lyo
referee	*juiz* m	joo·*ees*
striker	*atacante* m	aa·taa·*kang*·te
team	*time* m	*tee*·me
throw in	*bater a lateral*	baa·*terr* aa laa·te·*row*
yellow card	*cartão* m *amarelo*	kaarr·*towng* aa·maa·*re*·lo

water sports

Can I book a lesson?
Posso marcar uma   po·so maarr·*kaarr* oo·maa
aula?   ow·laa

Can I hire (a) ...	*Posso alugar ...*	po·so aa·loo·*gaarr* ...
boat	*um barco*	oom *baar*·ko
canoe	*uma canoa*	oo·maa ka·*no*·aa
kayak	*um caiaque*	oom kai·*aa*·ke
life jacket	*um colete*	oom ko·*le*·te
	salva-vidas	sow·vaa·*vee*·daas
snorkelling	*equipamento*	e·kee·paa·*meng*·to
gear	*para fazer*	*paa*·raa faa·*zerr*
	snorkel	ees·*norr*·kel
water-skis	*esqui*	es·*kee*
	aquático	aa·*kwaa*·tee·ko
wetsuit	*roupa de*	*ho*·paa de
	borracha	bo·*haa*·shaa

Are there any ...?	*Tem ...?*	teng ...
reefs	*recifes*	he·*see*·fes
rips	*corredeira*	ko·he·*day*·raa
water hazards	*algum risco*	ow·*goom* hees·ko
	na água	naa *aa*·gwaa
waves	*ondas*	*ong*·daas

boogie board	*morey* m *boogie*	*mo*·ray *boo*·gee
motorboat	*barco* m *a motor*	*baarr*·ko aa mo·*torr*
oars	*remos* m pl	*he*·mos
sailing boat	*barco* m *a vela*	*baarr*·ko aa *ve*·laa
surfboard	*prancha* f *de surfe*	*prang*·shaa de *soor*·fee
surfing	*surfe* m	*soorr*·fee
wave	*onda* f	*ong*·daa
wind	*vento* f	*veng*·to
windsurfing	*windsurf* m	weeng·dee·*soor*·fee

See also **diving**, page 129.

outdoors

hiking

caminhada

Where can I ...?	Onde posso ...?	ong·de po·so ...
buy supplies	comprar	kong·praarr
	mantimentos	mang·tee·meng·tos
find someone	encontrar	eng·kong·traarr
who knows	alguém que	ow·geng kê
this area	conheça esta	ko·nye·saa es·taa
	area	aa·re·aa
get a map	pegar um	pe·gaarr oom
	mapa	maa·paa
hire hiking gear	alugar	aa·loo·gaarr
	equipamento	e·kee·paa·meng·to
	de caminhada	de kaa·mee·nyaa·daa

How ...?	Qual é a ...?	kwow e aa ...
high is the	altura	ow·too·raa
climb	da subida?	daa soo·bee·daa
long is the trail	distância	dees·tang·syaa
	do caminho	do ka·mee·nyo

Do we need a guide?
Precisamos de um guia? — pre·see·za·mos de oom gee·aa

Are there guided treks?
Tem caminhadas — teng ka·mee·nyaa·daas
com guia? — kong gee·aa

Is it safe?
É seguro? — e se·goo·ro

Is there a hut?
Tem abrigo? — teng aa·bree·go

When does it get dark?
Quando escurece? — kwang·do es·koo·re·se

Do we need to take …?	Precisamos levar …?	pre·see·za·mos le·vaarr …
bedding	roupa de cama	ho·paa de ka·maa
food	comida	ko·mee·daa
water	água	aa·gwaa
Is the track …?	O caminho …?	o ka·mee·nyo …
(well-)marked	é (bem) marcado	e (beng) maarr·kaa·do
open	esta aberto	es·taa aa·berr·to
scenic	é pitoresco	e pee·to·res·ko
Which is the … route?	Qual é a rota mais …?	kwow e aa ho·taa mais …
easiest	fácil	faa·seel
most interesting	interessante	eeng·te·re·sang·te
shortest	curta	koorr·taa
Where can I find a/the …?	Onde posso encontrar …?	ong·de po·so eng·kong·traarr …
camping ground	a área de camping	aa aa·re·aa de kang·peeng
nearest village	cidade mais perto	see·daa·de mais perr·to
showers	um chuveiro	oom shoo·vay·ro
toilets	um banheiro	oom ba·nyay·ro

Where have you come from?
De onde você veio?   de ong·de vo·se vay·o

How long did it take?
Quanto tempo leva?   kwang·to teng·po le·vaa

Does this path go to …?
  Este caminho
  leva para …?

  es·te ka·*mee*·nyo
  le·vaa *paa*·raa …

Can I go through here?
  Posso ir por aqui?

  po·so eerr porr aa·*kee*

Is the water OK to drink?
  A água é boa para
  beber?

  a *aa*·gwaa e *bo*·aa *paa*·raa
  be·*berr*

I'm lost.
  Estou perdido/perdida. m/f

  es·*to* perr·*dee*·do/perr·*dee*·daa

---

listen for …

e pe·ree·*go*·zo
  É perigoso.   It's dangerous.

koo·ee·*daa*·do kom a he·*saa*·kaa
  Cuidado com a ressaca!   Be careful of the undertow!

---

beach

a praia

Where's the … beach?	Onde fica a …?	ong·de *fee*·kaa aa …
best	melhor praia	me·*lyorr* prai·aa
nearest	praia mais perto	*praa*·yaa mais *perr*·to
nudist	praia de nudismo	*praa*·yaa de noo·*dees*·mo
public	praia pública	*praa*·yaa *poo*·blee·kaa

outdoors

137

signs		
Proibido Mergulhar	pro·ee·*bee*·do mer·goo·*lyaarr*	No Diving
Proibido Nadar	pro·ee·*bee*·do naa·*daarr*	No Swimming

How much for a/an …?	*Quanto custa …?*	kwang·to koos·taa …
chair	*uma cadeira*	oo·maa kaa·*day*·raa
hut	*um abrigo*	oom aa·*bree*·go
umbrella	*um guarda sol*	oom *gwaarr*·daa sol

weather

tempo

What's the weather like?
Como está o tempo?   ko·mo es·*taa* o *teng*·po

What will the weather be like tomorrow?
Como estará o tempo amanhã?   ko·mo es·taa·*raa* o *teng*·po aa·ma·*nyang*

It's …	*Está …*	es·taa …
cloudy	*nublado*	noo·*blaa*·do
cold	*frio*	*free*·o
fine	*bom*	bong
freezing	*um gelo*	oom *zhe*·lo
hot	*quente*	*keng*·te
raining	*chovendo*	sho·*veng*·do
snowing	*nevando*	ne·*vang*·do
sunny	*ensolarado*	eng·so·laa·*raa*·do
warm	*ameno*	aa·*me*·no
windy	*ventando*	veng·*tang*·do

SOCIAL

138

Where can I buy ...?	Onde posso comprar um ...?	ong·de po·so kong·praarr oom ...
a rain jacket	casaco de chuva	kaa·zaa·ko de shoo·vaa
an umbrella	guarda-chuva	gwaarr·daa·shoo·vaa
dry season	época f de seca	e·po·kaa de se·kaa
wet season	época f de chuvas	e·po·kaa de shoo·vaas

flora & fauna

What ... is that?	O que é ...?	o ke e ...
animal	aquele animal	aa·ke·le aa·nee·mow
flower	aquela flor	aa·ke·laa florr
plant	aquela planta	aa·ke·laa plang·taa
tree	aquela árvore	aa·ke·laa aarr·vo·re

local plants & animals

arara (macaw)	arara f	aa·raa·raa
golden lion	mico leão m	mee·ko le·owng
parrot	papagaio m	paa·paa·gaa·yo
toucan	tucano m	too·ka·no

jacaranda (flowering Brazilian tree)

jacarandá f		zhaa·kaa·rang·daa

Victoria Amazonica (the national flower, a water lily)

vitória-régia f		vee·to·ree·a·he·gee·aa

What's it used for?
Para que serve?   paa·raa ke serr·ve

Can you eat the fruit?
Pode-se comer a fruta?   po·de·se ko·merr aa froo·taa

Is it …?	Isto …?	ees·to …
common	*é comum*	e ko·moom
dangerous	*é perigoso*	e pe·ree·go·zo
endangered	*está ameaçado/ ameaçada de extinção* m/f	es·taa aa·me·aa·saa·do/ aa·me·aa·saa·daa de es·teeng·sowng
poisonous	*é venenoso*	e ve·ne·no·zo
protected	*está protegido/ protegida* m/f	es·taa pro·te·zhee·do/ pro·te·zhee·daa

A typical breakfast consists of coffee, milk, juice, bread, jam, cheese, ham and fruit. Lunch is usually rice, beans (black or white depending on the region), vegetables and meat of some kind. Dinner is similar to lunch, though a lighter style of dinner, more akin to breakfast, is increasing in popularity.

key language

linguagem chave

breakfast	café m da manhã	kaa·fe daa ma·nyang
lunch	almoço m	ow·mo·so
dinner	jantar m	zhang·taarr
snack	lanche m	lang·she
eat	comer	ko·merr
drink	beber	be·berr
I'd like ...	Gostaria de ...	gos·taa·ree·aa de ...
Please.	Por favor.	porr faa·vorr
Thank you.	Obrigado/ Obrigada. m/f	o·bree·gaa·do/ o·bree·gaa·daa
I'm starving!	Estou faminto/ faminta! m/f	es·to faa·meeng·to/ faa·meeng·taa

finding a place to eat

encontrando um lugar para comer

Can you recommend a ...	Você pode recomendar um ...	vo·se po·de he·ko·meng·daarr oom ...
bar	bar	baarr
cafe	café	kaa·fe
restaurant	restaurante	hes·tow·rang·te

Where would you go for …?	Onde você iria para …?	ong·de vo·se ee·ree·aa paa·raa …
a celebration	uma comemoração	oo·maa ko·me·mo·ra·sowng
a cheap meal	uma refeição barata	oo·maa he·fay·sowng baa·raa·taa
local specialities	especialidades locais	es·pe·see·aa·lee·daa·des lo·kais

I'd like to reserve a table for …	Eu gostaria de reservar uma mesa para …	e·oo gos·taa·ree·aa de he·zer·vaarr oo·maa me·zaa paa·raa …
(two) people	(duas) pessoas	(doo·aas) pe·so·aas
(eight) o'clock	(às oito) horas	(aas oy·to) aw·raas

I'd like …, please.	Eu queria …, por favor.	e·oo ke·ree·aa … porr faa·vorr
a children's menu	o cardápio de crianças	o kaar·da·pyo de kree·ang·saas
a half portion	meia porção	me·yaa porr·sowng
a menu in English	o cardápio em inglês	o kaar·daa·pyo eng eeng·gles
a table for (five)	uma mesa para (cinco)	oo·maa me·zaa paa·raa (seeng·ko)
the drink list	a lista de bebidas	aa lees·taa de be·bee·daas
the menu	o cardápio	o kaar·daa·pyo
the (non-) smoking section	(não-) fumantes	(nowng·) foo·mang·tes

Are you still serving food?

Vocês ainda estão servindo comida? vo·ses aa·eeng·daa es·towng serr·veeng·do ko·mee·daa

How long is the wait?

A espera é de quanto tempo? aa es·pe·raa e de kwang·to teng·po

---

going nuts

There's no single word to translate 'nuts'. You have to say which kind of nut you mean, for example *noz* (walnut), *amendoin* (peanut), and *amêndoas* (almond).

aa·*kee* es·*taa* *Aqui está!*	**Here you go!**
es·*ta*·mos fe·*shaa*·dos *Estamos fechados.*	**We're closed.**
es·*ta*·mos lo·*taa*·dos *Estamos lotados.*	**We're full.**
o ke *po*·so serr·*vee*·los *O que posso serví-los?*	**What can I get for you?**

ong·de vo·*ses* gos·taa·*ree*·ang de seng·*taarr*
  *Onde vocês gostariam
  de sentar?*
	**Where would you
	like to sit?**

oom mo·*meng*·to *Um momento.*	**One moment.**

restaurant

restaurante

At a restaurant, use *senhor* or *senhora* when addressing the waiter or waitress.

What would you recommend?
  O que você recomenda? o ke vo·*se* he·ko·*meng*·daa

What's in that dish?
  O que tem neste prato? o ke teng *nes*·te *praa*·to

I'll have that.
  Eu quero isto. e·oo *ke*·ro *ees*·to

Does it take long to prepare?
  Leva muito tempo *le*·vaa *mweeng*·to *teng*·po
  para preparar? *paa*·raa pre·paa·*raar*

Is it self-serve?
  Nós mesmos nos servimos? nos *mes*·mos nos serr·*vee*·mos

Is service included in the bill?
  O serviço está o serr·*vee*·so es·*taa*
  incluído na conta? eeng·kloo·*ee*·do naa *kong*·taa

Are these complimentary?
  É cortesia da casa? e kor·te·*zee*·aa daa *kaa*·zaa

I'd like …	Eu quero …	e·oo ke·ro …
a local speciality	a especialidade local	aa es·pe·see·aa·lee·daa·de lo·kow
a meal fit for a king	uma refeição suntuosa	oo·maa he·fay·sowng soom·too·o·zaa
the chicken	o frango	o frang·go

I'd like it with/ without …	Eu queria com/ sem …	e·oo ke·ree·aa kong/ seng …
chilli	pimenta	pee·meng·taa
garlic	alho	aa·lyo
oil	óleo	o·lyo

at the table

à mesa

Please bring …	Por favor traga …	porr faa·vorr traa·gaa …
a cloth	uma toalha	oo·maa to·aa·lyaa
a serviette	um guardanapo	oom gwaar·daa·naa·po
a wineglass	uma taça de vinho	oo·maa taa·saa de vee·nyo
the bill	a conta	aa kong·taa

talking food

I love this dish.
Adorei este prato.   aa·do·*ray* es·te *praa*·to

I love the local cuisine.
Adorei a cozinha   aa·do·*ray* aa ko·*zee*·nyaa
local.   lo·*kow*

That was delicious!
Estava delicioso!   es·*taa*·vaa de·lee·see·o·zo

My compliments to the chef.
Meus cumprimentos   me·oos koom·pree·*meng*·tos
ao chefe.   ow *she*·fe

I'm full.
Estou satisfeito/   es·*to* saa·tees·*fay*·to/
satisfeita. m/f   saa·tees·*fay*·taa

This is ...	*Está ...*	es·*taa* ...
(too) cold	*(demais) frio*	(*zhee*·mais) *free*·o
spicy	*apimentado*	aa·pee·meng·*taa*·do
superb	*excelente*	e·se·*leng*·te

ashtray
cinzeiro m
seeng·*zay*·ro

spoon
colher f
ko·*lyer*

fork
garfo m
gaar·fo

plate
prato m
praa·to

knife
faca f
faa·kaa

wineglass
taça f *de vinho*
taa·saa de
vee·nyo

glass
copo m
ko·po

table
mesa f
me·zaa

aperitivos	aa·pe·ree·*tee*·vos	appetisers
sopas	so·paas	soups
entradas	eng·*traa*·daas	entrees
saladas	saa·*laa*·daas	salads
pratos	*praa*·tos	main courses
principais	preeng·see·*pais*	
sobremesas	so·bre·*me*·zaas	desserts
aperitivos	aa·pe·ree·*tee*·vos	aperitifs
refrigerantes	he·free·zhe·*rang*·tes	soft drinks
bebidas	be·*bee*·daas	spirits
destiladas	des·tee·*laa*·daas	
cervejas	serr·*ve*·zhaas	beers
vinhos	*vee*·nyos	sparkling wines
espumantes	es·poo·*mang*·tes	
vinhos brancos	*vee*·nyos *brang*·kos	white wines
vinhos tintos	*vee*·nyos *teeng*·tos	red wines
vinhos de	*vee*·nyos de	dessert wines
sobremesa	so·bre·*me*·zaa	
digestivos	dee·zhes·*tee*·vos	digestifs

breakfast

café da manhã

What's a typical breakfast?

Como é um típico ko·mo e oom *tee*·pee·ko
café da manhã? kaa·*fe* daa ma·*nyang*

bacon	*bacon* m	*bay*·kon
bread	*pão* m	powng
butter	*manteiga* f	mang·*tay*·gaa
cake	*bolo* m	*bo*·lo
cereal	*cereal* m	se·re·*ow*
cheese bread	*pão* m *de queijo*	powng de *kay*·zho
cold cuts	*frios* m	*free*·os
corn bread	*broa* f *de milho*	*bro*·aa de *mee*·lyo

... eggs	ovos ... m	o·vos ...
boiled	quentes	keng·tes
fried	fritos	free·tos
hard-boiled	cozidos duros	ko·zee·dos doo·ros
poached	pochés	po·shes
scrambled	mexidos	me·shee·dos

fruit juice	suco m de frutas	soo·ko de froo·taas
jam	geléia f	zhe·le·yaa
milk	leite m	lay·te
muesli	muesli m	moos·lee
omelette	omelete f	o·me·le·te
(oat/maize)	mingau m	meeng·gow
porridge	(de aveia/maizena)	(de aa·ve·yaa/mai·ze·naa)
toast	torrada f	to·haa·daa

For other breakfast items and related language, see **self-catering**, page 153, and the **culinary reader**, page 159.

light meals

refeições leves

What's that called?
Como se chama isso?   ko·mo se sha·maa ee·so

I'd like ..., please.	Eu queria ..., por favor.	e·oo ke·ree·aa ... porr faa·vorr
a piece	um pedaço	oom pe·daa·so
a sandwich	um sanduiche	oom sang·doo·ee·she
one slice	uma fatia	oo·maa faa·tee·aa
that one	aquele	aa·ke·le
two	dois	doys

condiments

Do you have ...?	Tem ...?	teng ...
chilli sauce	molho de pimenta	mo·lyo de pee·meng·taa
ketchup	ketchup	ket·shoo·pee
pepper	pimenta	pee·meng·taa
salt	sal	sow
tomato sauce	molho de tomate	mo·lyo de to·maa·te
vinegar	vinagre	vee·naa·gre

For additional items, see the **culinary reader**, page 159.

methods of preparation

métodos de preparo

I'd like it ...	Eu queria ...	e·oo ke·ree·aa ...
I don't want it ...	Eu não queria ...	e·oo nowng ke·ree·aa ...
boiled	cozido/ cozido m/f	ko·zee·do/ ko·zee·daa
broiled	na brasa	naa braa·zaa
deep-fried	frito/frita em recipiente m/f	free·to/free·taa eng he·see·pyeng·te
fried	frito/frita m/f	free·to/free·taa
grilled	grelhado/ grelhada m/f	gre·lyaa·do/ gre·lyaa·daa
medium	ao ponto	ow pong·to
rare	mal passado/ passada m/f	mow paa·saa·do/ paa·saa·daa
re-heated	requentado/ requentada m/f	he·keng·taa·do/ he·keng·taa·daa
steamed	ao vapor	ow vaa·porr
well-done	bem passado/ passado m/f	beng paa·saa·do/ paa·saa·daa
with the dressing on the side	com o molho separado	kong o mo·lyo se·paa·raa·do
without ...	sem ...	seng ...

in the bar

no bar

Excuse me!
Com licença! — kong lee·*seng*·saa

I'll have …
Eu queria … — e·oo ke·*ree*·aa …

I'm next.
Eu sou o próximo/ próxima. m/f — e·oo so o *pro*·see·mo/ *pro*·see·maa

Same again, please.
O mesmo, por favor. — o *mes*·mo porr faa·*vorr*

No ice, thanks.
Sem gelo, obrigado/ obrigada. m/f — seng *zhe*·lo o·bree·*gaa*·do/ o·bree·*gaa*·daa

I'll buy you a drink.
Eu te pago uma bebida. — e·oo te *paa*·go *oo*·maa be·*bee*·daa

What would you like?
O que você quer? — o ke vo·*se* kerr

It's my round.
É minha vez. e *mee*·nyaa ves

How much is that?
Quanto é? *kwang*·to e

Do you serve meals here?
Vocês servem refeições vo·*ses* serr·*veng* he·*fay*·*soyngs*
aqui? aa·kee

listen for ...

a·sho ke ja *she*·gaa *paa*·raa vo·*se* Acho que já chega para você.	**I think you've had enough.**
o ke vo·*se* es·*taa* be·*bang*·do O que você está bebendo?	**What are you having?**
ool·tee·mos pe·*dee*·dos Últimos pedidos.	**Last orders.**

nonalcoholic drinks

bebidas sem álcool

... mineral water	*água mineral ...*	aa·gwaa mee·ne·*row* ...
sparkling	*com gás*	kong gaas
still	*sem gás*	seng gaas
orange juice	*suco de laranja*	soo·ko de laa·*rang*·zhaa
soft drink	*refrigerante*	he·free·zhe·*rang*·te
(hot) water	*água (quente)*	aa·gwaa (*keng*·te)
(cup of) tea	*(xícara) de chá*	(shee·kaa·raa) de shaa
(cup of) coffee	*(xícara) de café*	(shee·kaa·raa) de kaa·*fe*
... with (milk)	*... com (leite)*	... kong (*lay*·te)
... without (sugar)	*... sem (açúcar)*	... seng (aa·*soo*·kaarr)

alcoholic drinks

beer	cerveja f	serr·ve·zhaa
brandy	brandy m	brang·dee
champagne	champagne f	shang·pa·nye
cocktail	coquetel m	ko·ke·tel

a shot of ...	uma dose de ...	oo·maa do·ze de ...
gin	gin	zheeng
rum	rum	hoom
tequila	tequila	te·kee·laa
vodka	vodka	vo·dee·kaa
whisky	whisky	oo·ees·kee
cachaça	cachaça	kaa·shaa·saa

a bottle/glass	uma garrafa/	oo·maa gaa·haa·faa/
of ... wine	taça de vinho ...	taa·saa de vee·nyo ...
dessert	de sobremesa	de so·bre·me·zaa
red	tinto	teeng·to
rosé	rosé	ho·ze
sparkling	espumante	es·poo·mang·te
white	branco	brang·ko

a ... of beer	... de cerveja	... de serr·ve·jaa
glass	um copo	oom ko·po
jug	uma jarra	oo·maa zhaa·haa
large bottle	uma garrafa	oo·maa gaa·haa·faa
	grande	grang·de
pint	um choppe	oom sho·pee
small bottle	uma garrafa	oo·maa gaa·haa·faa
	pequena	pe·ke·naa

drinking up

Cheers!
Saúde!
sa·*oo*·de

This is hitting the spot.
Caiu bem.
kaa·*ee*·oo beng

Pull my finger!
Puxe meu dedo!
poo·*she* me·oo *de*·do

I think I've had one too many.
Acho que bebi mais do que deveria.
a·sho ke be·*bee* mais do ke de·ve·*ree*·aa

I'm feeling drunk.
Estou me sentindo bêbado/bêbada. m/f
es·*to* me seng·*teeng*·do *be*·baa·do/*be*·baa·daa

I feel ill.
Estou me sentindo mal.
es·*to* me seng·*teeng*·do mow

Where's the toilet?
Onde é o banheiro?
ong·de e o ba·*nyay*·ro

Can you call a taxi for me?
Você pode chamar um táxi para mim?
vo·*se po*·de shaa·*maarr* oom *taak*·see *paa*·raa meeng

local drinks

água f *de côco*	aa·gwaa de *ko*·ko	coconut water
batida f	baa·*tee*·daa	pureed fruit and *cachaça* cocktail
cachaça f	kaa·*shaa*·saa	white spirit made from sugar cane
caipirinha f	kai·pee·*ree*·nyaa	lime and *cachaça* cocktail
caldo m *de cana*	*kow*·do de *ka*·naa	sugar cane juice
mate m	*maa*·te	iced tea

buying food

What's the local speciality?
Qual é a especialidade local?
kwow e a es·pe·see·aa·lee·*daa*·de lo·*kow*

What's that?
O que é aquilo?
o ke e aa·*kee*·lo

Can I taste it?
Posso experimentar?
po·so es·pe·ree·meng·*taarr*

Can I have a bag, please?
Pode me dar uma bolsa, por favor?
po·de me daarr oo·ma *bol*·sa porr faa·*vorr*

How much is (a kilo of cheese)?
Quanto é (o kilo do queijo)?
kwang·to e (o *kee*·lo do *kay*·zho)

How much is it?
Quanto custa?
kwang·to koos·taa

food stuff		
cooked	*cozido/cozida* m/f	ko·*zee*·do/ko·*zee*·daa
cured	*curado/curada* m/f	koo·*raa*·do/koo·*raa*·daa
dried	*seco/seca* m/f	*se*·ko
fresh	*fresco/fresca* m/f	*fres*·ko/*fres*·kaa
frozen	*congelado/ congelada* m/f	kong·zhe·*laa*·do kong·zhe·*laa*·daa
smoked	*defumado/ defumada* m/f	de·foo·*maa*·do de·foo·*maa*·daa
raw	*cru/crua* m/f	kroo/*kroo*·a

I'd like ...	Eu gostaria de ...	e·oo gos·taa·ree·aa de ...
(200) grams	(duzentas) gramas	(doo·zeng·taas) gra·maas
half a kilo	meio kilo	me·yo kee·lo
a kilo	um kilo	oom kee·lo
(two) kilos	(dois) kilos	(doys) kee·los
a bottle	uma garrafa	oo·maa gaa·haa·faa
a dozen	uma dúzia	oo·maa doo·zyaa
half a dozen	meia dúzia	me·yaa doo·zee·aa
a jar	um vidro	oom vee·dro
a packet	um pacote	oom paa·ko·te
a piece	um pedaço	oom pe·daa·so
(three) pieces	(três) pedaços	(tres) pe·daa·sos
a slice	uma fatia	oo·maa faa·tee·aa
(six) slices	(seis) fatias	(says) faa·tee·aas
a tin	uma lata	oo·maa laa·taa
(just) a little	(só) um pouco	(so) oom po·ko
more	mais	mais
some ...	um pouco ...	oom po·ko ...
that one	aquele	aa·ke·le
this one	este	es·te

listen for ...

mais ow·goo·maa koy·zaa *Mais alguma coisa?*	**Anything else?**
o ke vo·se gos·taa·ree·aa *O que você gostaria?*	**What would you like?**
po·so aa·zhoo·daa·lo/aa·zhoo·daa·laa *Posso ajudá-lo/ajudá-la?* m/f	**Can I help you?**
sowng (seeng·ko he·ais) *São (cinco Reais).*	**That's (five reals).**

Less.	Menos.	me·nos
A bit more.	Um pouco mais.	oom po·ko mais
Enough.	Chega.	she·gaa

Do you have …?	Vocês tem …?	vo·ses teng …
anything	algo mais	ow·go mais
cheaper	barato	baa·raa·to
other kinds	outros tipos	o·tros tee·pos

Where can I find the … section?	Onde posso encontrar a seção de …?	ong·de po·so eng·kong·traarr aa se·sowng de …
dairy	laticínios	laa·tee·see·nyos
fish	peixe	pay·she
frozen goods	congelados	kong·zhe·laa·dos
fruit and vegetable	frutas e legumes	froo·taas e le·goo·mes
meat	carne	kaar·ne
poultry	frango	frang·go

cooking utensils

Could I please borrow a/an ...?
Posso pegar um/uma ...   po·so pe·*gaarr* oom/*oo*·maa ...
emprestado/   eng·pres·*taa*·do/
emprestada? m/f   eng·pres·*taa*·daa

I need a/an ...
Preciso de um/uma ... m/f   pre·*see*·zo de oom/*oo*·maa ...

bottle opener	*abridor* m	aa·bree·*dor*
	de garrafas	de gaa·*haa*·faas
bowl	*tigela* f	tee·*zhe*·laa
can opener	*abridor* m	aa·bree·*dorr*
	de latas	de *laa*·taas
chopping board	*tábua* f *de*	*taa*·bwaa de
	cortar	korr·*taarr*
corkscrew	*abridor* m	aa·bree·*dorr*
cup	*xícara* f	*shee*·kaa·raa
fork	*garfo* m	*gaarr*·fo
fridge	*geladeira* f	zhe·laa·*day*·raa
frying pan	*frigideira* f	free·zhe·*day*·raa
glass	*copo* m	*ko*·po
knife	*faca* f	*faa*·kaa
microwave	*microondas* m	mee·kro·*ong*·daas
oven	*forno* m	*forr*·no
plate	*prato* m	*praa*·to
saucepan	*panela* f	paa·*ne*·laa
spoon	*colher* f	ko·*lyerr*
toaster	*torradeira* f	to·haa·*day*·raa

vegetarian & special meals
comida vegetariana & especial

ordering food

Is there a (vegetarian) restaurant near here?
Tem um restaurante   teng oom hes·tow·*rang*·te
(vegetariana) aqui   (ve·zhe·taa·ree·*a*·naa) aa·*kee*
por perto?   porr *perr*·to

Do you have ...	*Você tem*	vo·*se* teng
food?	*comida ...?*	ko·*mee*·daa ...
halal	*halal*	a·*low*
kosher	*kosher*	ko·sherr
vegetarian	*vegetariana*	ve·zhe·taa·ree·*a*·naa

I don't eat ...	*Eu não como ...*	e·oo nowng *ko*·mo ...
fish	*peixe*	*pay*·she
poultry	*frango*	*frang*·go
(red) meat	*carne (vermelha)*	*kaar*·ne (verr·*me*·lyaa)

Is it cooked	*Isto é feito em/*	ees·to e *fay*·to eng/
in/with ...?	*com ...?*	kong ...
butter	*manteiga*	mang·*te*·gaa
fish stock	*caldo de peixe*	kow·do de *pay*·she
meat stock	*caldo de carne*	kow·do de *kaarr*·ne

Could you	*Você poderia*	vo·*se* po·de·*ree*·aa
prepare a meal	*preparar uma*	pre·paa·*raarr* oo·maa
without ...?	*refeição sem ...?*	he·fay·*sowng* seng ...
eggs	*ovos*	*o*·vos
pork	*porco*	*porr*·ko
seafood	*frutos do mar*	*froo*·tos do maarr

Is this ...?	*Isto é ...?*	ees·to ee ...
free of animal	*sem derivados*	seng de·ree·*vaa*·dos
produce	*de animais*	de aa·nee·*mais*
free-range	*de caipira*	kai·pee·raa
genetically	*transgênico*	trans·*zhe*·nee·ko
modified		

vegetarian & special meals

157

decaffeinated	descafeinado	des·kaa·fe·ee·naa·do
gluten-free	sem glúten	seng *gloo*·teng
halal	halal	a·*low*
kosher	kosher	ko·sherr
low-fat	de baixo teor	de *bai*·sho te·*orr*
	de gordura	de gorr·*doo*·raa
low in sugar	de baixo teor	de *bai*·sho te·*orr*
	de açúcar	de aa·*soo*·kaarr
organic	orgânico	orr·*ga*·nee·ko
salt-free	sem sal	seng sow

special diets & allergies

dietas especiais & alergias

I'm on a special diet.

| Estou numa dieta | es·to *noo*·maa dee·*e*·taa |
| especial. | es·pe·see·*ow* |

I'm (a) ...	Eu sou ...	e·oo so ...
Buddhist	Budista	boo·*dees*·taa
Hindu	Hindu	*eeng*·doo
Jewish	Judeu/Judia m/f	zhoo·*de*·o/zhoo·*dee*·aa
Muslim	Muçulmano/	moo·sool·*ma*·no/
	Muçulmana m/f	moo·sool·*ma*·naa
vegan	vegitalista m&f	ve·zhe·ta·*lees*·taa
vegetarian	vegetariano/	ve·zhe·taa·ree·*a*·no/
	vegetariana m/f	ve·zhe·taa·ree·*a*·naa

I'm allergic to ...	Eu sou alérgico/	e·oo so aa·*lerr*·zhee·ko/
	alérgica à ... m/f	aa·*lerr*·zhee·kaa aa ...
dairy produce	laticínios	laa·tee·*see*·nyos
eggs	ovos	o·vos
gelatin	gelatina	zhe·laa·*tee*·naa
gluten	glúten	*gloo*·teng
honey	mel	mel
MSG	monoglutamato	mo·no·gloo·taa·*maa*·to
	de sódio	de *so*·dyo
peanuts	amendoims	aa·meng·do·*eengs*
seafood	frutos do mar	*froo*·tos do maarr

FOOD

158

A

abacate ⓜ a-baa-*kaa*-te *avocado*

abacaxi ⓜ aa-baa-kaa-*shee* *pineapple*

abóbora ⓕ aa-*bo*-bo-raa *pumpkin*

açafrão ⓜ aa-saa-*frowng* *saffron*

açaí ⓜ aa-saa-*ee* *deep purple fruit of a palm tree – it has a gritty taste*

acarajé ⓜ aa-kaa-raa-*zhe* a *Bahian street food made from mashed brown beans formed into balls & stuffed with* **vatapá**, *then fried in* **dendê** *oil*

acebolado/acebolada ⓜ/ⓕ aa-se-bo-*laa*-do/aa-se-bo-*laa*-daa *saute of onion, garlic, olive oil & sometimes a bay leaf served with steak*

acompanhamento ⓜ aa-kong-pa-nyaa-*meng*-to *accompaniment*

açúcar ⓜ aa-*soo*-kaarr *sugar*
    — **mascavo** maas-*kra*-vo *brown sugar*
    — **refinado** he-fee-*naa*-do/ he-fee-*naa*-daa *refined sugar*

adoçante ⓜ aa-do-*sang*-te *sugar substitute*

agrião ⓜ aa-gree-*owng* *watercress*

água ⓕ *aa*-gwaa *water*
    — **da nascente** daa naa-*seng*-te *spring water*
    — **da torneira** daa torr-*nay*-raa *tap water*
    — **mineral (com/sem gás)** mee-ne-*row* (kong/seng gas) *mineral water (still/sparkling)*

aguardente ⓜ aa-gwaarr-*deng*-te *strong sugar cane alcohol drunk throughout the country, also known as* **cachaça**

aipo ⓜ *ai*-po *celery*

alcachofra ⓕ ow-kaa-*sho*-fraa *artichoke*

alecrim ⓜ aa-le-*kreeng* *rosemary*

alface ⓕ ow-*faa*-se *lettuce*

alho ⓜ **porro** *aa*-lyo po-*ho* *garlic leek*

almoço ⓜ ow-*mo*-so *lunch*

almôndegas ⓕ pl ow-*mong*-de-gaas *meatballs, usually beef or pork, served in a tomato-based sauce*

ambrosia ⓕ ang-bro-*zee*-aa *sweetened egg yolks thickened to a soft creamy texture, eaten as a dessert*

amêijoa ⓕ aa-*may*-zho-aa *cockle*

ameixa ⓕ aa-*may*-shaa *plum*

amêndoa ⓕ aa-*meng*-dwaa *almond*

amendolm ⓜ aa-meng-doo-*eeng* *peanut*

amora ⓕ aa-*mo*-raa *blackberry*

angú ⓜ ang-*goo* *runny polenta (corn meal porridge)*

cordeiro ⓜ korr-*day*-ro *lamb*

arroz ⓜ aa-*hoz* *rice*
    — **cozido** ko-*zee*-do *cooked rice*
    — **de carreteiro** de kaa-he-*tay*-ro *rice mixed with fried salted beef, served with fried manioc*
    — **de marisco** de maa-*rees*-ko *casserole of seafood & rice in tomato sauce*
    — **integral** eeng-te-*grow* *brown rice*

asa ① *aa*·zaa wing
— **assada** aa·*saa*·daa *roasted wing*
— **de frango** de *fraug*·go
chicken wing
— **frita** *free*·taa *fried wing*
aspargo ⑩ aas·*paar*·go *asparagus*
atum ⑩ aa·*toong tuna*
avelã ① aa·ve·*lang hazelnut*
aves ① pl *aa*·ves *poultry*
avestruz ⑩ aa·ves·*troos ostrich*
azeite ⑩ aa·*zay*·te *olive oil*
azeitonas ① pl aa·zay·*to*·naas *olives*
— **pretas** *pre*·taas *black olives*
— **recheadas** re·she·*aa*·daas
stuffed olives
— **sem caroço** seng kaa·*ro*·so
pitted olives
— **verdes** *verr*·des *green olives*

B

bacaba ① baa·*kaa*·baa *Amazonian
fruit used in wines & syrups*
bacalhau ⑩ baa·kaa·*lyow
dried salted cod*
banha ① *ba*·nyaa *lard*
batata ① **doce** baa·*taa*·taa *do*·se
sweet potato
batatas ① pl baa·*taa*·taas *potatoes*
— **cozidas** ko·*zee*·daas
boiled potatoes
— **fritas** *free*·taas *potato chips
or crisps*
baunilha ① bow·*nee*·lyaa *vanilla*
bavaroise ① baa·vaa·hoo·*waa*·ze
*whipped gelatinous dessert made
with cream & pieces of fruit such as
strawberries or pineapple*
bebida ① be·*bee*·daa *beverage*
— **(sem) álcool** (seng) *ow*·kol
(non)alcoholic beverage
— **destilada** des·tee·*laa*·daa *spirits*
— **gelada** zhe·*laa*·daa *cold beverage*
— **quente** *keng*·te *hot beverage*

beringela ① be·reeng·*zhe*·laa
aubergine • eggplant
beterraba ① be·te·*haa*·baa *beetroot*
bicarbonato ⑩ **de sódio**
bee·kaa·borr·*naa*·to de *so*·dyo
baking soda • bicarbonate of soda
bife ⑩ *bee*·fe *steak of beef, other meats,
poultry or fish • fillet*
— **ao ponto** ow *pong*·to *steak that's
medium cooked*
— **bem passado** beng paa·*saa*·do
well-done steak
— **de alcatra** de ow·*kaa*·traa
rump steak
— **de atum** de aa·*toong tuna steak*
— **de filé** de fee·*le sirloin steak*
— **de lombinho** de long·*bee*·nyo
pork fillet steak
— **de vaca** de *vaa*·kaa *beef steak*
biscoitos ⑩ pl bees·*koy*·tos
biscuits • cookies
bobó ⑩ **de camarão** bo·*bo* de
kaa·maa·*rowng thick stew of fresh
prawns, coconut milk, **dendê** oil,
coriander & pureed manioc*
bolachas ① pl as bo·*laa*·shaas
crackers • biscuits
bolo ⑩ *bo*·lo *cake*
— **de aniversário**
de aa·nee·verr·*saa*·ryo *birthday cake*
— **de carne** de *kaar*·ne *meatloaf*
— **de casamento**
de kaa·zaa·*meng*·to *wedding cake*
— **de chocolate** de sho·ko·*laa*·te
chocolate cake
— **de laranja** de laa·*rang*·zhaa
orange cake
— **de nozes** de *no*·zes *walnut cake*
— **rei** hay *a Christmas bread in the
shape of a large ring, studded with
walnuts, pine nuts, almonds & raisins &
decorated with glazed fruit*
bombons ⑩ pl bong·*bongs bonbons*
brasa *braa*·zaa *see* **na brasa**
brócolis ⑩ pl *bro*·ko·lees *broccoli*

bucho ⓜ *boo*·sho tripe

bufet ⓜ **de saladas frias** boo·*fe* de saa·*laa*·daas *free*·aas *cold salad buffet with vegetable, pasta & bean salads*

buriti ⓜ boo·ree·*tee* *a palm-tree fruit with a mealy texture & a hint of peach*

C

cabidela, à kaa·bee·*de*·la, aa *any dish made with blood & giblets of poultry*

cabrito ⓜ kaa·*bree*·to *kid (goat)*

cacau ⓜ ka·*kow* cocoa · *pulp from cocoa pod*

— **chocolate quente** sho·ko·*laa*·te keng·te *hot cocoa (beverage)*

caça ① *kaa*·saa *game*

cação ⓜ kaa·*sowng* *shark meat*

cachaça ① kaa·*shaa*·saa *strong sugar cane spirit produced & drunk throughout the country*

café ⓜ kaa·*fe* coffee · *cafe*

— **com leite** kong *lay*·te *medium-sized cup of half milk & half filter coffee*

— **descafeinado** des·kaa·fe·ee·*naa*·do *decaffeinated coffee*

— **em grão** eng *growng* *coffee beans*

— **instantâneo** eengs·tang·*ta*·nyo *instant coffee*

— **moído** mo·*ee*·do *ground coffee*

— **pingado** peen·*gaa*·do *short black · espresso with a dash of cold milk*

cafeteria ① kaa·fe·te·*ree*·aa *coffee shop or cafeteria*

cafezinho kaa·fe·*zee*·nyo *short black · espresso topped with hot water*

caipirinha ① kai·pee·ree·*nyaa* *cocktail of lime, sugar & cachaça on ice*

cajú ⓜ kaa·*zhoo* cashew · *tart fruit of cashew (the nut is enclosed in the fruit), usually used in juices*

caldeirada ① kow·day·*raa*·daa *soup-like stew, usually made with fish*

caldo ⓜ *kow*·do soup · *broth*

— **de galinha** de gaa·*lee*·nyaa *chicken broth*

— **verde** *verr*·de *potato-based soup with* **couve** & **paio**

camarão ⓜ kaa·maa·*rowng* prawn

— **á paulista** aa pow·*lees*·taa *unshelled fresh prawn fried in olive oil with garlic & salt*

canela ① kaa·*ne*·la cinnamon

canja ① kang·zhaa *soup made with chicken broth, often a meal in itself*

— **de galinha** de gaa·*lee*·nyaa *chicken soup*

carambola ① kaa·rang·*bo*·laa starfruit

caramelo ⓜ kaa·raa·*me*·lo caramel · *hard candy*

carangueijada ① kaa·rang·ge·*zhaa*·daa *a feast of crab cooked whole on salt, accompanied by chilli &* **farofa**

camarão ⓜ ka·ma·*rowng* prawns

— **frito com alho** *free*·to kong *aa*·lyo *prawns sauteed in garlic, sometimes with chilli*

carne ① *kaar*·ne meat

— **assada** aa·*saa*·daa *roast meat*

— **de porco** de *porr*·ko *pork*

— **de sol** de sol *a tasty, salted meat, fried in oil*

— **de vaca** de *vaa*·kaa *beef*

— **picada** pee·*kaa*·daa *chopped meat*

carneiro ⓜ kaarr·*nay*·ro *mutton*

cardápio ⓜ kaar·*daa*·pyo *menu*

— **de vinhos** de *vee*·nyos *wine list*

carvão, no ⓜ&① kaar·*vowng*, no *char-grilled*

caruru ⓜ kaa·roo·*roo* *one of the most popular Brazilian dishes of African origin, made with okra, onions, salt, dried shrimp &* **dendê** *oil. Traditionally, a sea fish such as grouper is added.*

casa, à moda da ⓜ&ⓕ *kaa*-zaa, aa *mo*-daa daa house-style

casa ⓕ **de chá** *kaa*-zaa de shaa teahouse selling pastries, sweets, coffee as well as herbal & black teas

caseira/caseiro ⓕ/ⓜ *kaa-zay*-raa/ *kaa-zay*-ro home-style cooking

castanhas ⓕ pl **de cajú** kas-*ta*-nyaas de kaa-*zhoo* chestnuts

castanhas ⓕ pl **portuguesas** kas-*ta*-nyaas porr-*too-ge*-zaas chestnuts

cavalas ⓕ pl kaa-*vaa*-laas mackerel

casquinha ⓕ **de siri** kaas-*kee*-nyaa de see-*ree* stuffed crab

cebola ⓕ se-*bo*-la onion

cenoura ⓕ se-*no*-raa carrot

cereal ⓜ se-re-*ow* cereal, grains or breakfast cereal

cereja ⓕ se-re-*zhaa* (sweet) cherry

cerveja ⓕ serr-*ve*-zhaa beer

cervejaria ⓕ serr-ve-zhaa-*ree*-aa beer bar/brewery (also serves food)

chá ⓜ shaa tea
— **com limão** kong lee-*mowng* black tea with thick strip of lemon peel
— **de ervas** de *err*-vaas herb tea
— **de erva doce** de *err*-vaa *do*-se aniseed tea (very commonly given to children)
— **de limão** de lee-*mowng* glass or cup of hot water with a twist of lemon rind
— **preto** *pre*-to black tea
— **verde** *verr*-de green tea

champanhe ⓜ shang-*pa*-nye champagne

chef ⓜ&ⓕ *she*-fe chef

chocolate ⓜ sho-ko-*laa*-te chocolate
— **ao leite** ow *lay*-te milk chocolate
— **branco** *brang*-ko white chocolate
— **preto** *pre*-to dark chocolate

choppe ⓜ *sho*-pee large glass of draught beer
— **preto** *pre*-to dark beer • stout

chouriço ⓜ sho-*ree*-so garlicky pork sausage flavoured with red pepper paste
— **de sangue** de *sang*-ge blood sausage

churrasco ⓜ shoo-*haas*-ko barbecue

claras ⓕ pl **de ovos** *klaa*-raas de o-vos egg whites

côco ⓜ *ko*-ko coconut

codorna ⓕ ko-*dorr*-na quail

coelho ⓜ ko-e-*lyo* rabbit
— **à caçador** aa kaa-*saa-dorr* 'hunter's style rabbit' – rabbit stewed with red & white wine & tomato
— **ao vinha d'alho** ow vee-*nyaa daa-lyo* baked rabbit set atop slices of fried bread, covered with onion slices & drizzled with port or white wine

coentro ⓜ ko-*eng*-tro coriander

cogumelos ⓜ pl ko-goo-*me*-los mushrooms

colorau ⓜ ko-lo-*row* sweet paprika

com tudo kong *too*-do 'with everything' – a dish with the lot

compota ⓕ kong-*po*-taa fruit preserve

confeitaria ⓕ kong-fay-taa-*ree*-aa patisserie

congelado/congelada ⓜ/ⓕ kong-zhe-*laa*-do/kong-zhe-*laa*-daa frozen

conserva ⓕ kong-*serr*-vaa tinned/ canned goods

consomé ⓜ kong-so-*me* consomme

corante ⓜ ko-*rang*-te food colouring

cordeiro ⓜ korr-*day*-ro mutton

costeleta ⓕ **de porco** kos-te-*le*-taa de *porr*-ko pork chop

couve ⓕ *ko*-ve green edible leaf
— **de Bruxelas** de broo-*she*-laas Brussels sprout
— **flor** florr cauliflower

coxinha ⓕ **de galinha** ko-*shee*-nyaa de gaa-*lee*-nyaa fried, savoury chicken mixture in the form of a drumstick

cozido ⓜ **(à brasileira)** ko-*zee*-do (aa bra-*see*-le-*raa*) *Brazilian stew, full of meat, vegetables, beans & rice*

cozido/cozida ⓜ/ⓕ ko-*zee*-do/ ko-*zee*-daa *cooked*

cozinha ⓕ ko-*zee*-nyaa *kitchen*
— **tradicional** traa-dee-syo-*now* *traditional cooking*

cravo ⓜ *kraa*-vo *cloves*

creme ⓜ *kre*-me *whipped cream*
— **chantilly** shang-tee-*lee* *whipped cream*
— **de legumes** de le-*goo*-mes *cream of vegetable soup*
— **pasteleiro** paas-te-*lay*-ro *egg-based cream filling used in pastries*

croissant ⓜ krwaa-*sang croissant*
— **com chocolate** kong sho-ko-*laa*-te *chocolate-filled croissant*
— **com creme** kong *kre*-me *custard-filled croissant*
— **com presunto** kong pre-*zoong*-to *croissant with ham*
— **com queijo** kong *kay*-zho *croissant with cheese*
— **misto** *mees*-to *croissant with ham & cheese*

croquete ⓜ kro-*ke*-te *meat croquette*

cru/crua m/f kroo/*kroo*-a *raw*

curado/curada m/f koo-*raa*-do/ koo-*raa*-daa *cured*

D

damasco ⓜ daa-*maas*-ko *apricot*

defumado/defumada ⓜ/ⓕ de-foo-*maa*-do/de-foo-*maa*-daa *smoked*

dendê ⓜ deng-*de* palm oil

desossado/desossada ⓜ/ⓕ de-zo-*saa*-do/de-zo-*saa*-daa *boned*

digestivo ⓜ dee-zhes-*tee*-vo *after-dinner drink, usually a liqueur, brandy or port*

dobradinha ⓕ do-braa-*dee*-nyaa *tripe with white beans & rice*

doce ⓜ *do*-se *sweet • dessert • jam*
— **de abóbora com requeijão** de aa-*bo*-bo-raa kong he-kay-*zhowng* *pumpkin jam*
— **de goiaba** de go-*yaa*-baa *guava jam*
— **de ovos** de *o*-vos *egg yolk sweets*

doces ⓜ pl **regionais** *do*-ses he-zhyo-*nais* *regional sweets*

dourado ⓜ do-*raa*-do *freshwater fish found throughout Brazil*

E

empada ⓕ eng-*paa*-daa *miniature pot pie*
— **de carne** de *kaarr*-ne *with meat filling*
— **de camarão** dekaa-*maa*-*rowng*
— **de frango** de *fran*-go *with prawn filling*
— **de galinha** de gaa-*lee*-nyaa *with chicken filling*
— **de legumes** de le-*goo*-mes *with vegetable filling*

empadão ⓜ eng-paa-*downg* *a big* **empada**

enguia ⓕ eng-*gee*-aa *eel*

entrada ⓕ eng-*traa*-daa *entree*

erva-doce ⓕ err-vaa-*do*-se *aniseed*

ervas ⓕ pl *err*-vaas *herbs*
— **aromáticas** aa-ro-*maa*-tee-kaas *mixture of cooking herbs*

ervilhas ⓕ pl err-*vee*-lyaas *peas*

escabeche ⓜ es-kaa-*be*-she *tomato, onion, parsley & garlic fried with a dash of vinegar & poured over fried fish*

escalopinho ⓜ es-kaa-lo-*pee*-nyo *medallion-shaped, high quality cuts of boneless meat*

espada ⓕ es-*paa*-daa *swordfish*

espanhola, à es-pa-*nyo*-laa, aa *dish in tomato & onion sauce*

espaguete ⓜ es·paa·*ge*·te *spaghetti*
especialidade ⓕ **da casa**
es·pe·syaa·lee·*daa*·de daa *kaa*·zaa
house speciality
especiarias ⓕ pl es·pe·syaa·*ree*·aas
spices
espeto ⓜ es·*pe*·to *on a skewer*
— **de camarão** de kaa·maa·*rowng*
skewered prawn
— **de carne** de *kaar*·ne *skewered beef*
— **de lula** de *loo*·laa *skewered squid*
— **misto** *mees*·to *mixed grill* ·
*skewered chunks of veal and/or pork,
separated by bacon or sausage slices,
green capsicum & onion*
espinafre ⓜ es·pee·*naa*·fre *spinach*
espumante ⓜ&ⓕ es·poo·*mang*·te
sparkling wine

F

faisão ⓜ fai·*sowng* *pheasant*
farinha ⓕ **de trigo** fa·*ree*·nyaa de
tree·go *wheat flour*
farinha ⓕ **de mandioca** faa·*ree*·nyaa
de mang·dee·o·kaa *manioc flour*
farofa ⓕ faa·ro·faa *manioc flour fried
with oil, garlic, salt & sometimes
sausage & eggs*
favas ⓕ pl *faa*·vaas *broad beans*
feijão ⓜ fay·*zhowng* *bean*
— **branco** *brang*·ko *white bean*
— **fradinho** fraa·*dee*·nyo
black-eyed pea
— **manteiga** mang·*tay*·gaa
butter bean
— **preto** *pre*·to *black bean*
feijoada ⓕ fay·zho·*aa*·daa *the national
dish of Brazil – pork & black bean stew
served with rice*
fígado ⓜ *fee*·gaa·do *liver*
figo ⓜ *fee*·go *fig*
filé ⓜ fee·*le* *fish fillet*
— **de pescada** de pes·*kaa*·daa
breaded & fried whiting fillet

folhado ⓜ **de carne** fo·*lyaa*·do de
kaarr·ne *puff pastry with meat filling*
folhado ⓜ **de salsicha** fo·*lyaa*·do de
sow·*see*·shaa *puff pastry with sausage
filling*
forno, ao *forr*·no, ow *oven baked*
framboesa ⓕ frang·bo·e·zaa *raspberry*
frango ⓜ *frang*·go *chicken*
— **assado** aa·*saa*·do *roast chicken*
— **na brasa** naa *braa*·zaa *char-grilled
chicken seasoned with garlic, bay leaf,
paprika & olive oil*
fresco/fresca ⓜ/ⓕ fres·ko/fres·kaa
fresh · cool · cold
frigideira ⓕ free·zhee·*day*·raa *frying
pan or skillet*
frio/fria ⓜ/ⓕ free·o/free·aa *cold*
frito/frita ⓜ/ⓕ free·to/free·taa *fried*
frios ⓜ pl free·os *cold cuts of meat*
fruta ⓕ *froo*·taa *fruit*
— **cristalizada** krees·taa·lee·*zaa*·daa
candied/glazed fruit
— **da época** daa e·po·kaa
seasonal fruit
fruta-do-conde ⓕ froo·taa·do·*kong*·de
custard apple
frutas secas ⓕ pl *froo*·taas se·kaas
dried fruit & nuts
folha ⓜ **do funcho** fo·lyaa do
foong·sho *dill*

G

galinha ⓕ gaa·*lee*·nyaa *chicken*
— **caipira** kai·*pee*·raa *free-range
chicken*
garrafa ⓕ gaa·*haa*·faa *bottle*
— **de meio litro** de *me*·yo *lee*·tro
half-litre bottle
— **de um litro** de oom *lee*·tro
litre bottle
— **pequena** pe·*ke*·naa *small bottle*
gelatina ⓕ zhe·laa·*tee*·naa *gelatin*
geléia ⓕ zhe·*le*·yaa *jelly*
gelo ⓜ *zhe*·lo *ice*
gemas ⓕ pl *zhe*·maas *egg yolks*

gengibre ⓜ zheng·*zhee*·bre *ginger*

goiaba ⓕ go·*yaa*·baa *guava*

goiabada ⓕ go·yaa·*baa*·daa *guava jam*

grão (de bico) ⓜ growng (de *bee*·ko) *chickpeas • garbanzo beans*

gratinado/gratinada ⓜ/ⓕ graa·tee·*naa*·do/graa·tee·*naa*·daa *au gratin – topped with breadcrumbs & browned*

graviola ⓕ graa·vee·o·*laa custard apple*

grelhado/grelhada ⓜ/ⓕ gre·*lyaa*·do/gre·*lyaa*·daa *grilled*

groselha ⓕ gro·ze·*lyaa gooseberry • gooseberry syrup*

guarnecido/guarnecida ⓜ/ⓕ gwaar·ne·*see*·do/gwaar·ne·*see*·daa *garnished with pickled cauliflower, carrots, onion & sometimes olives*

guisado/guisada ⓜ/ⓕ gee·*zaa*·do/gee·*zaa*·daa *braised*

H

hortaliça ⓕ or·taa·*lee*·saa *green leafy vegetables*

— **cozida** ko·*zee*·daa *boiled green leafy vegetables*

— **refogada** he·fo·*gaa*·daa *sauteed green leafy vegetables*

hortelã ⓕ or·te·*lang mint*

I

inhame ⓜ ee·*nyaa*·me *yam*

iogurte ⓕ ee·o·*goorr*·te *yogurt*

— **líquido** *lee*·kee·do *liquid yogurt*

iscas ⓕ pl **de fígado** *ees*·kaas de *fee*·gaa·do *chopped liver*

J

jaca ⓕ *zhaa*·kaa *jackfruit*

jambu ⓜ zham·*boo a Brazilian herb*

jantar ⓜ zhang·*taarr dinner*

jardineira ⓕ zhaar·dee·*nay*·raa *hearty beef & vegetable stew*

javali ⓜ zhaa·vaa·*lee wild boar*

L

lagosta ⓕ laa·*gos*·taa *lobster*

lagostim ⓜ laa·gos·*teeng crayfish*

lanche ⓜ *lang*·she *afternoon snack*

laranja ⓕ laa·*rang*·zhaa *orange*

lata ⓕ *laa*·taa *can*

lebre ⓕ *le*·bre *hare*

legumes ⓜ pl le·*goo*·mes *vegetables*

leitão ⓜ lay·*towng suckling pig roasted in a wood-fired oven*

leite ⓜ *lay*·te *milk*

— **condensado** kong·deng·*saa*·do *condensed milk*

— **gordo** *gorr*·do *full cream milk*

— **desnatado** des·naa·*taa*·do *skim milk*

lesma ⓕ *les*·maa *snails*

licor ⓜ lee·*korr liqueur*

limão ⓜ lee·*mowng lime*

— **galego** gaa·*le*·go *lemon*

língua ⓕ *leeng*·gwaa *tongue*

linguado ⓜ leeng·*gwaa*·do *sole*

— **à (la) Meunière** aa (laa) mo·nee·*err lightly pan-fried sole sprinkled with parsley & lemon juice*

linguiça ⓕ leen·*gwee*·saa *thin, long garlicky pork sausage*

lombinho ⓜ **de porco** long·*bee*·nyo de *porr*·ko *thinly sliced pork tenderloin*

lombo ⓜ **de porco assado** *long*·bo de *porr*·ko aa·*saa*·do *roast pork loin*

louro ⓜ *lo*·ro *bay leaf*

lula ⓕ *loo*·laa *squid*

— **à Sevilhana** aa se·vee·*lya*·naa *fried squid rings served with mayonnaise*

— **recheada** he·she·*aa*·daa *small squid stuffed with rice, tomatoes & parsley*

M

maçã ⓕ maa·*sang* apple
— **assada** a·*saa*·daa baked apple

maduro/madura ⓜ/ⓕ
maa·*doo*·ro/maa·*doo*·raa
ripe (fruit) • mature (wine)

maionese ⓕ maa·yo·*ne*·ze mayonnaise

mamão ⓜ maa·*mowng* papaya

mandioca ⓕ mang·dee·*o*·kaa manioc •
cassava
— **frita** *free*·taa deep-fried cassava –
a common bar snack

moda, à mo·daa, aa in the manner of

manga ⓕ mang·gaa mango

manjerona ⓕ mang·zhe·ro·naa
marjoram

manteiga ⓕ mang·*tay*·gaa butter

maracujá ⓜ maa·raa·koo·*zhaa*
passionfruit

margarina ⓕ maarr·gaa·*ree*·naa
margarine

marisco ⓜ maa·*rees*·ko shellfish

marmelada ⓕ maarr·me·*laa*·daa
firm quince paste

marisqueira ⓕ maa·rees·*kay*·raa
seafood restaurant

massa ⓕ *maa*·saa pasta • dough
— **folhada** fo·*lyaa*·daa flaky pastry

medalhão ⓜ me·daa·*lyowng*
medallion of meat or fish

mel ⓜ mel honey

melaço ⓜ me·*laa*·so molasses

melancia ⓕ me·lang·*see*·aa
watermelon

melão ⓜ me·*lowng* melon
— **com presunto** kong pre·*zoong*·to
slices of honeydew melon topped with
thin slices of ham

mercado ⓜ merr·*kaa*·do market

merenda ⓕ me·*reng*·daa snack •
light lunch • picnic lunch

merengue ⓜ me·*reng*·ge meringue

mexilhões ⓜ pl me·shee·*lyoyngs*
mussels

mil folhas ⓜ pl meel fo·*lyaas* layers of
flaky pastry with custard filling

milho ⓜ **doce** *mee*·lyo do·se sweet corn

minimercado ⓜ mee·nee·merr·*kaa*·do
small convenience store

mini-prato ⓜ mee·nee·*praa*·to
very small serving

miolos ⓜ pl mee·o·los brains

miudos ⓜ pl mee·oo·dos giblets

moda ⓕ **da casa** mo·daa daa kaa·zaa
house-style – usually describes a meat
dish accompanied by rice, chips,
salad & a fried egg

moelas ⓕ pl as mo·e·laas
chicken gizzards

molho ⓜ mo·lyo sauce • gravy • dressing
— **branco** brang·ko white sauce
— **de caramelo** de kaa·raa·me·lo
caramel sauce
— **de cocktail** de ko·kee·tel sauce
made from mayonnaise, tomato
sauce & a dash of whisky
— **de manteiga** de mang·*tay*·gaa
butter sauce
— **verde** verr·de sauce for fish or
octopus made with chopped onion,
garlic, red capsicum, parsley, vinegar
& lots of olive oil

molusco ⓜ mo·*loos*·ko clam

moqueca ⓕ mo·ke·kaa style of cooking
from Bahia • a kind of sauce or stew
made from **dendê** oil & coconut milk,
cooked in a covered clay pot

moqueca ⓕ **(de peixe) capixaba**
mo·ke·kaa (de pay·she)
kaa·pee·*shaa*·baa fish stew
traditionally made in a clay pot

morangos ⓜ pl mo·*rang*·gos
strawberries

morcela ⓕ morr·se·laa blood sausage

moscatel ⓜ mos·kaa·*tel* sweet dessert
wine

mostarda ⓕ mos·*taarr*·daa mustard

N

na brasa naa *braa-zaa*
char-grilled

na chapa naa *shaa-paa* cooked on
a hot steel plate

na pedra naa *pe-draa* meat or fish
grilled on a hot stone at the table

nabo ⓜ *naa-bo* turnip

nêspera ⓕ *nes-pe-raa* loquat

novilho ⓜ *no-vee-lyo* veal

noz ⓕ *noz* walnut

O

óleo ⓜ *o-lyo* oil
— **de amendoim** de
aa-meng-do-*eeng* peanut oil
— **de cozinha** de ko-zee-*nyaa*
cooking oil
— **de girassol** de zhee-raa-*sol*
sunflower seed oil
— **de milho** de mee-lyo corn oil
— **de soja** de so-*zhaa* soybean oil
— **vegetal** ve-zhe-*tow* vegetable oil

omelete ⓜ *o-me-le-te* omelette

orégano ⓜ *o-re-ga-no* oregano

ostra ⓕ *os-traa* oyster

ovas ⓕ pl **(de pescada)** *o-vaas* (de
pes-*kaa-daa*) fish eggs, usually hake

ovo ⓜ *o-vo* egg
— **cozido** ko-*zee-do* boiled egg
— **frito** *free-to* fried egg
— **mexido** me-*shee-do*
scrambled egg
— **poché** po-*she* poached egg

P

pá ⓕ *paa* beef cut

padaria ⓕ *paa-daa-ree-aa* bakery

paio ⓜ *paa-yo* smoked pork tenderloin
sausage

palmier ⓜ *pow-mee-err* flat, palm-
shaped puff pastry

panqueca ⓕ *pang-ke-kaa* crepe
— **de galinha** de gaa-lee-*nyaa*
chicken crepe
— **de legumes** de le-*goo-mes*
vegetable crepe

pão ⓜ *powng* bread
— **com linguiça**
kong leeng-*gwee-saa*
bread roll with sausage
— **da casa** daa *kaa-zaa* 'house bread'
— **de centeio** de seng-*te-yo*
light rye bread
— **de forma** de *forr-maa*
loaf of bread
— **de-ló** de *lo* collapsed sponge cake
— **de milho** de *mee-lyo* corn bread
— **de trigo integral** de *tree-go*
eeng-te-*grow* wheat-flour bread
— **doce** *do-se* sweetened bread roll
with cream, icing or sugar
— **integral** eeng-te-*grow* wholegrain
bread

papa ⓕ **de milho** *paa-paa* de *mee-lyo*
cornmeal porridge

papos-de-anjo ⓜ pl *paa-pos-de-ang-*zho
little egg-based puffs in a sugar syrup

passas ⓕ pl *paa-saas* raisins

pastéis ⓜ pl pas-*tays* pastries • small
savoury fritters or something that
looks more like a pie
— **de bacalhau** de baa-kaa-*lyow*
deep-fried, oval-shaped savouries
made of mashed potato, onion,
parsley & salt cod

pastel ⓜ paas-*tel* pastry

pastelaria ⓕ paas-te-laa-*ree-aa*
pastry shop • coffee shop • pastries

pato ⓜ *paa-to* duck
— **no tucupi** no too-koo-*pee*
roast duck flavoured with garlic &
cooked in *tucupi*

pé ⓜ **de porco com feijão branco** pe
de *porr-ko* kong fay-*zowng* *brang-ko*
stew made from pig's feet and white
beans

peito ⓜ **de frango** *pay*·to de *frang*·go chicken breast

peixada ⓕ pay·*shaa*·daa *fish cooked in broth with vegetables & tomatoes*

peixe ⓜ *pay*·she *fish*
  — **assado no forno** aa·*saa*·do no *forr*·no *baked fish*
  — **frito** *free*·to *fried fish*

pepino ⓜ pe·*pee*·no *cucumber*

pêra ⓕ *pe*·raa *pear*

peru ⓜ pe·*roo* *turkey*

pescada ⓕ pes·*kaa*·daa *whiting*

pescadinhas ⓕ pl pes·kaa·*dee*·nyaas *fried small whiting*

pêssego ⓜ *pe*·se·go *peach*

petiscos ⓜ pl pe·*tees*·kos *appetisers including sausages, cheese & olives, fried manioc, French fries*

picanha ⓕ pee·*ka*·nyaa *thin cut of rump steak*

picante pee·*kang*·te *describes any spicy or hot sauce*

pimenta ⓕ pee·*meng*·taa *pepper*
  — **branca** *brang*·kaa *white pepper*
  — **do reino** do *hay*·no *black pepper*

pimentão ⓜ pee·meng·*towng* (sweet) *pepper • capsicum*
  — **assado** aa·*saa*·do *roast capsicum*
  — **verde** *verr*·de *green capsicum*
  — **vermelho** verr·*me*·lyo *red capsicum*

pinhão ⓜ pee·*nyowng* *pine nut*

pirarucu ⓜ pee·raa·hoo·*koo* *common Amazonian river fish*
  — **ao forno** ow *forr*·no *oven-cooked* **pirarucu** *with lemon & other seasonings*

poché ⓜ po·*she* *poached*

polpa ⓕ *pol*·paa *fruit or vegetable pulp*
  — **de fruta** de *froo*·taa *fruit pulp*
  — **de tomate** de to·*maa*·te *tomato pulp*

polvo ⓜ *pol*·vo *octopus*

porco ⓜ *porr*·ko *pork*

posta ⓕ *pos*·taa *fish steak*

prato ⓜ *praa*·to *dish*
  — **de verão** de ve·*rowng* *fruit salad common in Rio de Janeiro*
  — **do dia** do *dee*·aa *the daily special*
  — **feito (PF)** *fay*·to (pe·e·fe) *set meal*
  — **principal** preeng·*seee*·*pow* *main dish*

presunto ⓜ pre·*zoong*·to *smoked ham*

pudim ⓜ poo·*deeng* *pudding*
  — **de leite condensado** de *lay*·te kong·deng·*saa*·do *a desert similar to creme caramel*
  — **de ovos** de o·vos *baked egg-custard pudding*

pupunha ⓕ poo·*poo*·nyaa *a fatty, vitamin-rich Amazonian fruit eaten with coffee*

Q

queijo ⓜ *kay*·zho *cheese*
  — **de cabra** de *kaa*·braa *goat's milk cheese*
  — **de ovelha** de o·*ve*·lyaa *sheep's milk cheese*
  — **de vaca** de *vaa*·kaa *cow's milk cheese*
  — **quente** *keng*·te *cheese melt*

quibe ⓜ *kee*·be *deep-fried meatballs*

R

recheado/recheada ⓜ/ⓕ he·she·*aa*·do/he·she·*aa*·daa *stuffed*

recheio ⓜ he·*shay*·o *stuffing or filling*

refeição ⓕ he·fay·*sowng* *meal*
  — **rápida** *haa*·pee·daa *quick meal • fast food*

refogado ⓜ he·fo·*gaa*·do *quick fry*

refrigerante ⓜ he·free·zhe·*rang*·te *soft drink*

repolho ⓜ he·*po*·lyo *variety of cabbage with crinkly leaves*
  — **roxo** *ho*·sho *purple cabbage*

rim ⓜ *heeng* *kidney*

risole ⓜ hee-*zo*-le *rissole • fried pasty*
— **de camarão** de-kaa-maa-*rowng* *pasty or rissole with prawn filling*
— **de carne** de-*kaarr*-ne *pasty or rissole with meat filling*
— **de frango** de *frang*-go *pasty or rissole with chicken filling*
rodízio ⓜ ho-*dee*-zyo *Brazilian barbecue featuring various grilled meats on skewers and a cold salad buffet*
rosbife ⓜ hos-*bee*-fe *roast beef*

S

sal ⓜ sow *salt*
salada ⓕ saa-*laa*-daa *salad*
— **de alface** de ow-*faa*-se *lettuce salad*
— **de atum** de aa-*toong* *salad of tuna, potato, peas, carrots, boiled eggs with an olive oil & vinegar dressing*
— **de bacalhau com feijão fradinho** de baa-kaa-*lyow* kong fay-*zhowng* fraa-*dee*-nyo *salad of shredded, uncooked salt cod & black-eyed peas with olive oil & vinegar dressing*
— **de feijão fradinho** de fay-*zhowng* fraa-*dee*-nyo *black-eyed pea salad flavoured with onion, garlic, olive oil & vinegar, sprinkled with chopped boiled egg & parsley*
— **de tomate** de to-*maa*-te *tomato & onion salad, often flavoured with oregano*
— **mista** *mees*-taa *tomato, lettuce & onion salad*
— **palmito** pow-*mee*-to *palm heart salad*
— **russa** hoo-*saa* *potato salad with peas, carrots mayonnaise*
salgadinho ⓜ sow-gaa-*dee*-nyos *small savoury pastry*

salgado/salgada ⓜ/ⓕ sow-*gaa*-do/ sow-*gaa*-daa *small savoury pastry*
salmão ⓜ sow-*mowng* *salmon*
— **defumado** de-foo-*maa*-do *smoked salmon*
salpicão ⓜ sow-pee-*kowng* *smoked pork sausage flavoured with garlic, bay leaf & sometimes wine*
salsa ⓕ sow-*saa* *parsley*
salsicha ⓕ sow-*see*-shaa *sausage*
sálvia ⓕ *sow*-vyaa *sage*
sanduíche ⓜ *sang*-doo-ee-she *sandwich*
sardinha ⓕ saarr-*dee*-nyaa *sardine*
seco/seca ⓜ/ⓕ *se*-ko/*se*-kaa *dry • dried*
sobremesa ⓕ so-bre-*me*-zaa *sweet • dessert • jam*
sonhos ⓜ pl *so*-nyos *doughnut-like pastry sprinkled with sugar & cinnamon*
sopa ⓕ *so*-paa *soup*
— **de feijão** de fay-*zhowng* *soup made from dried pulses or beans*
— **de feijão fradinho** de fay-*zwong* fraa-*dee*-nyo *black-eyed pea soup flavoured with sausages*
— **de legumes** de le-*goo*-mes *vegetable soup*
— **de peixe** de *pay*-she *fish in a tomato & onion broth, served over chunks of bread*
— **do dia** do *dee*-aa *soup of the day*
— **juliana** zhoo-lee-*a*-naa *soup made with mixed, julienned vegetables*
sorvete ⓜ sorr-*ve*-te *ice cream*
suco ⓜ *soo*-ko *juice*
— **de laranja natural** de laa-*rang*-zhaa naa-too-*row* *freshly squeezed orange juice*

T

tacacá ⓕ taa-kaa-*kaa* *an Indian dish of dried shrimp cooked with pepper, jambu & manioc*

tamboril ⓜ tang·bo·*reel* monkfish

tamarindo ⓜ taa·maa·*reeng*·do tamarind

torta ⓕ **de amêndoaa** torr·taa de aa·*meng*·dwaa almond tart

torta ⓕ **de maçã** torr·taa de maa·*sang* apple tart

tomate ⓜ to·*maa*·te tomato

tomilho ⓜ to·*mee*·lyo thyme

torrada ⓕ to·*haa*·daa toast

torresmo ⓜ to·*hes*·mo pork cracklings served hot or cold as a snack

toucinho ⓜ too·*see*·nyo bacon
— **defumado** de·foo·*maa*·do smoked bacon
— **salgado** sow·*gaa*·do salt-cured bacon

trança ⓕ *trang*·saa pastry topped with coconut mixture & chopped nuts

tremoços ⓜ pl tre·*mo*·sos salted, preserved yellow beans eaten as a snack

tripa ⓕ *tree*·pa tripe

truta ⓕ *troo*·taa trout

tucupi ⓜ too·koo·*pee* sauce made from the juice of the manioc plant & **jambu**

tutu ⓜ **á mineira** too·too aa mee·*nay*·raa a bean paste with toasted bacon & manioc flour, often served with cooked cabbage

U

uvas ⓕ pl *oo*·vaas grapes

V

vatapá ⓜ vaa·taa·*paa* dried shrimp, cashew, fish, pepper & tomato sauce

veado ⓜ ve·*aa*·do venison

vinagre ⓜ vee·*naa*·gre vinegar

vinha ⓕ **d'alho** vee·nyaa daa·lyo meat marinated in wine or vinegar, olive oil, garlic & bay leaf

vinho ⓜ *vee*·nyo wine
— **branco** *brang*·ko white wine
— **da casa** daa *kaa*·zaa house wine
— **da região** daa he·zhee·*owng* local wine
— **quente** *keng*·te mulled wine
— **rosé** ho·ze rosé wine
— **tinto** *teeng*·to red wine
— **verde** *verr*·de 'green wine' – light sparkling red, white or rosé wine

vitamina ⓕ vee·taa·*mee*·naa milk & fruit shake

vitela ⓕ vee·*te*·laa veal

X

xerém chouriço ⓜ she·*reng* sho·*ree*·so cornmeal porridge served with shellfish, pork or other meat

xinxim de galinha ⓜ sheeng·*sheeng* de gaa·*lee*·nyaa chicken pieces flavoured with garlic, salt & lemon

emergencies

emergências

Help, I'm being robbed!
Socorro, estou sendo   so·ko·ho es·to *seng*·do
assaltado/assaltada! m/f   aa·sow·*taa*·do/aa·sow·*taa*·daa

Stop, thief!
Pega ladrão!   pe·gaa la·*drowng*

Can I use your phone?
Posso usar seu telefone?   po·so oo·*zaarr* se·oo te·le·fo·ne

It's an emergency.
É uma emergência.   e *oo*·maa e·merr·*zheng*·see·aa

Call the police!
Chame a polícia!   *sha*·me aa po·*lee*·syaa

Call a doctor!
Chame um médico!   *sha*·me oom *me*·dee·ko

Call an ambulance!
Chame uma   *sha*·me oo·maa
ambulância!   am·boo·*lang*·see·aa

Could you please help?
Você pode ajudar,   vo·*se* po·de aa·zhoo·*daarr*
por favor?   porr faa·*vorr*

I'm lost.
Estou perdido/   es·to perr·*dee*·do/
perdida. m/f   perr·*dee*·daa

Is it dangerous here?
Aqui é perigoso?   a·*kee* e pe·ree·*go*·zo

Where are the toilets?
Onde tem um banheiro?   on·de teng oom ba·*nyay*·ro

I'm ill.
Estou doente. es·*to* do·*eng*·te

She's having a baby.
Ela está tendo um bebê e·laa es·*taa* teng·do oom be·*be*

My ... is ill.	... *está doente.*	... es·*taa* do·*eng*·te
daughter	*Minha filha*	mee·nyaa *fee*·lyaa
friend (female)	*Minha amiga*	mee·nyaa aa·*mee*·gaa
friend (male)	*Meu amigo*	me·oo aa·*mee*·go
son	*Meu filho*	me·oo *fee*·lyo

He/She is	*Ele/Ela está*	e·le/e·laa es·*taa*
having a/an ...	*tendo ...*	teng·do ...
allergic reaction	*uma reação alérgica*	*oo*·maa he·aa·*sowng* aa·*lerr*·zhee·kaa
asthma attack	*um ataque de asma*	oom aa·*taa*·ke de *aas*·maa
epileptic fit	*um ataque epilético*	oom aa·*taa*·ke e·pee·*le*·tee·ko
heart attack	*um ataque cardíaco*	oom aa·*taa*·ke kaarr·*dee*·aa·ko

signs

Delegacia de Polícia	de·le·gaa·*see*·aa de po·*lee*·syaa	Police Station
Hospital	os·pee·*tow*	Hospital
Polícia	po·*lee*·syaa	Police
Pronto Socorro	*prong*·to so·*ko*·ho	Emergency Department

police

Where's the police station?
Onde é a delegacia   ong·de e aa de·le·gaa·*see*·aa
de polícia?   de po·*lee*·syaa

Please telephone the Tourist Police.
Por favor telefone para   porr faa·*vorr* te·le·*fo*·ne *paa*·raa
a Polícia de Turistas.   aa po·*lee*·syaa de too·*rees*·taas

I want to report an offence.
Eu quero fazer uma   *e*·oo *ke*·ro faa·*zerr* oo·maa
queixa.   *kay*·shaa

He/She tried	Ele/Ela tentou	*e*·le/*e*·laa teng·*to*
to … me.	me …	me …
rape	estrupar	es·troo·*paarr*
rob	roubar	ho·*baarr*

I've been …	Eu fui …	*e*·oo foo·*ee* …
He/She has been …	Ele/Ela foi …	*e*·le/*e*·laa foy …
assaulted	agredido/	aa·gre·*dee*·do/
	agredida m/f	aa·gre·*dee*·daa
raped	estrupado/	es·troo·*paa*·do/
	estrupada m/f	es·troo·*paa*·daa
robbed	assaltado/	aa·sow·*taa*·do/
	assaltada m/f	aa·sow·*taa*·daa

My … was stolen.	… foi roubado/	… foy ho·*baa*·do/
	roubada. m/f	ho·*baa*·daa
credit card	Meu cartão m	*me*·oo kaarr·*towng*
	de crédito	de *kre*·dee·to
money	Meu dinheiro m	*me*·oo dee·*nyay*·ro
wallet	Minha	*mee*·nyaa
	carteira f	kaar·*tay*·raa

My ... were stolen.	... foram roubados/ roubadas. m/f pl	... fo·rang ho·baa·dos/ ho·baa·daas
bags	Minhas bolsas f pl	mee·nyaas bol·saas
papers	Meus papéis m pl	me·oos paa·peys
travellers cheques	Meus travellers cheques m pl	me·oos traa·ve·ler she·kes

the police may say ...

You're charged with ...
Você está sendo acusado/ acusada de ... m/f
vo·se es·taa seng·do aa·koo·zaa·do/ aa·koo·zaa·daa de ...

He/She is charged with ...
Ele/Ela está sendo acusado/ acusada de ... m/f
e·le/e·laa es·taa seng·do aa·koo·zaa·do/ aa·koo·zaa·daa de ...

assault	agressão	aa·gre·sowng
disturbing the peace	perturbar a paz	perr·toor·baarr aa pas
not having a visa	não ter visto	nowng terr vees·to
overstaying your visa	ter ultrapassado o seu visto	terr ool·traa·paa·saa·do o se·oo vees·to
possession (of illegal substances)	posse (de substâncias ilegais)	po·se (de soo·bees·tang·syaas ee·le·gais)
shoplifting	furto	foor·to
theft	roubo	ho·bo
It's a ... fine.	É uma multa de ...	e oo·maa mool·taa de ...
parking	estacionamento	es·taa·see·o·naa·meng·to
speeding	velocidade	ve·lo·see·daa·de

I've lost my ...	*Perdi ...*	perr·dee ...
backpack	*minha mochila*	mee·nyaa mo·shee·laa
handbag	*minha bolsa*	mee·nyaa bol·saa
	de mão	de mowng
passport	*meu passaporte*	me·oo paa·saa·porr·te

It was him/her.
Foi ele/ela. foy e·le/e·laa

I have insurance.
Eu tenho seguro. e·oo te·nyo se·goo·ro

What am I accused of?
Do que estou sendo do ke es·to seng·do
acusado/acusada? m/f aa·koo·zaa·do/aa·koo·zaa·daa

I'm sorry.
Desculpe. des·kool·pe

I didn't realise I was doing anything wrong.
Eu não sabia que e·oo nowng saa·bee·aa ke
estava fazendo algo es·taa·vaa faa·zeng·do ow·go
errado. e·haa·do

I didn't do it.
Eu não fiz isso. e·oo nowng fees ee·so

Can I pay an on-the-spot fine?
Posso pagar a multa po·so paa·gaarr aa mool·taa
na hora? naa aw·raa

Can I make a phone call?
Posso fazer uma po·so faa·zerr oo·maa
ligação? lee·gaa·sowng

Can I have a lawyer (who speaks English?)
Posso ter um advogado po·so terr oom ad·vo·gaa·do
(que fale inglês?) (ke faa·le eeng·gles)

essentials

175

This medication is for personal use.

Esta medicação é   es·taa me·dee·ka·*sowng* e
para uso pessoal.   paa·raa oo·zo pe·so·ow

I have a prescription for this drug.

Eu tenho receita médica   e·oo te·nyo he·*say*·taa me·dee·kaa
para esta droga.   paa·raa es·taa dro·gaa

I (don't) understand.

Eu (não) entendo.   e·oo (nowng) eng·*teng*·do

I want to	*Eu quero entrar em*	e·oo ke·ro eng·*traarr* eng
contact my ...	*contato com a ...*	kong·*taa*·to kong aa ...
consulate	*meu*	me·oo
	consulado	kong·soo·*laa*·do
embassy	*minha*	mee·nyaa
	embaixada	eng·bai·*shaa*·daa

---

as the saying goes ...

A mentira tem pernas curtas.
  aa meng·*tee*·ra perr·naas   A lie has short legs.
  koor·taas

Mais vale um pássaro na mâo que dois voando.
  mais vaa·le oom paa·saa·ro na   A bird in the hand
  mowng ke doys vwang·do   is worth two in the bush.

doctor

o médico

Where's the nearest ...?	*Onde fica ... mais perto?*	ong·de *fee*·kaa ... mais *perr*·to
(night) chemist	*a farmácia (noturna)*	aa faarr·*maa*·syaa (no·*toor*·naa)
dentist	*o dentista*	o deng·*tees*·taa
doctor	*o médico*	o *me*·dee·ko
emergency department	*o pronto socorro*	o *prong*·to so·*ko*·ho
hospital	*o hospital*	o os·pee·*tow*
medical centre	*a clínica médica*	aa *klee*·nee·kaa *me*·dee·kaa
optometrist	*o optometrista*	o op·to·me·*trees*·taa

I need a doctor (who speaks English).
Eu preciso de um médico (que fale inglês).
e·oo pre·*see*·zo de oom *me*·dee·ko (ke *faa*·le eeng·*gles*)

Could I see a female doctor?
Posso ver uma médica?
po·so verr *oo*·maa *me*·dee·kaa

Could the doctor come here?
O médico pode vir aqui?
o *me*·dee·ko *po*·de veerr aa·*kee*

Is there an after-hours emergency number?
Tem um número para emergência?
teng oom *noo*·me·ro *paa*·raa e·merr·*zheng*·syaa

the doctor may say ...

What's the problem?
Qual é o problema? kwow e o pro·*ble*·maa

Where does it hurt?
Onde dói? ong·de doy

Do you have a temperature?
Você tem febre? vo·*se* teng *fe*·bre

How long have you been like this?
Há quanto tempo você aa *kwang*·to *teng*·po vo·*se*
está assim? es·*taa* aa·*seeng*

Have you had this before?
Você já teve isso antes? vo·*se* jaa *te*·ve *ee*·so ang·*tes*

Are you sexually active?
Você está sexualmente vo·*se* es·*taa* sek·soo·ow·*meng*·te
ativo/ativa? m/f aa·*tee*·vo/aa·*tee*·vaa

Have you had unprotected sex?
Você fez sexo sem vo·*se* fes *sek*·so seng
proteção? pro·te·*sowng*

Do you ...?	*Você ...?*	vo·*se* ...
drink	*bebe*	*be*·be
smoke	*fuma*	*foo*·maa
take drugs	*usa drogas*	oo·zaa *dro*·gaas

Are you ...?	*Você ...?*	vo·*se* ...
allergic to	*é alérgico/*	e aa·*lerr*·zhee·ko/
anything	*alérgica*	aa·*lerr*·zhee·kaa
	à alguma	aa ow·*goo*·maa
	coisa m/f	*koy*·zaa
on medication	*está tomando*	es·*taa* to·*mang*·do
	remédio	he·*me*·dyo

How long are you travelling for?
Quanto tempo você *kwang*·to *teng*·po vo·*se*
vai viajar? vai vee·aa·*zhaarr*

You need to be admitted to hospital.
Você precisa ser vo·*se* pre·*see*·zaa serr
internado/internada eeng·terr·*naa*·do/eeng·terr·*naa*·daa
num hospital. m/f noom os·pee·*tow*

the doctor may say ...

You should have it checked when you go home.

Você deverá checar isto quando voltar para casa.	vo·*se* de·ve·*raa* she·*kaarr* ees·to kwang·do vol·*taarr* paa·raa kaa·zaa

You should return home for treatment.

Você deveria voltar para casa para tratamento.	vo·*se* de·ve·*ree*·aa vol·*taarr* paa·raa kaa·zaa paa·raa traa·taa·*meng*·to

You're a hypochondriac.

Você é hipocondríaco/ hipocondríaca. m/f	vo·*se* e ee·po·kong·*dree*·aa·ko/ ee·po·kong·*dree*·aa·kaa

I've run out of my medication.

Estou sem remédio.	es·*to* seng he·*me*·dee·yo

This is my usual medicine.

Este é meu remédio habitual.	es·te e *me*·oo he·*me*·dyo aa·bee·too·*ow*

My son weighs (20 kilos).

Meu filho pesa (vinte kilos).	me·oo fee·lyo pe·zaa (veeng·te kee·los)

My daughter weighs (20 kilos).

Minha filha pesa (vinte kilos).	mee·nyaa fee·lyaa pe·zaa (veeng·te kee·los)

What's the correct dosage?

Qual é a dosagem correta?	kwow e aa do·zaa·*zheng* ko·*he*·taa

I don't want a blood transfusion.

Eu não quero uma transfusão de sangue.	e·oo nowng *ke*·ro oo·maa trans·foo·*zowng* de sang·ge

Please use a new syringe.

Por favor use uma seringa nova.	porr faa·*vorr* oo·ze oo·maa se·*reeng*·gaa *no*·vaa

I have my own syringe.

Eu tenho minha própria seringa.	e·oo te·nyo mee·nyaa pro·pree·ya se·*reeng*·gaa

I've been vaccinated against ...	Eu fui vacinado/ vacinada contra ... m/f	e·oo foo·ee vaa·see·naa·do/ vaa·see·naa·daa kong·traa ...
hepatitis A/B/C	hepatite A/B/C	e·paa·tee·te aa/be/se
yellow fever	febre amarela	fe·bre aa·maa·re·laa
He/She has been vaccinated against ...	Ele/Ela foi vacinado/ vacinada contra ...	e·le/e·laa foy vaa·see·naa·do/ vaa·see·naa·daa kong·traa ...
tetanus	tétano	te·ta·no
typhoid	tifo	tee·fo
I need new ...	Eu preciso de ...	e·oo pre·see·zo de ...
contact lenses	novas lentes de contato	no·vaas leng·tes de kong·taa·to
glasses	novos óculos	no·vos o·koo·los

My prescription is ...
Minha receita
médica é ...
mee·nyaa he·say·taa
me·dee·kaa e ...

How much will it cost?
Quanto vai custar?
kwang·to vai koos·tarr

Can I have a receipt for my insurance?
Posso pegar um recibo
para meu seguro?
po·so pe·gaarr oom he·see·bo
paa·raa me·oo se·goo·ro

symptoms & conditions

I'm ill.
Estou doente.   es·*to* do·*eng*·te

My friend is ill.
Meu amigo está   me·oo aa·*mee*·go es·*taa*
doente. m   do·*eng*·te
Minha amiga está   mee·nyaa aa·*mee*·gaa es·*taa*
doente. f   do·*eng*·te

My son is ill.
Meu filho está doente.   me·oo fee·lyo es·*taa* do·*eng*·te

My daughter is ill.
Minha filha está   mee·nyaa fee·lyaa es·*taa*
doente.   do·*eng*·te

It hurts here.
Aqui dói.   aa·*kee* doy

I'm dehydrated.
Estou desidratado/   es·to de·zee·draa·*taa*·do/
desidratada. m/f   de·zee·draa·*taa*·daa

I can't sleep.
Eu não consigo   e·oo nowng kong·*see*·go
dormir.   dorr·*meerr*

I've been …	*Fui …*	*foo*·ee …
He/She has been …	*Ele/Ela está …*	e·le/e·laa es·*taa* …
injured	*machucado/*	maa·shoo·*kaa*·do/
	machucada m/f	maa·shoo·*kaa*·daa
vomiting	*vomitando*	vo·mee·*tang*·do

I feel …	Estou me sentindo …	es·to me seng·teeng·do …
anxious	ansioso/ ansiosa m/f	ang·see·o·zo/ ang·see·o·zaa
better	melhor	me·lyorr
depressed	deprimido/ deprimida m/f	de·pree·mee·do/ de·pree·mee·daa
dizzy	tonto/tonta m/f	tong·to/tong·taa
hot and cold	com calor e com frio	kong kaa·lorr e kong free·o
nauseous	enjoado/ enjoada m/f	eng·zho·aa·do/ en·zho·aa·daa
shivery	com tremedeira	kong tre·me·day·raa
strange	estranho/ estranha m/f	es·tra·nyo/ es·tra·nyaa
weak	fraco/fraca m/f	fraa·ko/fraa·kaa
worse	pior	pee·orr

I think it's the medication I'm on.

Acho que é este remédio que estou tomando. a·sho ke e es·te he·me·dyo ke es·to to·mang·do

I'm on medication for …

Estou tomando remédio para … es·to to·mang·do he·me·dyo paa·raa …

He/She is on medication for …

Ele/Ela está tomando remédio para … e·le/e·laa es·taa to·mang·do he·me·dyo paa·raa …

I have …

Tenho … te·nyo …

He/She has …

Ele/Ela tem … e·le/e·laa teng …

I've (recently) had …

(Recentemente) Tive … (he·seng·te·meng·te) tee·ve …

He/She has (recently) had …

Ele/Ela (recentemente) teve … e·le/e·laa (he·seng·te·meng·te) te·ve …

asthma	*asma* f	aas·maa
cold	*resfriado* f	hes·free·aa·do
headache	*dor* f *de cabeça*	dorr de kaa·be·saa
diabetes	*diabete* f	dee·aa·be·te
diarrhoea	*diarréia* f	dee·aa·he·yaa
fever	*febre* f	fe·bre
nausea	*náusea* f	now·ze·aa
pain	*dor* f	dorr
sore throat	*dor* f *de garganta*	dorr de gaar·gang·taa

women's health

saúde da mulher

(I think) I'm pregnant.
(Acho que) Estou grávida. (aa·sho ke) es·to graa·vee·daa

I'm on the Pill.
Estou tomando a pílula. es·to to·mang·do a pee·loo·laa

I haven't had my period for (six) days/weeks.
Não fico menstruada nowng fee·ko mengs·troo·aa·daa
há (seis) dias/semanas. aa (says) dee·aas/se·ma·naas

I've noticed a lump here.
Notei um caroço aqui. no·tay oom kaa·ro·so aa·kee

the doctor may say ...

Are you using contraception?
Você está usando vo·se es·taa oo·zang·do
algum método ow·goom me·to·do
anticoncepcional? an·tee·kong·sep·syo·now

Are you menstruating?
Você está vo·se es·taa
menstruando? mengs·troo·ang·do

Are you pregnant?
Você está grávida? vo·se es·taa graa·vee·daa

When did you last have your period?
Quando foi sua kwang·do foy soo·aa
última menstruação? ool·tee·maa mengs·troo·aa·sowng

You're pregnant.
Você está grávida. vo·se es·taa graa·vee·daa

I need ...	Eu preciso ...	e·oo pre·see·zo ...
a pregnancy test	fazer um teste de gravidez	faa·zerr oom tes·te de graa·vee·dez
contraception	de anticoncep-cional	de ang·tee·kong·sep·syo·now
the morning-after pill	a pílula do dia seguinte	aa pee·loo·laa do dee·aa se·geeng·te

allergies

alergias

For food-related allergies, see **vegetarian & special meals**, page 158.

I have a skin allergy.

Eu tenho alergia de pele.   e·oo te·nyo aa·lerr·zhee·aa de pe·le

I'm allergic to ...	Tenho alergia à ...	te·nyo aa·lerr·zhee·aa aa ...
He/She is allergic to ...	Ele/Ela é alérgico/ alérgica à ... m/f	e·le/e·laa e aa·lerr·zhee·ko/ aa·lerr·zhee·kaa aa ...
antibiotics	antibióticos	ang·tee·bee·o·tee·kos
anti-inflammatories	anti-inflamatórios	ang·tee·eeng·fla·ma·to·ree·os
aspirin	aspirina	aas·pee·ree·naa
bees	abelhas	aa·be·lyaas
codeine	codeína	ko·de·ee·naa
penicillin	penicilina	pe·nee·see·lee·naa
pollen	pólem	po·leng
sulphur-based drugs	drogas à base de súlfura	dro·gaas aa baa·ze de sool·foo·raa
inhaler	respirador m	hes·pee·raa·dorr
injection	injeção f	eeng·zhe·sowng
antihistamines	antiestamínico m	ang·tee·es·ta·mee·nee·ko

parts of the body

My ... hurts.
  Meu/Minha ... dói. m/f   me·oo/mee·nyaa ... doy

I can't move my ...
  Não consigo mover   nowng kong·see·go mo·verr
  meu/minha ... m/f   me·oo/mee·nyaa ...

My ... is swollen.
  Meu ... está inchado. m   me·oo ... es·taa eeng·shaa·do
  Minha ... está inchada. f   mee·nyaa ... es·taa eeng·shaa·daa

eye
olho m
o·lyo

nose
nariz m
naa·rees

ear
~relha f
~·re·lyaa

mouth
boca f
bo·kaa

head
cabeça f
kaa·be·saa

hand
mão f
mowng

arm
braço m
braa·so

chest
peito m
pay·to

stomach
estômago m
es·to·maa·go

bum
bunda f
boom·daa

leg
perna f
perr·naa

foot
pé m
pe

alternative treatments

I don't use (Western medicine).
Eu não uso   e·oo nowng oo·zo
(medicina ocidental).   (me·dee·see·naa o·see·deng·tow)

I prefer ...	*Eu prefiro ...*	e·oo pre·fee·ro ...
Can I see	*Posso ver alguém*	po·so verr ow·geng
someone who	*que pratica ...*	ke pra·tee·kaa ...
practices ...?		
acupuncture	*acupuntura*	aa·koo·poom·too·raa
naturopathy	*naturapatia*	naa·too·ro·paa·tee·aa
reflexology	*reflexologia*	he·flek·so·lo·zhee·aa

chemist

I need something for ...
Preciso de alguma   pre·see·zo de ow·goo·maa
coisa para ...   koy·zaa paa·raa ...

Do I need a prescription for ...?
Preciso de receita   pre·see·zo de he·say·taa
médica para ...?   me·dee·kaa paa·raa ...

I have a prescription.
Eu tenho receita médica.   e·oo te·nyo he·say·taa me·dee·kaa

How many times a day?
Quantas vezes ao dia?   kwang·taas ve·zes ow dee·aa

Will it make me drowsy?
Isto vai me deixar   ees·to vai me day·shaarr
tonto/tonta? m/f   tong·to/tong·taa

antiseptic	*anti-séptico* m	ang·tee·*sep*·tee·ko
contraceptive	*anti-concepcional* m	ang·tee·kong·*sep*·syo·now
painkillers	*analgésicos* m pl	aa·now·*zhe*·zee·kos
thermometer	*termômetro* m	terr·*mo*·me·tro
rehydration salts	*sais* m pl *de hidratação*	sais de ee·draa·taa·*sowng*

listen for ...

doo·aas *ve*·zes porr *dee*·aa (aas he·fay·*soyngs*)
*Duas vezes por dia
(às refeições).*
**Twice a day
(with food).**

vo·*se* zhaa to·*mo* ee·*so* ang·tes
Você já tomou isso antes?
**Have you taken this
before?**

vo·*se* teng ke to·*maarr too*·do
Você tem que tomar tudo.
**You must complete
the course.**

dentist

dentista

I have a ...	*Eu tenho ...*	e·oo *te*·nyo ...
broken tooth	*um dente quebrado*	oom *deng*·te ke·*braa*·do
cavity	*uma cárie*	oo·maa *kaa*·ree·e
toothache	*dor de dente*	dorr de *deng*·te

I've lost a filling.
Perdi uma obturação.   perr·*dee* oo·maa ob·too·raa·*sowng*

My dentures are broken.
*Minha dentadura
está quebrada.*   mee·nyaa deng·taa·*doo*·raa
es·taa ke·*braa*·daa

My gums hurt.
   Minha gengivas dói.   mee·nyaa zheng·*zhee*·vaas doy

I don't want it extracted.
   Eu não quero extrair.   e·oo nowng *ke*·ro es·traa·*eerr*

Ouch!
   Au!   ow

I need ...	*Preciso ...*	pre·*see*·zo ...
an anaesthetic	*de analgésico*	de aa·now·*zhe*·zee·ko
a filling	*de uma*	de *oo*·maa
	obturação	ob·too·ra·*sowng*

listen for ...	
aa·bre beng	
Abra bem.	**Open wide.**
eng·*shaa*·gwe	
Enxágue.	**Rinse.**
morr·de	
Morde.	**Bite down on this.**
nowng se *me*·shaa	
Não se mexa.	**Don't move.**
nowng vai do·*err naa*·daa	
Não vai doer nada.	**This won't hurt a bit.**

SUSTAINABLE TRAVEL

As the climate change debate heats up, the matter of sustainability becomes an important part of the travel vernacular. In practical terms, this means assessing our impact on the environment and local cultures and economies – and acting to make that impact as positive as possible. Here are some basic phrases to get you on your way …

communication & cultural differences

I'd like to learn some of your local dialects.
Eu gostaria de   e·oo gos·taa·*ree*·aa de
aprender algo do seu   aa·preng·*derr* ow·go do *se*·oo
dialeto local.   dee·aa·*le*·to lo·*kow*

Would you like me to teach you some English?
Você gostaria que eu te   vo·*se* gos·taa·*ree*·aa ke *e*·oo te
ensine algo em inglês?   en·*see*·ne ow·go eng eeng·*gles*

I respect your customs.
Eu respeito os seus   e·oo hes·*pay*·to os *se*·oos
costumes.   kos·*too*·mes

community benefit & involvement

What sorts of issues is this community facing?
Que tipo de problemas   ke *tee*·po de pro·*ble*·mas
a comunidade está   aa ko·moo·nee·*da*·de es·*taa*
enfrentando?   eng·freng·*tang*·do

literacy	*analfabetismo* m	aa·nal·fa·be·*tees*·mo
poverty	*pobreza* f	po·*bre*·zaa
tree-logging	*desmatamento* m	des·ma·ta·*meng*·to

sustainable travel

189

Are there any volunteer programs available in the area?

Tem algum programa   teng ow·*goong* pro·*gra*·maa
voluntário a   vo·loong·*taa*·ryo aa
disposição   dees·po·zee·*sowng*
na redondeza?   naa he·downg·*de*·zaa

I'd like to volunteer my skills.

Eu gostaria de   e·oo gos·taa·*ree*·aa de
voluntariar com minha   vo·loong·taa·ree·*aarr* kong *meen*·ya
especialização.   es·pe·syaa·lee·zaa·*sowng*

environment

Does your company have a green policy?

A sua empresa tem   aa *soo*·aa eng·*pre*·zaa teng
algum acordo de   ow·*goong* aa·*korr*·do de
preservação do   pre·zerr·vaa·*sowng* do
meio-ambiente?   *may*·o ang·bee·*eng*·te

Where can I recycle this?

Onde posso reciclar isto?   ong·de *po*·so he·see·*klaarr* ees·to

transport

Can we get there by public transport?

Podemos chegar lá de   po·*de*·mos she·*gaarr* laa de
transporte público?   trans·*porr*·te *poob*·lee·ko

Can we get there by bicycle?

Podemos ir até lá   po·*de*·mos eerr aa·*te* laa
de bicicleta?   de bee·see·*kle*·taa

I'd prefer to walk there.

Eu prefiro caminhar   e·oo pre·*fee*·ro ka·meeng·*nyarr*
até lá.   aa·*te* laa

accommodation

Are there any ecolodges here?

Tem algum hospedagem   teng ow·*goong* os·pe·*daa*·zheng
ecológica por aqui?   e·ko·*lo*·zhee·ka porr aa·*kee*

I'd like to stay at a locally-run hotel.

Eu gostaria de me	e·oo gos·taa·ree·aa de me
hospedar em um hotel	os·pe·daarr eng oong o·tel
de proprietários locais.	de pro·pree·e·taa·ryos lo·kais

Can I turn the air conditioning off and open the window?

Posso desligar o	po·so des·lee·garr o
ar condicionado	aarr kong·dee·syo·naa·do
e abrir a janela?	e aa·breerr aa zhaa·ne·laa

There's no need to change my sheets, they're still clean.

Não precisa trocar	nowng pre·see·zaa tro·kaarr
os meus lençóis,	os me·oos len·soys
ainda estão limpos.	aa·eeng·da es·towng leeng·pos

shopping

Where can I buy locally produced goods/souvenirs?

Onde posso comprar	ong·de po·so kong·praarr
produtos/souvenirs	pro·doo·tos/soo·ve·neers
produzidos localmente?	pro·doo·zee·dos lo·kow·meng·te

Do you sell Fair Trade products?

Você vende produtos	vo·se veng·de pro·doo·tos
de comércio justo?	de ko·merr·syo zhoos·to

Is this made	Isto é feito	ee·sto e fay·to
from ...?	com ...?	kong ...
coral	coral	ko·row
local wood	madeira	maa·day·raa
products	local	lo·kow

food

Can you tell me what traditional foods I should try?

Você pode me dizer	vo·se po·de me dee·zherr
quais comidas	kwais ko·mee·das
tradicionais eu devo	traa·dee·syo·nais e·oo de·vo
esperimentar?	es·pe·ree·meng·taarr

Do you sell …?	Você vende …?	vo·se veng·de …
locally	alimentos	a·lee·meng·tos
produced	produzidos	pro·doo·zee·dos
food	localmente	lo·kow·meng·te
organic	produtos	pro·doo·tos
produce	orgânicos	orr·ga·nee·kos

sightseeing

Does your company …?	A sua empresa …?	aa soo·aa eng·pre·zaa …
donate money to charity	doa dinheiro para a comunidade	do·aa dee·nyay·ro paa·raa aa ko·moo·nee·daa·de
hire local guides	tem guias turísticos locais	teng gee·aas too·rees·tee·kos lo·kais
visit local businesses	leva a estabele- cimentos de proprietarios locais	le·va aa es·ta·be·le- see·meng·tos de pro·pree·e·taa·ryos lo·kais

Does the guide speak …?	O guia fala …?	o gee·aa faa·la …
Apalai	Apalai	aa·pa·lai
Arara	Arara	aa·raa·ra
Bororo	Bororó	bo·ro·ro
Canela	Canela	ka·ne·la
Caraja	Carajá	ka·raa·zhaa
Guarani	Guaraní	gwaa·ra·nee
Terena	Terena	te·re·naa
Tucano	Tucano	too·ka·no

I'd like to hire a local guide.

Eu gostaria de
contratar um
guia local.

e·oo gos·taa·ree·aa de
kong·traa·taarr oong
gee·aa lo·kow

Are cultural tours available?

Tem excursões
culturais?

teng es·koorr·soyngs
kool·too·rais

Nouns in the dictionary have their gender indicated by ⓜ or ①. If it's a plural noun, you'll also see pl. Where a word that could be either a noun or a verb has no gender indicated, it's the verb. For all words relating to local food, see the **culinary reader**, page 159.

A

aboard *a bordo* aa·borr·do
abortion *aborto* ⓜ aa·borr·to
about *sobre* so·bre
above *sobre* so·bre
abroad *exterior* es·te·ree·orr
accident *acidente* ⓜ aa·see·deng·te
accommodation *hospedagem* ①
  os·pe·daa·zheng
across *através* aa·traa·ves
activist *ativista* ⓜ&① aa·tee·vees·taa
acupuncture *acupuntura* ①
  aa·koo·poom·too·raa
adaptor *adaptador* ⓜ aa·daa·pee·taa·dorr
addiction *vício* ⓜ vee·syo
address *endereço* ⓜ eng·de·re·so
administration *administração* ①
  aa·dee·mee·nees·traa·sowng
admission price *preço* ⓜ *da entrada*
  pre·so daa eng·traa·daa
admit (acknowledge) *admitir*
  aa·dee·mee·teerr
adult *adulto/adulta* ⓜ/①
  aa·dool·to/aa·dool·taa
advertisement *anúncio* ⓜ aa·noom·see·o
advice *conselho* ⓜ kong·se·lyo
aerobics *aeróbica* ① aa·e·ro·bee·kaa
aeroplane *aeroplano* ⓜ aa·e·ro·pla·no
Africa *África* ① aa·free·kaa
after *depois de*·poys
(this) afternoon *(esta) tarde* ①
  (es·taa) taarr·de
aftershave *pós barba* ⓜ pos baarr·baa
again *novamente* no·vaa·meng·te
age *idade* ① ee·daa·de
(three days) ago *há (três dias)*
  aa (tres dee·aas)
agree *concordar* kong·korr·daarr

agriculture *agricultura* ①
  aa·gree·kool·too·raa
ahead *em frente* eng freng·te
AIDS *Aids* ① ai·dees
air *ar* ⓜ aarr
air-conditioning *ar condicionado*
  aarr kong·dee·syo·naa·do
airline *linha aérea* ① pl lee·nyaa aa·e·re·aa
airmail *via* ① *aérea* vee·aa aa·e·re·aa
airplane *avião* ⓜ aa·vee·owng
airport *aeroporto* ⓜ aa·e·ro·porr·to
airport tax *taxa* ① *de aeroporto*
  taa·shaa de aa·e·ro·porr·to
aisle *corredor* ⓜ ko·he·dorr
alarm clock *despertador* ⓜ
  des·perr·taa·dorr
alcohol *álcool* ⓜ ow·kol
all *tudo/tuda* ⓜ/① too·do/too·daa
allergy *alergia* ① aa·lerr·zhee·aa
almond *amêndoa* ① aa·meng·dwaa
almost *quase* kwaa·ze
alone *sozinho/sozinha* ⓜ/① so·zee·nyo/
  so·zee·nyaa
already *já* zhaa
also *também* tang·beng
altar *altar* ⓜ ow·taarr
altitude *altitude* ① ow·tee·too·de
always *sempre* seng·pre
ambassador *embaixador/*
  embaixadora ⓜ/①
  eng·bai·shaa·dorr/eng·bai·shaa·do·raa
American football *futebol* ⓜ *americano*
  foo·te·bol aa·me·ree·ka·no
anaemia *anemia* ① aa·ne·mee·aa
anarchist *anarquista* ⓜ&①
  aa·naarr·kees·taa
ancient *ancião/anciã* ⓜ/①
  ang·see·owng/ang·see·ang
and *e* e

angry *zangado/zangada* ⓜ/ⓕ
zang-*gaa*-do/zang-*gaa*-daa
animal *animal* ⓜ&ⓕ aa-nee-*mow*
ankle *tornozelo* torr-no-ze-lo
answer *resposta* ⓕ hes-*pos*-taa
ant *formiga* ⓕ forr-*mee*-gaa
antibiotics *antibióticos* ⓜ pl
ang-tee-bee-o-tee-kos
antinuclear *antinuclear*
ang-tee-noo-kle-*aarr*
antique *antigo/antiga* ⓜ/ⓕ ang-*tee*-go/
ang-*tee*-gaa
antiseptic *anti-séptico* ⓜ
ang-tee-*sep*-tee-ko
any *qualquer* kwow-*kerr*
apartment *apartamento* ⓜ
aa-paarr-taa-*meng*-to
appendix (body) *apêndice* ⓜ
aa-*peng*-dee-se
apple *maçã* ⓕ maa-*sang*
appointment *consulta* ⓕ kong-*sool*-taa
apricot *damasco* ⓜ daa-*maas*-ko
April *abril* aa-*breel*
archaeological *arqueológico/
arqueológica* ⓜ/ⓕ aarr-ke-o-lo-zhee-ko/
aarr-ke-o-lo-zhee-kaa
architect *arquiteto/arquiteta* ⓜ/ⓕ
aarr-kee-*te*-to/aarr-kee-*te*-taa
architecture *arquitetura* ⓕ
aar-kee-te-*too*-raa
argue *discutir* dees-koo-*teerr*
arm *braço* ⓜ *braa*-so
aromatherapy *aromaterapia* ⓕ aa-
aa-ro-maa-te-raa-*pee*-aa
arrest *prender* preng-*derr*
arrival *chegada* ⓕ she-*gaa*-daa
arrivals *chegadas* ⓕ pl she-*gaa*-daas
arrive *chegar* she-*gaarr*
art *arte* ⓕ *aarr*-te
art gallery *galeria* ⓕ *de arte* gaa-le-*ree*-aa
de *aarr*-te
artist *artista* ⓜ&ⓕ aar-*tees*-taa
ashtray *cinzeiro* ⓜ seen-*zay*-ro
Asia *Ásia* ⓕ *aa*-zyaa
ask (a question) *perguntar*
perr-goong-*taarr*
ask (for something) *pedir* pe-*deerr*
asparagus *aspargo* ⓜ aas-*paarr*-go
aspirin *aspirina* ⓕ aas-pee-*ree*-naa

asthma *asma* ⓕ *aas*-maa
athletics *atletismo* ⓜ aat-le-*tees*-mo
atmosphere *atmosfera* ⓕ
aa-tee-mos-fe-raa
aubergine *beringela* ⓕ be-reeng-*zhe*-la
August *agosto* aa-*gos*-to
aunt *tia* ⓕ *tee*-aa
Australia *austrália* ⓕ ows-*traa*-lya
Australian Rules Football *Futebol* ⓜ
Australian Rules foo-te-*bol*
ows-*tra*-lee-ang roo-les
automatic teller machine (ATM) *caixa* ⓜ
automático kai-shaa ow-to-*maa*-tee-ko
autumn *outono* o-*to*-no
avenue *avenida* ⓕ aa-ve-*nee*-daa
avocado *abacate* ⓜ aa-baa-*kaa*-te
awful *horrível* o-*hee*-vel

B

B&W (film) *preto e branco*
pre-to e brang-ko
baby *bebê* ⓜ&ⓕ be-*be*
baby food *comida* ⓕ *de bebê*
ko-*mee*-daa de be-*be*
baby powder *talco* ⓜ *tow*-ko
babysitter *babá* ⓕ baa-*baa*
back (position) *de costas* de *kos*-taas
back (body) *costas* ⓕ *kos*-taas
backpack *mochila* ⓕ mo-*shee*-la
bacon *bacon* ⓜ *bay*-kong
bad *ruim* hoo-*eeng*
bag *saco* ⓜ *saa*-ko
baggage *bagagem* ⓕ baa-*gaa*-zheng
baggage allowance *limité* ⓜ *de peso*
lee-*mee*-te de *pe*-zo
baggage claim *requerimento* ⓜ *de
bagagem* he-ke-ree-*meng*-to de
baa-*gaa*-zheng
bakery *padaria* ⓕ paa-daa-*ree*-aa
balance (account) *balanço* ⓜ baa-*lang*-so
balcony *varanda* ⓕ vaa-*rang*-daa
ball *bola* ⓕ *bo*-laa
ballet *balé* ⓜ ba-*le*
banana *banana* ⓕ baa-*na*-naa
band (music) *banda* ⓕ (*de música*)
bang-daa (de moo-ze-*kaa*)
bandage *curativo* ⓜ koo-raa-*tee*-vo
Band-Aid *band-aid* ⓜ bang-*day*-dee

bank *banco* ⓜ *bang*·ko
bank account *conta* ⓕ *bancária*
  kong·taa bang·*kaa*·rya
banknote *nota* ⓕ *no*·taa
baptism *batismo* ⓜ baa·*tees*·mo
bar *bar* ⓜ baarr
bar work *trabalho* ⓜ *em bar*
  traa·*ba*·lyo eng baarr
barber *barbeiro* ⓜ baar·*bay*·ro
baseball *baseball* ⓜ *bay*·ze·bol
basket *cesta* ⓕ *ses*·taa
basketball *basquete* ⓜ baas·*ke*·te
bath *banheira* ⓕ ba·*nyay*·raa
bathing suit *roupa* ⓕ *de banho*
  ho·paa de *ba*·nyo
bathroom *banheiro* ⓜ ba·*nyay*·ro
battery *pilha* ⓕ *pee*·lyaa
be (temporary) *estar* es·*taarr*
be (ongoing) *ser* serr
beach *praia* ⓕ *prai*·aa
beach volleyball *vôlei* ⓜ *de praia*
  vo·lay de *praa*·yaa
bean *feijão* ⓜ fay·*zhowng*
beansprout *broto* ⓜ *de feijão*
  bro·to de fay·*zhowng*
beautiful *bonito/bonita* ⓜ/ⓕ
  bo·*nee*·to/bo·*nee*·taa
beauty salon *salão* ⓜ *de beleza*
  saa·*lowng* de be·*le*·zaa
because *por que* porr·*ke*
bed *cama* ⓕ *ka*·maa
bedding *roupa* ⓕ *de cama*
  ho·paa de *ka*·maa
bedroom *quarto* ⓜ *kwaarr*·to
bee *abelha* ⓕ aa·*be*·lyaa
beef *bife* ⓜ *bee*·fe
beer *cerveja* ⓕ serr·*ve*·zhaa
beetroot *beterraba* ⓕ be·te·*haa*·baa
before *antes* ang·tes
beggar *pedinte* ⓜ&ⓕ pe·*deeng*·te
behind *atrás* aa·*traas*
below *abaixo* aa·*bai*·sho
best *melhor* me·*lyorr*
bet *aposta* ⓕ aa·*pos*·taa
better *melhor* me·*lyorr*
between *entre* eng·tre
bible *bíblia* ⓕ *bee*·blyaa
bicycle *bicicleta* ⓕ bee·see·*kle*·taa
big *grande* grang·de

bike *bicicleta* ⓕ bee·see·*kle*·taa
bike chain *corrente* ⓕ *de bicicleta*
  ko·*heng*·te de bee·see·*kle*·taa
bike lock *tranca* ⓕ *de bicicleta* trang·*kaa*
  de bee·see·*kle*·taa
bike path *rota* ⓕ *de bicicleta*
  ho·ta de bee·see·*kle*·taa
bike shop *loja* ⓕ *de bicicleta*
  lo·zhaa de bee·see·*kle*·taa
bill (account) *conta* ⓕ *kong*·taa
binoculars *binóculos* ⓜ pl bee·no·koo·los
bird *pássaro* ⓜ paa·saa·ro
birth certificate *certidão* ⓕ *de nascimento*
  serr·tee·*downg* de naa·see·*meng*·to
birthday *aniversário* ⓜ aa·nee·verr·*saa*·ryo
biscuit *biscoito* ⓜ bees·*koy*·to
bite (dog) *mordida* ⓕ morr·*dee*·daa
bite (insect) *mordida* ⓕ morr·*dee*·daa
black *preto/preta* ⓜ/ⓕ *pre*·to/*pre*·taa
bladder *bexiga* ⓕ be·*shee*·gaa
blanket *cobertor* ⓜ ko·berr·*torr*
blind *cego/cega* ⓜ/ⓕ *se*·go/*se*·gaa
blister *bolha* ⓕ *bo*·lyaa
blocked *bloqueado/bloqueada* ⓜ/ⓕ
  blo·ke·*aa*·do/blo·ke·*aa*·daa
blood *sangue* ⓜ *sang*·ge
blood group *grupo* ⓜ *sanguíneo*
  groo·po sang·*gwee*·ne·o
blood pressure *pressão* ⓕ *arterial*
  pre·*sowng* aar·te·ree·*ow*
blood test *exame* ⓜ *de sangue*
  e·*za*·me de *sang*·ge
blue *azul* aa·*zool*
board (a plane, ship, etc) *subir a bordo*
  soo·*beerr* aa borr·do
boarding house *casa* ⓕ *de cômodos* ·
  pensão ⓕ *kaa*·zaa de *ko*·mo·dos ·
  peng·*sowng*
boarding pass *boarding pass* ⓜ
  borr·deeng paas
boat *barco* ⓜ *baar*·ko
body *corpo* ⓜ *korr*·po
bone *osso* ⓜ *o*·so
book *livro* ⓜ *lee*·vro
book (make a booking) *reservar*
  he·zerr·*vaarr*
booked out *esgotado/esgotada* ⓜ/ⓕ
  es·go·*taa*·do/es·go·*taa*·daa
book shop *livraria* ⓕ lee·vraa·*ree*·aa

boot (footwear) *bota* ① bo·taa
boots (footwear) *botas* ① pl bo·taas
border *borda* ① borr·daa
bored *entediado/entediada* ⑩/①
eng·te·dee·*aa*·do/eng·te·dee·*aa*·daa
boring *entediante* eng·te·dee·*ang*·te
borrow *emprestar* eng·pres·*taarr*
botanic garden *jardim* ⑩ *botânico*
zharr·*deeng* bo·*ta*·nee·ko
both *ambos/ambas* ⑩/①
ang·bos/*ang*·baas
bottle *garrafa* ① gaa·*haa*·faa
bottle opener *abridor* ⑩ *de garrafas*
aa·bree·*dorr* de gaa·*haa*·faas
bottle shop *loja* ① *de bebidas*
lo·zhaa de be·*bee*·daas
bottom (position) *fundo* *foong*·do
bottom (body) *traseiro* ⑩ traa·*zay*·ro
bowl *tigela* ① tee·*zhe*·laa
box *caixa* ① *kai*·shaa
boxer shorts *ciroula* ① se·ro·*laa*
boxing *boxe* ⑩ bo·kee·see
boy *menino* ⑩ me·*nee*·no
boyfriend *namorado* ⑩ na·mo·*raa*·do
bra *sutiã* ① soo·tee·*ang*
brake *freio* ⑩ *fray*·o
brandy *brandy* ⑩ *brang*·dee
brave *corajoso/corajosa* ⑩/①
ko·raa·*zho*·zo/ko·raa·*zho*·zaa
bread *pão* ⑩ *powng*
bread rolls *pães* ⑩ pl *payngs*
break *quebrar* ke·*braarr*
break down *pifar* • *enguiçar*
pee·*faarr* • eng·gee·*saarr*
breakfast *café* ⑩ *da manhã*
ka·*fe* da ma·*nyang*
breast (body) *peito* ⑩ sg *pay*·to
breasts (body) *seios* ⑩ pl *say*·os
breathe *respirar* hes·pee·*raarr*
bribe *suborno* ⑩ soo·*bor*·no
bridge *ponte* ① *pong*·te
briefcase *pasta* ① *pas*·taa
brilliant *brilhante* bree·*lyang*·te
bring *trazer* traa·*zerr*
broccoli *brócolis* ⑩ pl *bro*·ko·lees
brochure *brochura* ① bro·*shoo*·raa
broken *quebrado/quebrada* ⑩/①
ke·*braa*·do/ke·*braa*·daa
bronchitis *bronquite* ① brong·*kee*·te

brother *irmão* ⑩ eerr·*mowng*
brown *marron* maa·*hong*
bruise *hematoma* ① e·maa·*to*·maa
brush (hair) *escova* ① es·ko·vaa
bucket *balde* ⑩ bow·de
Buddhist *Budista* boo·dees·taa
buffet *buffet* ⑩ boo·fe
bug *bicho* ⑩ *bee*·sho
build *construir* kongs·troo·*eerr*
builder *construtor* ⑩ kongs·troo·*tor*
building *prédio* ⑩ *pre*·dyo
bumbag *pochete* ① po·*she*·te
burn *queimadura* ① kay·maa·doo·raa
burnt *queimado/queimada* ⑩/①
kay·*maa*·do/kay·*maa*·daa
bus (city) *ônibus* ⑩ o·nee·boos
bus (intercity) *ônibus* ⑩ o·nee·boos
bus station *rodoviária* ①
ho·do·vee·*aa*·ryaa
bus stop *ponto* ⑩ *de ônibus*
pong·to de o·nee·boos
business *negócios* ⑩ pl ne·*go*·syos
business class *business class* ①
bee·zee·*nes* klaas
business person *homem/mulher* ⑩/①
de negócios o·meng/moo·*lyerr* de
ne·*go*·syos
business trip *viagem* ① *de negócios*
vee·*aa*·zheng de ne·*go*·syos
busker *artista* ⑩&① *de rua*
aar·*tees*·taa de hoo·aa
busy *ocupado/ocupada* ⑩/①
oo·koo·*paa*·do/o·koo·*paa*·daa
but *mas* maas
butcher *açougueiro/açougueira* ⑩/①
aa·so·*gay*·ro/aa·so·*gay*·raa
butcher's shop *açougue* ⑩ aa·so·ge
butter *manteiga* ① man·*tay*·gaa
butterfly *borboleta* ① borr·bo·le·taa
buttons *botões* ⑩ pl bo·*toyngs*
buy *comprar* kong·*praarr*

C

cabbage *repolho* ⑩ he·*po*·lyo
cable car *bonde* ⑩ *bong*·de
cafe *café* ⑩ kaa·fe
cake *bolo* ⑩ *bo*·lo

cake shop *confeitaria* ① kong·fay·taa·ree·aa
calculator *calculadora* ① kow·koo·laa·do·raa
calendar *calendário* ⑩ kaa·leng·daa·ryo
camera *câmera* ① ka·me·raa
camera shop *loja* ① *de equipamentos fotográficos* lo·zhaa de e·kee·pa·meng·tos fo·to·graa·fee·kos
camp *acampar* aa·kang·paarr
camp site *local* ⑩ *para acampar* lo·kow paa·raa aa·kang·paarr
camping ground *acampamento* ⑩ aa·kang·paa·meng·to
camping store *loja* ⑩ *de acampamento* lo·zhaa de aa·kam·paa·meng·to
can (be able) *poder* po·derr
can (have permission) *poder* po·derr
can (tin) *lata* ① laa·taa
can opener *abridor* ⑩ *de lata* aa·bree·dorr de laa·taa
Canada *Canadá* ⑩ kaa·naa·daa
cancel *cancelar* kang·se·laarr
cancer *câncer* ⑩ kang·serr
candle *vela* ① ve·laa
candy *bala* ① baa·laa
cantaloupe *melão* ⑩ me·lowng
capsicum *pimentão* ⑩ pee·meng·towng
car *carro* ⑩ kaa·ho
car hire *aluguel* ⑩ *de carro* aa·loo·gel de kaa·ho
car registration *registro* ⑩ *de carro* he·zhees·tro de kaa·ho
caravan *caravan* ① kaa·raa·vang
cardiac arrest *parada* ① *cardíaca* paa·raa·daa kaarr·dee·aa·kaa
cards (playing) *cartas* ① pl *kaarr·tas*
care (for someone) *gostar (de alguém)* gos·taarr (de ow·geng)
car park *estacionamento* ⑩ es·taa·syo·naa·meng·to
carpenter *carpinteiro* ⑩ karr·peeng·tay·ro
carrot *cenoura* ① se·no·raa
carry *carregar* kaa·he·gaarr
carton *caixa* ① *de papelão* kai·shaa de paa·pe·lowng
cash *em espécie* eng es·pe·sye
cash (a cheque) *descontar (um cheque)* des·kong·taarr (oom she·ke)

cash register *caixa* ① *registradora* kai·shaa he·gees·traa·do·raa
cashew *castanha* ① *de cajú* kas·ta·nyaa de kaa·zhoo
cashier *caixa* ⑩&① kai·sha
casino *casino* ⑩ kaa·see·no
cassette *fita* ① *cassete* fee·taa kaa·se·te
castle *castelo* ⑩ kaas·te·lo
casual work *trabalho* ⑩ *ocasional* traa·baa·lyo o·kaa·zee·o·now
cat *gato/gata* ⑩/① gaa·to/gaa·taa
cathedral *catedral* ① kaa·te·drow
Catholic *Católico/Católica* ⑩/① kaa·to·lee·ko/kaa·to·lee·kaa
cauliflower *couve flor* ① ko·ve florr
cave *caverna* ① kaa·verr·naa
CD *CD* ⑩ se·de
celebration *comemoração* ① ko·me·mo·raa·sowng
cent *centavos* ⑩ pl seng·taa·vos
centimetre *centímetro* ⑩ seng·tee·me·tro
centre *centro* ⑩ seng·tro
ceramics *cerâmica* ① se·ra·mee·kaa
cereal *cereal* ⑩ se·re·ow
certificate *certificado* ⑩ serr·tee·fee·kaa·do
chain *corrente* ① ko·heng·te
chair *cadeira* ① kaa·day·raa
chairlift (skiing) *teleférico* ⑩ te·le·fe·ree·ko
championships *campeonatos* ⑩ pl kang·pe·o·naa·tos
chance *oportunidade* ① o·porr·too·nee·daa·de
change *trocar* tro·kaarr
change (coins) *troco* ⑩ tro·ko
changing room *provador* ⑩ pro·vaa·dorr
charming *charmoso/charmosa* ⑩/① shaarr·mo·zo/shaarr·mo·zaa
chat up *conversar* kong·verr·saarr
cheap *barato/barata* ⑩/① baa·raa·to/baa·raa·taa
cheat *traição* ① tra·ee·sowng
check *checar* she·kaarr
check-in (desk) *check in* ① she·keeng
checkpoint (border) *ponto* ⑩ *de controle* pong·to de kong·tro·le
cheque (banking) *cheque* ⑩ she·ke
cheque (bill) *conta* ① kong·taa
cheese *queijo* ⑩ kay·zho

cheese shop *queijaria* ① kay·zhaa·ree·aa
chef *chefe* ⑩&① *de cozinha*
she·fe de ko·zee·nyaa
chemist *pharmacista* ⑩&①
faarr·maa·sees·taa
cherry *cereja* ① se·re·zhaa
chess *xadrez* ⑩ shaa·dres
chess board *tabuleiro* ⑩ *de xadrez*
taa·boo·lay·ro de shaa·dres
chest (body) *peito* ⑩ pay·to
chestnut *castanha* ① *portuguesa*
kaas·ta·nyaa porr·too·ge·zaa
chewing gum *goma* ① *de mascar*
go·maa de maas·kaarr
chicken *galinha* ① gaa·lee·nyaa
chicken pox *catapora* ① kaa·taa·po·raa
chickpea *grão* ⑩ *de bico*
growng de bee·ko
child *criança* ⑩&① kree·ang·saa
child seat *cadeira* ① *de criança*
kaa·day·raa de kree·ang·saa
childminding *cuidado* ⑩ *da criança*
kooy·daa·do de kree·ang·saa
children *crianças* ⑩&① pl kree·ang·saas
chilli *pimenta* ① pee·meng·taa
chilli sauce *molho* ⑩ *de pimenta* mo·lyo
de pee·meng·taa
chiropractor *quiroprático/*
quiroprática ⑩/① kee·ro·praa·tee·ko/
kee·ro·praa·tee·kaa
chocolate *chocolate* ⑩ sho·ko·laa·te
choose *escolher* es·ko·lyerr
Christian *Cristão/Cristã* ⑩/① krees·towng/
krees·tayng
Christian name *nome* ⑩ *Cristão* ·
primeiro nome ⑩ no·me krees·towng ·
pree·may·ro no·me
Christmas Day *Dia* ⑩ *de Natal*
dee·aa de naa·tow
Christmas Eve *Noite* ① *de Natal* noy·te
de na·tow
church *igreja* ① ee·gre·zhaa
cider *cidra* ① see·draa
cigar *charuto* ⑩ shaa·roo·to
cigarette *cigarro* ⑩ see·gaa·ho
cigarette lighter *isqueiro* ⑩ ees·kay·ro
cinema *cinema* ⑩ see·ne·maa
circus *circo* ⑩ seerr·ko
citizenship *cidadania* ① see·daa·da·nee·aa

city *cidade* ① see·daa·de
city centre *centro* ⑩ *da cidade*
seng·tro daa see·daa·de
civil rights *direitos* ⑩ pl *civis*
dee·ray·tos see·vees
class (category) *classe* ① klaa·se
class system *sistema* ① *de classes*
sees·te·maa de klaa·ses
classical *clássico/clássica* ⑩/①
klaa·see·ko/klaa·see·kaa
clean *limpo/limpa* ⑩/①
leeng·po/leeng·paa
client *cliente* ⑩&① klee·eng·te
cliff *penhasco* ① pe·nyaas·ko
climb *subir* soo·beerr
cloakroom *guarda* ⑩ *volumes* gwaarr·daa
vo·loo·mes
clock *relógio* ⑩ he·lo·zhyo
close *fechar* fe·shaarr
closed *fechado/fechada* ⑩/① fe·shaa·do/
fe·shaa·daa
clothesline *corda* ① *de roupa*
korr·daa de ho·paa
clothing *roupas* ① pl ho·paas
clothing store *loja* ① *de roupas*
lo·zhaa de ho·paas
cloud *nuvem* ① noo·veng
cloudy *nublado/nublada* ⑩/①
noo·blaa·do/noo·blaa·daa
clutch (car) *embreagem* ①
eng·bre·aa·zheng
coach *técnico/técnica* ⑩/①
te·kee·nee·ko/te·kee·nee·kaa
coast *costa* ① kos·taa
coat *casaco* ⑩ kaa·zaa·ko
cocaine *cocaína* ① ko·kaa·ee·naa
cockroach *barata* ① baa·raa·taa
cocoa *cacau* ⑩ ka·kow
coconut *côco* ⑩ ko·ko
coffee *café* ⑩ kaa·fe
coins *moedas* ① pl mo·e·daas
cold *frio* ⑩ free·o
cold *frio/fria* ⑩/① free·o/free·aa
colleague *colega* ⑩&① ko·le·gaa
collect call *ligação* ① *à cobrar*
lee·gaa·sowng aa ko·braarr
college *academia* ① ·
universidade ① aa·kaa·de·mee·aa ·
oo·nee·verr·see·daa·de

colour *cor* ① korr
comb *pente* ⓜ peng·te
come *vir* veerr
comedy *comédia* ① ko·me·dyaa
comfortable *confortável* kong·forr·taa·vel
communications (profession)
comunicação ① ko·moo·nee·kaa·sowng
communion *comunhão* ①
ko·moo·nyowng
communist *comunista* ⓜ&①
ko·moo·nees·taa
companion *companheiro/companheira*
ⓜ/① kong·pa·nyay·ro/kong·pa·nyay·raa
company *companhia* ⓜ&①
kong·paa·nyaa
compass *compasso* ⓜ kong·paa·so
complain *reclamar* he·klaa·marr
computer *computador* ⓜ
kong·poo·taa·dorr
computer game *jogo* ⓜ *de computador*
zho·go de kong·poo·taa·dorr
concert *show* ⓜ show
conditioner *condicionador* ⓜ
kong·dee·syo·naa·dorr
condom *camisinha* ① kaa·mee·zee·nyaa
confession *confissão* ① kong·fee·sowng
conjunctivitis *conjuntivite* ①
kong·zhoong·tee·vee·te
confirm (a booking) *confirmar*
kong·feerr·marr
connection (phone) *conecção* ①
ko·ne·kee·sowng
conservative *conservador/conservadora*
ⓜ/① kong·serr·vaa·dorr/
kong·serr·vaa·do·raa
constipation *constipação* ①
kongs·tee·paa·sowng
consulate *consulado* ⓜ kong·soo·laa·do
contact lens solution *colírio* ⓜ *para lentes
de contato* ko·lee·ryo paa·raa leng·tes de
kong·taa·to
contact lenses *lentes* ⓜ pl *de contato*
leng·tes de kong·taa·to
contraceptives *anticoncepcional* ⓜ
ang·tee·kong·sep·syo·now
contract *contrato* ⓜ kong·traa·to
convenience store *mercearia* ①
merr·se·aa·ree·aa
convent *convento* ⓜ kong·veng·to

cook *cozinheiro/cozinheira* ⓜ/①
ko·zee·nyay·ro/ko·zee·nyay·raa
cook *cozinhar* ko·zee·nyaarr
cookie *biscoito* ⓜ bees·koy·to
corn *milho* ⓜ mee·lyo
cornflakes *cereal* ⓜ se·re·ow
corner *esquina* ① es·kee·naa
corrupt *corrupto/corrupta* ⓜ/①
koo·hoo·pee·to/koo·hoo·pee·taa
cost *custar* koos·taarr
cotton *algodão* ⓜ ow·go·downg
cotton balls *bolas* ① pl *de algodão*
bo·laas de ow·go·downg
cotton buds *cotonete* ⓜ ko·to·ne·te
cough *tossir* to·seerr
cough medicine *xarope* ⓜ shaa·ro·pe
count *contar* kong·taarr
counter (at bar) *balcão* ⓜ bow·kowng
country *país* ⓜ paa·ees
countryside *interior* ⓜ eeng·te·ree·orr
coupon *cupom* ⓜ koo·pong
courgette *abobrinha* ① aa·bo·bree·nyaa
court (legal) *corte* ① korr·te
court (tennis) *quadra* ① kwaa·draa
couscous *cuscuz* ⓜ marroquino
koos·koos maa·ho·kee·no
cover charge *couvert* ⓜ *artístico*
koo·verr aarr·tees·tee·ko
cow *vaca* ① vaa·kaa
cracker *biscoito* ⓜ *d'água*
bees·koy·to daa·gwaa
crafts *artesanato* ⓜ aarr·te·zaa·naa·to
crash *batida* ① baa·tee·daa
crazy *louco/louca* ⓜ/① lo·ko/lo·kaa
cream *creme* ⓜ kre·me
creche *creche* ① kre·she
credit card *cartão* ⓜ *de crédito*
kaarr·towng de kre·dee·to
cricket (sport) *cricket* ⓜ kree·ke·tee
crop *tosa* ① to·zaa
cross (religious) *cruz* ① kroos
crowded *lotado/lotada* ⓜ/① lo·taa·do/
lo·taa·daa
cucumber *pepino* ⓜ pe·pee·no
cup *xícara* ① shee·kaa·raa
cupboard *armário* ⓜ aarr·maa·ryo
currency exchange *câmbio* ⓜ *de valores*
kang·byo de vaa·lo·res
current (electricity) *corrente* ① ko·heng·te

current affairs *assuntos* ⓜ pl *atuais* aa-*soong*-tos aa-too-*ais*
curry *caril* ⓜ kaa-*reel*
customs *alfândega* ⓕ aal-*fang*-de-gaa
cut *cortar* korr-*taarr*
cutlery *talheres* ⓜ pl taa-*lye*-res
CV *CV* ⓜ se-ve
cycle *andar de bicicleta* ang-*daarr* de bee-see-*kle*-taa
cycling *ciclismo* ⓜ see-*klees*-mo
cyclist *ciclista* ⓜ&ⓕ see-*klees*-taa
cystitis *cistite* ⓕ sees-*tee*-te

D

dad *pai* ⓜ pai
dance *dançar* dang-*saarr*
dancing *dança* ⓕ *dang*-saa
dangerous *perigoso/perigosa* ⓜ/ⓕ pe-ree-*go*-zo/pe-ree-*go*-zaa
dark *escuro/escura* ⓜ/ⓕ es-*koo*-ro/ es-*koo*-raa
date (appointment) *hora* ⓕ *marcada* *aw*-raa maarr-*kaa*-daa
date (day) *data* ⓕ *daa*-taa
date (fruit) *tâmara* ⓕ ta-*maa*-raa
date (a person) *namorar* naa-mo-*raarr*
date of birth *data* ⓕ *de nascimento* *daa*-taa de naa-see-*meng*-to
daughter *filha* ⓕ *fee*-lyaa
dawn *madrugada* ⓕ maa-droo-*gaa*-daa
day *dia* ⓕ *dee*-aa
day after tomorrow *depois* ⓜ *de amanhã* de-*poys* de aa-*maa*-*nyang*
day before yesterday *antes* ⓜ *de ontem* *ang*-tes de *ong*-teng
dead *morto/morta* ⓜ/ⓕ morr-to/morr-taa
deaf *surdo/surda* ⓜ/ⓕ *soor*-do/*soor*-daa
deal (cards) *dar* daarr
December *dezembro* de-*zeng*-bro
decide *decidir* de-see-*deer*
deep *profundo/profunda* ⓜ/ⓕ pro-*foong*-do/pro-*foong*-daa
deforestation *desflorestamento* ⓜ des-flo-res-taa-*meng*-to
degrees (temperature) *graus* ⓜ pl grows
delay *atraso* ⓜ aa-*traa*-zo

delicatessen *delicatessen* ⓕ de-lee-kaa-te-seng
deliver *entregar* eng-tre-*gaarr*
democracy *democracia* ⓕ de-mo-kraa-*see*-aa
demonstration *demonstração* ⓕ de-mongs-traa-*sowng*
Denmark *Dinamarca* ⓕ dee-naa-*maarr*-kaa
dental floss *fio* ⓜ *dental* *fee*-o deng-*tow*
dentist *dentista* ⓜ&ⓕ deng-*tees*-taa
deodorant *desodorante* ⓜ de-zo-do-*rang*-te
depart (leave) *partir* paarr-*teerr*
department store *loja* ⓕ *de departamentos* lo-*zhaa* de de-paarr-taa-*meng*-tos
departure *partida* ⓕ paarr-*tee*-daa
departure gate *portão* ⓜ *de partida* porr-*towng* de paarr-*tee*-daa
deposit *depósito* ⓜ de-po-zee-to
derailleur *câmbio* ⓜ *de marcha* kang-byo de *maarr*-shaa
descendent *descendente* ⓜ&ⓕ de-seng-*deng*-te
desert *deserto* ⓜ de-*zerr*-to
design *design* ⓜ design
dessert *sobremesa* ⓕ so-bre-*me*-zaa
destination *destino* ⓜ des-*tee*-no
details *detalhes* ⓜ pl de-*taa*-lyes
diabetes *diabetes* ⓕ dee-aa-*be*-tes
dial tone *linha* ⓕ *lee*-nyaa
diaper *fralda* ⓕ *frow*-daa
diaphragm *diafragma* ⓜ dee-aa-*fraa*-gee-maa
diarrhoea *diarréia* ⓕ dee-aa-*hay*-aa
diary *diário* ⓜ dee-*aa*-ryo
dice *dados* ⓜ pl *daa*-dos
dictionary *dicionário* ⓜ dee-syo-*naa*-ryo
die *morrer* mo-*herr*
diet *dieta* ⓕ dee-*e*-taa
different *diferente* dee-fe-*reng*-te
difficult *difícil* dee-*fee*-seel
dining car *vagão* ⓜ *restaurante* vaa-*gowng* hes-tow-*rang*-te
dinner *jantar* ⓜ zhang-*taarr*
direct *direto/direita* ⓜ/ⓕ dee-*re*-to/dee-*re*-taa

direct-dial *ligação* ① *direta*
lee·gaa·*sowng* dee·re·taa

director *diretor/diretora* ⓜ/①
dee·re·*torr*/dee·re·*to*·raa

dirty *sujo/suja* ⓜ/① *soo*·zho/*soo*·zhaa

disabled *deficiente* de·fee·see·*eng*·te

disco *disco* ⓜ *dees*·ko

discount *desconto* ⓜ des·*kong*·to

discrimination *discriminação* ①
dees·kree·mee·naa·*sowng*

disease *doença* ① do·*eng*·saa

disk (computer) *disk* ⓜ deesk

diving *mergulho* ⓜ merr·*goo*·lyo

diving equipment *equipamento* ①
de mergulho e·kee·paa·*meng*·to de
merr·*goo*·lyo

dizzy *tonto/tonta* ⓜ/①
tong·to/*tong*·taa

do *fazer* faa·*zerr*

doctor *médico/médica* ⓜ/① *me*·dee·ko/
me·dee·kaa

documentary *documentário* ⓜ
do·koo·meng·*taa*·ryo

dog *cachorro* ⓜ/① kaa·*sho*·ho

dole *seguro social* ⓜ se·goo·ro so·see·*ow*

doll *boneco/boneca* ⓜ/①
bo·*ne*·ko/bo·*ne*·kaa

dollar *dólar* ⓜ *do*·laarr

door *porta* ① *porr*·taa

dope (drugs) *bagulho* ⓜ baa·*goo*·lyo

double *duplo/dupla* ⓜ/①
doo·plo/*doo*·plaa

double bed *cama* ① *de casal*
ka·maa de kaa·*zow*

double room *quarto* ⓜ *de casa kwaarr*·to
de kaa·*zow*

down *baixo* bai·sho

downhill *para baixo* paa·raa bai·sho

dozen *dúzia* ① *doo*·zyaa

drama *drama* ⓜ *dra*·maa

dream *sonho* ⓜ *so*·nyo

dress *vestido* ves·*tee*·do

dried *seco/seca* ⓜ/① *se*·ko/*se*·kaa

dried fruit *frutas* ① pl *secas*
froo·taas *se*·kaas

drink *bebida* ① be·*bee*·daa

drive *dirigir* dee·ree·*zherr*

drivers licence *carteira* ① *de motorista*
kaar·*tay*·raa de mo·to·*rees*·taa

drug *droga* ① *dro*·gaa

drug addiction *vício* ⓜ *de drogas*
vee·syo de *dro*·gaas

drug dealer *traficante* ⓜ&①
tra·fee·*kang*·te

drug user *usuário/usuária* ⓜ/① *de*
drogas oo·zoo·*aa*·ryo/oo·zoo·*aa*·ryaa
de *dro*·gaas

drugs *drogas* ① pl *dro*·gaas

drum *bateria* ① baa·te·*ree*·aa

drunk *bêbado/bêbada* ⓜ/①
be·baa·do/*be*·baa·daa

dry *secar* se·*kaarr*

dry *seco/seca* ⓜ/① *se*·ko/*se*·kaa

duck *pato/pata* ⓜ/① *paa*·to/*paa*·taa

dummy (for baby) *chupeta* ① shoo·*pe*·taa

DVD *DVD* ⓜ de·ve·*de*

E

each *cada* kaa·daa

ear *orelha* ① o·re·lyaa

early *cedo* se·do

earn *ganhar* ga·*nyaarr*

earplugs *tampões* ⓜ *de ouvido*
tang·*powng* de o·*vee*·do

earrings *brincos* ⓜ pl *breeng*·kos

Earth *Terra* ① *te*·haa

earthquake *terremoto* ⓜ te·he·*mo*·to

east *leste* ⓜ *les*·te

Easter *Páscoa* ① *paas*·kwaa

easy *fácil* faa·seel

eat *comer* ko·*merr*

economy class *classe* ① *econômica*
klaa·se e·ko·no·mee·kaa

ecstacy (drug) *êxtase* ⓜ *es*·taa·ze

eczema *eczema* ① e·kee·ze·maa

editor *editor/editora* ⓜ/①
e·dee·*torr*/e·dee·*to*·raa

education *educação* ① e·doo·ka·*sowng*

egg *ovo* ⓜ o·vo

eggplant *beringela* ① be·reeng·*zhe*·laa

election *eleição* ① e·lay·*sowng*

electrical store *loja* ① *de aparelhos*
elétricos lo·zhaa de aa·paa·*re*·lyos
e·*le*·tree·kos

electricity *eletricidade* ①
e·*le*·tree·see·*daa*·de

elevator *elevador* ⓜ e·le·vaa·*dorr*

embarrassed *envergonhado/ envergonhada* ⓜ/ⓕ en·verr·go·*nyaa*·do/en·verr·go·*nyaa*·daa
embassy *embaixada* ⓕ eng·bai·*shaa*·daa
emergency *emergência* ⓕ e·merr·*zheng*·syaa
emotional *sensível* seng·*see*·vel
employee *empregado/ empregada* ⓜ/ⓕ eng·pre·*gaa*·do/ eng·pre·*gaa*·daa
employer *empregador/ empregadora* ⓜ/ⓕ eng·pre·gaa·*dorr*/ eng·pre·gaa·*do*·raa
empty *vazio/vazia* ⓜ/ⓕ vaa·*zee*·o/vaa·*zee*·aa
end *fim* ⓜ feeng
endangered species *espécies* ⓕ pl *ameaçadas de extinção* es·*pe*·syes aa·me·aa·*saa*·daas de es·teeng·*sowng*
engagement *noivado* ⓜ noy·*vaa*·do
engine *motor* ⓜ mo·*torr*
engineer *engenheiro/engenheira* ⓜ/ⓕ eng·zhe·*nyay*·ro/eng·zhe·*nyay*·raa
engineering *engenharia* ⓕ eng·zhe·nya·*ree*·aa
England *Inglaterra* ⓕ eeng·glaa·*te*·haa
English (language) *Inglês* ⓜ eeng·*gles*
enjoy (oneself) *aproveitar* aa·pro·vay·*taarr*
enough *suficiente* soo·fee·see·*eng*·te
enter *entrar* eng·*traarr*
entertainment guide *guia* ⓜ *de entretenimento* gee·aa de eng·tre·te·nee·*meng*·to
envelope *envelope* ⓜ eng·ve·*lo*·pe
environment *meio* ⓜ *ambiente* *may*·o ang·bee·*eng*·te
epilepsy *epilepsia* ⓕ e·pee·le·pee·*see*·aa
equal opportunity *oportunidades* ⓕ pl *iguais* o·porr·too·nee·*daa*·des ee·*gwaa*·ees
equality *igualdade* ⓕ ee·gwow·*daa*·de
equipment *equipamento* ⓜ e·kee·paa·*meng*·to
escalator *escada rolante* ⓕ es·*kaa*·daa ho·*lang*·te
euro *euro* ⓜ *e·oo·ro*
Europe *Europa* ⓕ e·oo·ro·paa
euthanasia *eutanásia* ⓕ e·oo·taa·*naa*·zyaa
evening *noite* ⓕ *noy*·te

everything *tudo* too·do
example *exemplo* ⓜ e·*zeng*·plo
excellent *excelente* e·se·*leng*·te
exchange *troca* ⓕ *tro*·kaa
exchange *trocar* tro·*kaarr*
exchange rate *taxa* ⓕ *de câmbio* taa·shaa de *kang*·byo
excluded *excluído/excluída* ⓜ/ⓕ es·kloo·*ee*·do/es·kloo·*ee*·daa
exhaust (car) *exaustor* ⓜ e·zows·*torr*
exhibition *exposição* ⓕ es·po·zee·*sowng*
exit *saída* ⓕ saa·*ee*·daa
expensive *caro/cara* ⓜ/ⓕ *kaa*·ro/*kaa*·raa
experience *experiência* ⓕ es·pe·ree·*eng*·syaa
exploitation *exploração* ⓕ es·plo·raa·*sowng*
express *expresso/expressa* ⓜ/ⓕ es·*pre*·so/ es·*pre*·saa
express mail *serviço* ⓜ *postal rápido* serr·*vee*·so pos·*tow haa·pee*·do
extension (visa) *extensão* ⓕ es·teng·*sowng*
eye *olho* ⓜ *o*·lyo
eye drops *colírio* ⓕ ko·*lee*·ryo

F

fabric *tecido* ⓜ te·*see*·do
face *rosto* ⓜ *hos*·to
face cloth *toalha* ⓕ *de rosto* to·*aa*·lyaa de *hos*·to
factory *fábrica* ⓕ *faa*·bree·kaa
factory worker *operário/operária* ⓜ/ⓕ o·pe·*raa*·ryo/o·pe·*raa*·ryaa
fall (autumn) *outono* ⓜ o·*to*·no
fall (down) *queda* ⓕ *ke*·daa
family *família* ⓕ faa·*mee*·lyaa
family name *sobrenome* ⓜ so·bre·*no*·me
famous *famoso/famosa* ⓜ/ⓕ faa·*mo*·zo/faa·*mo*·zaa
fan (machine) *ventilador* ⓜ veng·tee·laa·*dorr*
fan (sport, etc) *fã* ⓜ&ⓕ fang
fanbelt *correia* ⓕ ko·*hay*·aa
far *longe* *long*·zhe
farm *fazenda* ⓕ faa·*zeng*·daa

farmer *fazendeiro/fazendeira* ⓜ/ⓕ
faa·zeng·*day*·ro/faa·zeng·*day*·raa

fast *rápido/rápida* ⓜ/ⓕ
haa·pee·do/*haa*·pee·daa

fat *gordo/gorda* ⓜ/ⓕ *gorr*·do/*gorr*·daa

father *pai* ⓜ pai

father-in-law *sogro* ⓜ *so*·gro

faucet *torneira* ⓕ torr·*nay*·raa

fault (someone's) *culpa* ⓕ *kool*·paa

faulty *defeituoso/defeituosa* ⓜ/ⓕ
de·fay·too·o·zo/de·fay·too·o·zaa

February *fevereiro* fe·ve·*ray*·ro

feed *alimentar* aa·lee·meng·*taarr*

feel *sentir* seng·*teerr*

feelings *sentimentos* ⓜ pl
seng·tee·*meng*·tos

fence *cerca* ⓕ *serr*·kaa

fencing (sport) *esgrima* ⓕ es·*gree*·maa

festival *festival* ⓜ fes·tee·*vow*

fever *febre* ⓕ *fe*·bre

few *alguns/algumas* ⓜ/ⓕ
ow·*goons*/ow·goo·maas

fiance *noivo* ⓜ *noy*·vo

fiancee *noiva* ⓕ *noy*·vaa

fiction *ficção* ⓕ feek·*sowng*

fig *figo* ⓕ *fee*·go

fight *luta* ⓕ *loo*·ta

fill *encher* eng·*sherr*

fillet *filé* ⓕ *fee*·le

film (cinema) *filme* ⓜ *feel*·me

film (photography) *filme* ⓜ *fotográfico*
feel·me fo·to·*graa*·fee·ko

film speed *velocidade* ⓕ *do filme*
ve·lo·see·*daa*·de do *feel*·me

filtered *filtrado/filtrada* ⓜ/ⓕ
feel·*traa*·do/feel·*traa*·daa

find *encontrar* eng·kong·*traarr*

fine (payment) *multa* ⓕ *mool*·taa

fine *bom/boa* ⓜ/ⓕ bong/*bo*·aa

finger *dedo* ⓜ *de*·do

finish *término* ⓜ *terr*·mee·no

finish *terminar* terr·mee·*naarr*

fire *fogo* ⓜ *fo*·go

firewood *lenha* ⓕ *le*·nyaa

first *primeiro/primeira* ⓜ/ⓕ
pree·*may*·ro/pree·*may*·raa

first class *primeira classe* ⓕ
pree·*may*·raa *klaa*·se

first-aid kit *kit* ⓜ *de primeiros socorros*
kee·tee de pree·*may*·ros so·*ko*·hos

fish *peixe* ⓜ *pay*·she

fish monger *peixeiro/peixeira* ⓜ/ⓕ
pay·*shay*·ro/pay·*shay*·raa

fish shop *peixaria* ⓕ pay·sha·*ree*·aa

fishing *pesca* ⓕ *pes*·kaa

flag *bandeira* ⓕ bang·*day*·raa

flannel *flanela* ⓕ fla·*ne*·laa

flashlight *flash* ⓜ *luminoso*
flash loo·mee·*no*·zo

flat (apartment) *apartamento* ⓜ
aa·paarr·taa·*meng*·to

flat *plano/plana* ⓜ/ⓕ *pla*·no/*pla*·naa

flea *pulga* ⓕ *pool*·gaa

flight *vôo* ⓜ *vo*·o

flood *enchente* ⓕ eng·*sheng*·te

floor *chão* ⓜ showng

floor (storey) *andar* ⓜ ang·*daarr*

florist (person) *florista* ⓜ&ⓕ flo·*rees*·taa

florist (shop) *floricultura* ⓕ
flo·ree·kool·*too*·raa

flour *farinha* ⓕ faa·*ree*·nyaa

flower *flor* ⓕ florr

fly *voar* vo·*aarr*

foggy *nebuloso/nebulosa* ⓜ/ⓕ
ne·boo·*lo*·zo/ne·boo·*lo*·zaa

follow *seguir* se·*geerr*

food *comida* ⓕ ko·*mee*·daa

foot *pé* ⓜ pe

football (soccer) *futebol* ⓜ foo·te·*bol*

footpath *calçada* ⓕ kow·*saa*·daa

foreign *estrangeiro/estrangeira* ⓜ/ⓕ
es·trang·*zhay*·ro/es·trang·*zhay*·raa

forest *floresta* ⓕ flo·*res*·taa

forever *para sempre* paa·raa *seng*·pre

forget *esquecer* es·ke·*serr*

forgive *perdoar* perr·do·*aarr*

fork *garfo* ⓜ *gaarr*·fo

fortnight *quinzena* ⓕ keeng·*ze*·naa

fortune teller *vidente* ⓜ&ⓕ vee·*deng*·te

foul *falta* ⓕ *fow*·taa

foyer *saguão* ⓜ saag·*wowng*

fragile *frágil* fraa·zheel

free (gratis) *gratuito/gratuita* ⓜ/ⓕ
graa·*too*·ee·to/graa·*too*·ee·taa

free (not bound) *livre* *lee*·vre

freeze *congelar* kong·zhe·*laarr*

Friday *sexta-feira* ⓕ *ses*·taa·*fay*·raa

fried *frito/frita* ⓜ/ⓕ *free*·to/*free*·taa
friend *amigo/amiga* ⓜ/ⓕ
aa·*mee*·go/aa·*mee*·gaa
frost *geada* ⓕ zhe·*aa*·daa
fruit *fruta* ⓕ *froo*·taa
fruit picking *colheita* ⓕ *de frutas*
ko·*lyay*·taa de *froo*·taas
fry *fritar* free·*taarr*
frying pan *frigideira* ⓕ free·zhee·*day*·raa
full *cheio/cheia* ⓜ/ⓕ *shay*·o/*shay*·aa
full-time *tempo* ⓜ *integral*
teng·po eeng·te·*grow*
fun *divertido/divertida* ⓜ/ⓕ
dee·verr·*tee*·do/dee·verr·*tee*·daa
funeral *enterro* ⓜ eng·*te*·ho
funny *engraçado/engraçada* ⓜ/ⓕ
eng·graa·*saa*·do/eng·graa·*saa*·daa
furniture *móveis* ⓜ pl *mo*·vays
future *futuro* ⓜ foo·*too*·ro

G

game (sport) *jogo* ⓜ *zho*·go
garage *oficina* ⓕ o·fee·*see*·naa
garbage *lixo* ⓜ *lee*·sho
garden *jardim* ⓜ zhaarr·*deeng*
gardener *jardineiro/jardineira* ⓜ/ⓕ
zhaarr·dee·*nay*·ro/zhaarr·dee·*nay*·raa
gardening *jardinagem* ⓕ
zhaarr·dee·*naa*·zheng
garlic *alho* ⓜ *aa*·lyo
gas (for cooking) *gás* ⓜ gas
gas (petrol) *gasolina* ⓕ gaa·zo·*lee*·na
gas cartridge *cartucho* ⓜ *de gás*
kaarr·*too*·sho de gaas
gastroenteritis *gastrenterite* ⓕ
gaas·treng·te·*ree*·te
gate (airport, etc) *portão* ⓜ porr·*towng*
gauze *gaze* ⓕ *gaa*·ze
gay *gay* gay
Germany *Alemanha* ⓕ aa·le·*ma*·nyaa
get *pegar* pe·*gaarr*
gift *presente* ⓜ pre·*zeng*·te
gig *apresentação* ⓕ
aa·pre·seng·taa·*sowng*
gin *gin* ⓜ zheen
girl *menina* ⓕ me·*nee*·naa
girlfriend *namorada* ⓕ naa·mo·*raa*·daa
give *dar* daarr

glandular fever *febre* ⓕ *glandular*
fe·bre glang·doo·*laar*
glass *vidro* ⓜ *vee*·dro
glasses (spectacles) *óculos* ⓜ pl o·koo·los
gloves *luvas* ⓕ pl *loo*·vaas
glue *cola* ⓕ *ko*·laa
go *ir* eerr
go out with *sair* saa·*eerr*
goal *objetivo* ⓜ o·bee·zhe·*tee*·vo
goal (sport) *gol* ⓜ gol
goalkeeper *goleiro/goleira* ⓜ/ⓕ
go·*lay*·ro/go·*lay*·raa
goat *bode* ⓜ *bo*·de
god (general) *deus* ⓜ *de*·oos
goggles (skiing) *óculos* ⓜ pl *de ski*
o·koo·los de es·*kee*
goggles (swimming) *óculos* ⓜ pl *de*
natação o·koo·los de naa·taa·*sowng*
gold *ouro* ⓜ *o*·ro
golf ball *bola* ⓕ *de golfe*
bo·laa de *gol*·fee
golf course *campo* ⓕ *de golfe*
kang·po de *gol*·fee
good *bom/boa* ⓜ/ⓕ bong/*bo*·aa
Goodbye. *Tchau/Adeus* ⓜ
tee·*show*/ aa·*de*·oos
government *governo* ⓜ go·*verr*·no
gram *grama* ⓕ *graa*·maa
grandchild *neto/neta* ⓜ/ⓕ
ne·to/*ne*·taa
grandfather *avô* ⓜ aa·*vo*
grandmother *avó* ⓕ aa·*vaw*
grapefruit *pomelo* ⓜ po·*me*·lo
grapes *uvas* ⓕ pl *oo*·vaas
grass *grama* ⓕ *gra*·maa
grave *túmulo* ⓜ *too*·moo·lo
gray *cinza* *seeng*·zaa
great *ótimo/ótima* ⓜ/ⓕ
o·tee·mo/o·tee·maa
green *verde* *verr*·de
greengrocer *verdureiro/verdureira* ⓜ/ⓕ
verr·doo·*ray*·ro/verr·doo·*ray*·raa
grey *cinza* *seeng*·zaa
grocery *mantimentos* ⓜ pl
mang·tee·*meng*·tos
groundnut *amendoim* ⓜ
aa·meng·do·*eeng*
grow *crescer* kres·*serr*

g-string *biquíni* ⓜ *fio dental*
bee-*kee*-nee fyo deng-*tow*
guess *adivinhar* aa-dee-vee-*nyaarr*
guide (audio) *guia* ⓜ *auditivo*
gee-aa ow-dee-tee-vo
guide (person) *guia* ⓜ&ⓕ gee-aa
guide dog *cão-guia* ⓜ kowng-*gee*-aa
guidebook *guia* ⓜ *gee*-aa
guided tour *excursão* ⓕ *guiada*
es-koor-*sowng* gee-*aa*-daa
guilty *culpado/culpa* ⓜ/ⓕ kool-*paa*-do/
kool-*paa*-daa
guitar *violão* ⓜ vee-o-*lowng*
gum *gengiva* ⓕ zheng-*zhee*-vaa
gun *arma* ⓕ *aarr*-maa
gym *ginástica* ⓕ zhee-*naas*-tee-kaa
gymnastics *ginástica* ⓕ *olímpica*
gee-*naas*-tee-kaa o-*leeng*-pee-kaa
gynaecologist *ginecologista* ⓜ&ⓕ
zhee-ne-ko-lo-*zhees*-taa

H

hair *cabelo* ⓜ kaa-*be*-lo
hairbrush *escova* ⓕ es-*ko*-vaa
hairdresser *cabeleireiro/cabeleireira* ⓜ/ⓕ
kaa-be-lay-*ray*-ro/kaa-be-lay-*ray*-raa
halal *halal* aa-*low*
half *metade* ⓕ me-*taa*-de
hallucination *alucinação* ⓕ
aa-loo-see-naa-*sowng*
ham *presunto* ⓜ pre-*zoong*-to
hammer *martelo* ⓜ maarr-*te*-lo
hammock *rede* ⓕ *he*-de
hand *mão* ⓕ mowng
handbag *bolsa* ⓕ *de mão*
bol-saa de mowng
handball *handebol* ⓜ heng-de-bol
handicrafts *artesanato* ⓜ
aarr-te-zaa-*naa*-to
handlebars *corrimão* ⓜ ko-hee-*mowng*
handmade *feito à mão*
fay-to aa mowng
handsome *bonito/bonita* ⓜ/ⓕ
bo-*nee*-to/bo-*nee*-taa
happy *feliz* fe-*lees*
harassment *molestamento* ⓜ
mo-les-taa-*meng*-to
harbour *baía* ⓕ baa-*ee*-aa

hard *duro/dura* ⓜ/ⓕ *doo*-ro/doo-raa
hard-boiled *cozido/cozida* ⓜ/ⓕ
ko-*zee*-do/ko-*zee*-daa
hardware store *loja* ⓕ *de ferramentas*
lo-zhaa de fe-haa-*meng*-taas
hat *chapéu* ⓜ shaa-*pe*-oo
have *ter* terr
have a cold *estar resfriado* ⓜ/ⓕ
es-*taarr* hes-free-*aa*-do
have fun *divertir-se* dee-verr-*teerr*-se
hay fever *febre* ⓕ *do feno*
fe-bre do *fe*-no
hazelnut *avelã* ⓕ aa-ve-*lang*
he *ele* *e*-le
head *cabeça* ⓕ kaa-*be*-saa
headache *dor* ⓕ *de cabeça*
dorr de kaa-*be*-saa
headlight *faróis* ⓜ pl faa-*roys*
health *saúde* ⓕ sa-oo-de
hear *escutar* es-koo-*taarr*
hearing aid *aparelho* ⓜ *de surdez*
aa-paa-*re*-lyo de soorr-*des*
heart *coração* ⓜ ko-ra-*sowng*
heart attack *ataque* ⓜ *de coração*
aa-*taa*-ke de ko-ra-*sowng*
heart condition *problema* ⓜ *de coração*
pro-*ble*-maa de ko-ra-*sowng*
heating *aquecimento* ⓜ
aa-ke-see-*meng*-to
heater *estufa* ⓕ es-*too*-faa
heavy *pesado/pesada* ⓜ/ⓕ
pe-*zaa*-do/pe-*zaa*-daa
Hello. *Olá.* o-*laa*
Hello. (answering telephone) *Alô.* aa-*lo*
helmet *capacete* ⓜ kaa-paa-*se*-te
help *ajuda* ⓕ aa-*zhoo*-daa
help *ajudar* aa-zhoo-*daarr*
Help! *Socorro!* so-*ko*-ho
hepatitis *hepatite* ⓕ e-paa-*tee*-te
her *dela* de-laa
herbalist *botânico/botânica* ⓜ/ⓕ
bo-*ta*-nee-ko/bo-*ta*-nee-kaa
herb *erva* ⓕ *err*-vaa
here *aqui* aa-*kee*
heroin *heroína* ⓕ e-ro-*ee*-naa
herring *arenque* ⓜ aa-*reng*-ke
high *alto/alta* ⓜ/ⓕ *ow*-to/*ow*-taa
high school *segundo grau* ⓜ
se-*goong*-do grow

highchair *cadeira* ① *para refeição*
kaa·*day*·raa paa·raa he·fay·*sowng*
hike *caminhar* kaa·mee·*nyaarr*
hiking *caminhada* ① kaa·mee·*nyaa*·daa
hiking boots *botas* ① *para caminhadas*
bo·taas paa·raa kaa·mee·*nyaa*·daas
hiking route *rota* ① *de caminhada*
ho·taa de kaa·mee·*nyaa*·daa
hill *morro* ⓜ mo·ho
Hindu *Hindu* eeng·*doo*
hire *alugar* aa·loo·*gaarr*
his *dele* de·le
historical *histórico/histórica* ⓜ/①
ees·to·ree·ko/ees·to·ree·kaa
history *história* ① ees·to·rya
hitchhike *pegar carona*
pe·gaarr kaa·ro·naa
HIV *HIV* ⓜ aa·gaa ee ve
hockey *hockey* ⓜ ho·kay
holiday *férias* ① pl fe·ryaas
home *casa* ① kaa·zaa
homeless *desabrigado/*
desabrigada ⓜ/① de·zaa·bree·*gaa*·do/
de·zaa·bree·*gaa*·daa
homemaker *dona* ① *de casa*
do·naa de kaa·zaa
homeopathy *homeopatia* ①
o·me·o·paa·*tee*·aa
homosexual *homosexual* o·mo·sek·soo·ow
honey *mel* ⓜ mel
honeymoon *lua* ① *de mel*
loo·aa de mel
horoscope *horóscopo* ⓜ o·ros·ko·po
horse *cavalo* ⓜ kaa·vaa·lo
horse riding *cavalgada* ①
kaa·vaal·*gaa*·daa
hospital *hospital* ⓜ os·pee·tow
hospitality *hospitalidade* ①
os·pee·taa·lee·*daa*·de
hot *quente* keng·te
hot water *água* ① *quente*
aa·gwaa keng·te
hotel *hotel* ⓜ o·tel
house *casa* ① kaa·zaa
housework *trabalho* ⓜ *de casa*
traa·*baa*·lyo de kaa·zaa
how *como* ko·mo
how much *quanto* kwang·to
hug *abraçar* aa·braa·*saarr*

huge *enorme* e·norr·me
human resources *recursos* ⓜ pl *humanos*
he·koor·sos oo·*ma*·nos
human rights *direitos* ⓜ pl *humanos*
dee·ray·tos oo·*ma*·nos
humanities *humanidades* ① pl
oo·ma·nee·*daa*·des
hundred *cem* seng
hungry *faminto/faminta* ⓜ/①
faa·meeng·to/faa·meeng·taa
hunting *caça* ① kaa·saa
hurt *machucar* maa·shoo·*kaarr*
husband *marido* ⓜ maa·*ree*·do

I

I *eu* e·oo
ice *gelo* ⓜ zhe·lo
ice axe *quebrador* ⓜ *de gelo*
ke·braa·dorr de zhe·lo
ice cream *sorvete* ⓜ sorr·ve·te
ice-cream parlour *sorveteria* ①
sorr·ve·te·*ree*·aa
ice hockey *hockey* ⓜ *de gelo*
ho·kay de zhe·lo
identification *identificação* ①
ee·deng·tee·fee·kaa·*sowng*
identification card *carteira* ① *de*
identidade kaar·*tay*·raa de
ee·deng·tee·*daa*·de
idiot *idiota* ⓜ&① ee·dee·o·taa
if *se* se
ill *mal* mal
immigration *imigração* ①
ee·mee·graa·*sowng*
important *importante* eeng·porr·*tang*·te
in a hurry *com pressa* kong pre·saa
in front of *na frente de* naa freng·te de
included *incluso/inclusa* ⓜ/①
eeng·*kloo*·zo/eeng·*kloo*·zaa
income tax *imposto* ⓜ *de renda*
eeng·*pos*·to de heng·daa
India *Índia* ① eeng·dyaa
indicator *indicador* ⓜ eeng·dee·kaa·*dorr*
indigestion *indigestão* ①
eeng·dee·zhes·*towng*
indoors *adentro* aa·*deng*·tro
industry *indústria* ① eeng·*doos*·tryaa
infection *infecção* ① eeng·fek·*sowng*

inflammation *inflamação* ①
eeng·fla·maa·sowng
influenza *gripe* ① gree·pe
ingredient *ingrediente* ⓜ
eeng·gre·dee·eng·te
inject *injetar* eeng·zhe·taarr
injection *injeção* ① eeng·zhe·sowng
injury *ferimento* ⓜ fe·ree·meng·to
inner tube *câmara* ① de ar
ka·ma·raa de aarr
innocent *inocente* ee·no·seng·te
inside *dentro* deng·tro
instructor *instrutor/instrutora* ⓜ/①
eengs·troo·torr/eengs·troo·to·raa
insurance *seguro* ⓜ se·goo·ro
interesting *interessante* eeng·te·re·sang·te
intermission *intervalo* ⓜ eeng·terr·vaa·lo
international *internacional*
eeng·terr·naa·syo·now
Internet *Internet* ① eeng·terr·ne·tee
Internet cafe *Internet café* ⓜ
eeng·terr·ne·tee kaa·fe
interpreter *intérprete* ⓜ&①
eeng·terr·pre·te
interview *entrevista* ① eeng·tre·vees·taa
invite *convidar* kong·vee·daar
Ireland *Irlanda* ① eerr·lang·daa
iron (clothes) *ferro* ⓜ de passa roupas
fe·ho de paa·saarr ho·paas
island *ilha* ① ee·lyaa
Israel *Israel* ① ees·haa·el
it *coisa* ① koy·zaa
IT (information technology)
IT ⓜ ai·tee
itch *coceira* ① ko·say·raa
itemised *listado/listada* ⓜ/①
lees·taa·do/lees·taa·daa
itinerary *itinerário* ① ee·tee·ne·raa·ryo
IUD *DIU* ⓜ dee·oo

J

jacket *jaqueta* ① zhaa·ke·taa
jail *prisão* ① pree·zowng
jam *geléia* ① zhe·le·yaa
January *janeiro* ⓜ zhaa·nay·ro
Japan *Japão* ⓜ zhaa·powng
jar *vidro* ⓜ vee·dro

jaw *mandíbula* ① mang·dee·boo·laa
jealous *ciumento/ciumenta* ⓜ/①
see·oo·meng·to/see·oo·meng·taa
jeans *jeans* ⓜ zheens
jeep *jeep* ⓜ zhee·pe
jewellery *joalheria* ① zho·a·lye·ree·aa
Jewish *Judeu/Judia* ⓜ/①
zhoo·de·oo/zhoo·dee·aa
job *emprego* ⓜ eng·pre·go
jogging *corrida* ① ko·hee·daa
joke *piada* ① pee·aa·daa
journalist *jornalista* ⓜ&①
zhorr·naa·lees·taa
journey *viagem* ① vee·aa·zheng
judge *juiz/juiza* ①
zhoo·ees/zhoo·ee·zaa
juice *suco* ⓜ soo·ko
July *julho* ⓜ zhoo·lyo
jump *pular* poo·laarr
jumper (sweater) *suéter* ① soo·e·terr
jumper leads *recarregador* ⓜ de bateria
he·kaa·he·gaa·dorr de baa·te·ree·aa
June *junho* ⓜ zhoo·nyoo

K

ketchup *ketchup* ⓜ ke·tee·shoo·pee
key *chave* ① shaa·ve
keyboard *teclado* ⓜ te·klaa·do
kick (a ball) *chutar* shoo·taarr
kidney *rin* ⓜ pl heeng
kill *matar* maa·taarr
kilogram *kilograma* ⓜ kee·lo·gra·maa
kilometre *kilômetro* ⓜ kee·lo·me·tro
kind *bom/boa* ⓜ/① bong/bo·aa
kindergarten *jardim* ⓜ de infância
zhaarr·deeng de eeng·fang·syaa
king *rei* ⓜ hay
kiss *beijo* ⓜ bay·zho
kiss *beijar* bay·zhaarr
kitchen *cozinha* ① ko·zee·nyaa
kiwifruit *kiwi* ⓜ kee·wee
knee *joelho* ⓜ zho·e·lyo
knife *faca* ① faa·kaa
know *saber* saa·berr
kosher *kosher* ko·sherr

L

labourer *trabalhador/trabalhadora* ⓜ/ⓕ
de obra traa·baa·lyaa·*dorr*/
traa·baa·lyaa·*do*·raa de o·braa
lace *renda* ⓕ *heng*·daa
lake *lago* ⓜ *laa*·go
lamb *ovelha* ⓕ o·ve·lyaa
land *terra* ⓕ *te*·haa
landlady *proprietária* ⓕ
pro·pree·e·*taa*·ryaa
landlord *proprietário* ⓜ pro·pree·e·*taa*·ryo
language *língua* ⓕ *leeng*·gwaa
laptop *laptop* ⓜ le·pee·to·*pee*
large *grande* grang·de
last *último/última* ⓜ/ⓕ
ool·tee·mo/*ool*·tee·maa
last (week) *passada (semana)* ⓕ
paa·*saa*·daa (se·*ma*·naa)
late *atrasado/atrasada* ⓜ/ⓕ
aa·traa·*zaa*·do/aa·traa·*zaa*·daa
laugh *rir* heerr
laundrette *lavanderia* ⓕ
laa·vang·de·*ree*·aa
laundry (room) *área* ⓕ *de serviço*
aa·re·aa de serr·*vee*·so
law *lei* ⓕ lay
lawyer *advogado/advogada* ⓜ/ⓕ
aa·dee·vo·*gaa*·do/aa·dee·vo·*gaa*·daa
laxative *laxante* ⓜ la·*shang*·te
lazy *preguiçoso/preguiçosa* ⓜ/ⓕ
pre·gee·so·zo/pre·gee·so·zaa
leader *líder* ⓜ&ⓕ *lee*·derr
leaf *folha* ⓕ *fo*·lyaa
learn *aprender* aa·preng·*derr*
leather *couro* ⓜ *ko*·ro
lecturer *professor/professora* ⓜ/ⓕ
pro·fe·*sorr*/pro·fe·so·raa
ledge *parapeito* ⓜ paa·raa·*pay*·to
leek *alho* ⓜ *porró* aa·lyo po·ho
left (direction) *(à) esquerda* ⓕ
(aa) es·*kerr*·daa
left luggage *achados e perdidos* ⓜ pl
aa·*shaa*·dos e perr·*dee*·dos
left-wing *esquerdista* es·kerr·*dees*·taa
leg *perna* ⓕ *perr*·naa
legal *legal* le·gow
legislation *legislação* ⓕ le·zhees·la·*sowng*
legume *legumes* ⓜ pl le·*goo*·mes

lemon *limão* ⓜ lee·*mowng*
lemonade *limonada* ⓕ lee·mo·*naa*·daa
lens *lentes* ⓕ pl leng·tes
lentil *lentilha* ⓕ leng·*tee*·lyaa
lesbian *lésbica* ⓕ *les*·bee·kaa
less *menos* ⓜ *me*·nos
letter (mail) *carta* ⓕ *kaarr*·taa
lettuce *alface* ⓕ ow·*faa*·se
liar *mentiroso/mentirosa* ⓜ/ⓕ
meng·tee·ro·zo/meng·tee·ro·zaa
library *biblioteca* ⓕ bee·blee·o·*te*·kaa
lice *piolho* ⓜ pee·*o*·lyo
licence *licença* ⓕ lee·*seng*·saa
license plate number *número* ⓜ *da placa*
noo·me·ro daa *plaa*·kaa
lie (not stand) *deitar* day·*taarr*
life *vida* ⓕ *vee*·daa
life jacket *colete salva-vidas* ⓜ
ko·*le*·te sow·vaa·*vee*·daas
lift (elevator) *elevador* ⓜ e·le·vaa·*dorr*
light *luz* ⓕ looz
light (not heavy) *leve* le·ve
light bulb *lâmpada* ⓕ *lang*·paa·daa
light meter *fotômetro* ⓜ fo·to·me·tro
lighter (cigarette) *isqueiro* ⓜ ees·*kay*·ro
like *gostar* gos·*taarr*
lime *limão* ⓜ lee·*mowng*
lip balm *bálsamo* ⓜ *para lábios*
bow·sa·mo paa·raa *laa*·byos
lips *lábios* ⓜ pl *laa*·byos
lipstick *batom* ⓜ ba·*tong*
liquor store *loja* ⓕ *de bebidas*
lo·zhaa de be·*bee*·daas
listen *escutar* es·koo·*taarr*
little (not much) *pouco/pouca* ⓜ/ⓕ
po·ko/*po*·kaa
little (small) *pequeno/pequena* ⓜ/ⓕ
pe·*ke*·no/pe·*ke*·naa
live (somewhere) *morar* mo·*raarr*
liver *fígado* ⓜ *fee*·gaa·do
lizard *lagarto* ⓜ laa·*gaarr*·to
local *local* lo·*kow*
lock *tranca* ⓕ *trang*·kaa
lock *trancar* trang·*kaarr*
locked *trancado/trancada* ⓜ/ⓕ
trang·*kaa*·do/trang·*kaa*·daa
lollies *balas* ⓕ pl *baa*·laas
long *longo/longa* ⓜ/ⓕ
long·go/*long*·gaa

look *ver* verr
look after *cuidar* kooy-*daarr*
look for *procurar* pro-koo-*raarr*
lookout *mirante* ① mee-*rang*-te
loose *solto/solta* ⑩/① *sol*-to/*sol*-taa
loose change *trocado* ⑩ tro-*kaa*-do
lose *perder* perr-*derr*
lost *perdido/perdida* ⑩/①
    perr-*dee*-do/perr-*dee*-daa
lost property office *escritório* ⑩ *de*
    achados e perdidos es-kree-to-ryo de
    aa-*shaa*-dos e perr-*dee*-dos
(a) lot *muito/muita* ⑩/①
    mweeng-to/*mweeng*-taa
loud *alto/alta* ⑩/① ow-to/ow-taa
love *amor* ⑩ aa-*morr*
love *amar* aa-*maarr*
lover *amante* ⑩&① aa-*mang*-te
low *baixo/baixa* ⑩/① bai-sho/bai-shaa
lubricant *lubrificante* ⑩
    loo-bree-fee-*kang*-te
luck *sorte* ① *sorr*-te
lucky *sortudo/sortuda* ⑩/①
    sorr-*too*-do/sorr-*too*-daa
luggage *bagagem* ① baa-*gaa*-zheng
luggage locker *guarda* ⑩ *volumes*
    gwaar-daa vo-loo-mes
luggage tag *etiqueta* ① *de bagagem*
    e-tee-*ke*-taa de baa-*gaa*-zheng
lump *nódulo* ⑩ *no*-doo-lo
lunch *almoço* ⑩ ow-mo-so
lung *pulmão* ⑩ pool-*mowng*
luxury *luxo* ⑩ *loo*-sho

M

machine *máquina* ① *maa*-kee-naa
magazine *revista* ① he-*vees*-taa
mail *correspondência* ①
    ko-hes-pong-*deng*-syaa
mailbox *caixa* ① *de correio*
    kai-shaa de ko-*hay*-o
main *principal* preeng-see-*pow*
main road *rua* ① *principal*
    hoo-aa preeng-see-*pow*
make *fazer* faa-*zerr*
make-up *maquiagem* ①
    maa-kee-*aa*-zheng

mammogram *mamograma* ⑩
    maa-mo-*gra*-maa
man *homem* ⑩ o-meng
manager *gerente* zhe-*reng*-te
mandarin *tangerina* ① tang-zhe-*ree*-naa
mango *manga* ① *mang*-gaa
manual worker *trabalhador/trabalhadora*
    ⑩/① *manual* traa-baa-lyaa-*dorr*/
    traa-baa-lyaa-*do*-raa maa-noo-ow
many *vários/várias* ⑩/①
    vaa-ryos/*vaa*-ryaas
map *mapa* ① *maa*-paa
March *março* maar-so
margarine *margarina* ①
    maarr-gaa-*ree*-naa
marijuana *maconha* ① maa-ko-nyaa
marital status *estado civil*
    es-*taa*-do see-*veel*
market *mercado* ⑩ merr-*kaa*-do
marmalade *marmelada* ①
    maarr-me-*laa*-daa
marriage *casamento* ⑩ kaa-zaa-*meng*-to
marry *casar* kaa-*zaarr*
martial arts *artes* ① pl *marciais*
    aarr-tes maar-see-*ais*
mass (Catholic) *missa* ① *mee*-saa
massage *massagem* ① maa-*saa*-zheng
masseur *massagista* ⑩&①
    maa-saa-*zhees*-taa
mat *capacho* ⑩ kaa-*paa*-sho
match (sport) *partida* ① paarr-*tee*-daa
matches *fósforos* ⑩ pl *fos*-fo-ros
mattress *colchão* ⑩ kol-*showng*
May *maio* *maa*-yo
maybe *talvez* tow-*ves*
mayonnaise *maionese* ① maa-yo-*ne*-ze
mayor *prefeito/prefeita* ⑩/①
    pre-*fay*-to/pre-*fay*-taa
measles *sarampo* ① saa-*rang*-po
meat *carne* ① *kaar*-ne
mechanic *mecânico/mecânica* ⑩/①
    me-*ka*-nee-ko/me-*ka*-nee-kaa
media *mídia* ① *mee*-dyaa
medicine *medicina* ① me-dee-*see*-naa
meditation *meditação* ①
    me-dee-taa-*sowng*
meet *encontrar* eng-kong-*traarr*
melon *melão* ⑩ me-*lowng*
member *membro* ⑩&① *meng*-bro

menstruation *menstruação* ⓕ
mengs·troo·aa·*sowng*

menu *cardápio* ⓜ kaarr·*daa*·pyo

message *mensagem* ⓕ meng·*sa*·zheng

metal *metal* ⓜ me·tow

metre *metro* ⓜ *me*·tro

microwave *microondas* ⓕ
mee·kro·*ong*·daas

midnight *meia-noite* ⓕ may·aa·*noy*·te

migraine *enxaqueca* ⓕ en·shaa·*ke*·kaa

military *militar* mee·lee·*taarr*

military service *serviço* ⓜ *militar*
serr·*vee*·so mee·lee·*taarr*

milk *leite* ⓜ *lay*·te

millimetre *milímetro* ⓜ mee·*lee*·me·tro

million *milhão* ⓜ mee·*lowng*

mince *carne* ⓕ *moída*
kaarr·ne mo·*ee*·daa

mineral water *água* ⓕ *mineral*
aa·gwaa mee·ne·row

minute *minuto* ⓜ mee·*noo*·to

mirror *espelho* ⓜ es·*pe*·lyo

miscarriage *aborto* ⓜ *espontâneo*
aa·*borr*·to es·pong·*ta*·ne·o

miss (feel absence of) *sentir falta*
seng·*teerr* fow·taa

mistake *erro* ⓜ *e*·ho

mix *misturar* mees·too·raar

mobile phone *celular* ⓜ se·loo·*laarr*

modem *modem* ⓜ mo·deng

moisturiser *hidratante* ⓕ
ee·draa·*tang*·te

monastery *monastério* ⓜ mo·naas·*te*·ryo

Monday *segunda-feira* ⓕ
se·*goong*·daa·*fay*·raa

money *dinheiro* ⓜ dee·*nyay*·ro

monk *monge* ⓜ *mong*·zhe

month *mês* ⓜ mes

monument *monumento* ⓜ
mo·noo·*meng*·to

moon *lua* ⓕ *loo*·aa

more *mais* mais

morning *manhã* ⓕ ma·*nyang*

morning sickness *enjôo* ⓜ en·*zho*·o

mosque *mosteiro* ⓜ mos·*tay*·ro

mosquito *mosquito* ⓜ mos·*kee*·to

mosquito coil *repelente* ⓜ *em aspiral*
he·pe·*leng*·te eng aas·pee·row

mosquito net *mosquiteiro* ⓜ
mos·kee·*tay*·ro

mother *mamãe* ⓕ ma·*mayng*

mother-in-law *sogra* ⓕ *so*·graa

motorbike *motocicleta* ⓕ
mo·to·see·*kle*·taa

motorboat *barco* ⓜ *à motor*
baar·ko aa mo·*torr*

motorway (tollway) *auto estrada* ⓕ
ow·to es·*traa*·daa

mountain *montanha* ⓕ mong·*ta*·nyaa

mountain bike *mountain bike* ⓜ
maa·oong·tayng *bai*·kee

mountain path *trilha* ⓕ *tree*·lyaa

mountain range *cordilheira* ⓕ
korr·dee·*lyay*·raa

mountaineering *montanhismo* ⓜ
mong·ta·*nyees*·mo

mouse *camundongo* ⓜ
ka·moong·*dong*·go

mouth *boca* ⓕ *bo*·kaa

movie *cinema* ⓜ see·ne·maa

mud *lama* ⓕ *la*·maa

muesli *muesli* ⓜ *mues*·lee

mum *mãe* ⓕ mayng

mumps *caxumba* ⓕ kaa·*shoong*·baa

murder *assassinato* ⓜ aa·saa·see·*naa*·to

murder *assassinar* aa·saa·see·*naarr*

muscle *músculo* ⓜ *moos*·koo·lo

museum *museu* ⓜ mo·*se*·oo

mushroom *cogumelo* ⓜ ko·goo·*me*·lo

music *música* ⓕ *moo*·zee·kaa

music shop *loja* ⓕ *de música*
lo·zhaa de *moo*·zee·kaa

musician *músico/música* ⓜ/ⓕ
moo·zee·ko/*moo*·zee·kaa

Muslim *Muçulmano/Muçulmana* ⓜ/ⓕ
moo·sool·*ma*·no/moo·sool·*ma*·naa

mussel *mexilhão* ⓜ me·shee·*lyowng*

mustard *mustarda* ⓕ moos·*taarr*·daa

mute *mudo/muda* ⓜ/ⓕ
moo·do/*moo*·daa

my *meu/minha* ⓜ/ⓕ *me*·oo/*mee*·nyaa

N

nail clippers *cortador* ⓜ *de unhas*
korr·taa·*dorr* de oo·nyaas

name *nome* ⓜ *no*·me

napkin *guardanapo* ⓜ gwaar·daa·*naa*·po

nappy *fralda* ⓕ *frow*·daa

nappy rash *irritação* ① *à fralda*
ee·hee·ta·sowng aa frow·daa

national park *parque* ⓜ *nacional*
paar·ke naa·syo·now

nationality *nacionalidade* ①
naa·syo·naa·lee·daa·de

nature *natureza* ① naa·too·re·zaa

naturopathy *naturopatia* ①
naa·too·ro·paa·tee·a

nausea *náusea* ① now·se·aa

near *perto/perta* ① perr·to/perr·taa

nearby *por perto/perta* ⓜ/①
porr perr·to/perr·taa

nearest *mais perto/perta* ⓜ/①
mals perr·to/perr·taa

necessary *necessário/necessária* ⓜ/①
ne·se·sa·ryo/ne·se·sa·ryaa

necklace *colar* ⓜ ko·laarr

nectarine *pessego* ⓜ pe·se·go

need *precisar* pre·see·zaarr

needle (sewing) *agulha* ① aa·goo·lyaa

needle (syringe) *agulha* ① aa·goo·lyaa

negative *negativo/negativa* ⓜ/①
ne·gaa·tee·vo/ne·gaa·tee·vaa

neither *nenhum deles* ne·yoom de·les

net *rede* ① he·de

Netherlands *Países* ⓜ pl *Baixos*
paa·ee·zes bai·shos

never *nunca* noong·kaa

new *novo/nova* ⓜ/① no·vo/no·vaa

New Year's Day *Dia* ⓜ *de Ano Novo* dee·aa
de a·no no·vo

New Year's Eve *Véspera* ① *de Ano Novo*
ves·pe·raa de a·no no·vo

New Zealand *Nova Zelândia* ①
no·vaa ze·lang·dyaa

news *novidades · notícias* ① pl
no·vee·daa·des · no·tee·syaas

news stand *jornaleiro* ⓜ zhorr·na·lay·ro

newsagency *jornaleiro* ⓜ zhorr·naa·lay·ro

newspaper *jornal* ⓜ zhorr·now

next *próximo/próxima* ⓜ/①
pro·see·mo/pro·see·maa

next to *ao lado de* ow laa·do de

nice *bacana* baa·ka·naa

nickname *apelido* ⓜ aa·pe·lee·do

night *noite* ① noy·te

no *não* nowng

noisy *barulhento/barulhenta* ⓜ/①
baa·roo·lyeng·to/baa·roo·lyeng·taa

none *nenhum* ne·yoom

non-smoking *não-fumante*
nowng·foo·mang·te

noodles *macarrão* ⓜ *chinês*
maa·kaa·howng shee·nes

noon *meio-dia* ⓜ may·o dee·aa

Norway *Noruega* ① no·roo·e·gaa

north *norte* ⓜ norr·te

nose *nariz* ① naa·rees

not *não* nowng

notebook *caderno* ⓜ kaa·derr·no

nothing *nada* naa·daa

November *novembro* no·veng·bro

now *agora* aa·go·raa

nuclear energy *energia* ① *nuclear*
e·nerr·zhee·aa noo·kle·aarr

nuclear testing *teste* ⓜ *nuclear*
tes·te noo·kle·aarr

nuclear waste *resíduo* ⓜ *nuclear*
he·zee·doo·o noo·kle·aarr

number *número* ⓜ noo·me·ro

numberplate *número* ⓜ *da placa*
noo·me·ro daa plaa·kaa

nun *freira* ① fray·raa

nurse *enfermeira* ① eng·ferr·may·raa

nut *noz* ① noz

O

oats *aveia* ① aa·ve·aa

ocean *oceano* ① o·se·a·no

October *outubro* o·too·bro

off (food) *estragado/estragada* ⓜ/①
es·traa·gaa·do/es·traa·gaa·daa

office *escritório* ⓜ es·kree·to·ryo

office worker *escriturário/escriturária*
ⓜ/① es·kree·too·raa·ryo/
es·kree·too·raa·ryaa

often *frequentemente*
fre·kweng·te·meng·te

oil *óleo* ⓜ o·lyo

old *velho/velha* ⓜ/① ve·lyo/ve·lyaa

olive *azeitona* ① aa·zay·to·naa

olive oil *azeite* ⓜ aa·zay·te

Olympic Games *Jogos Olímpicos* ⓜ pl
zho·gos o·leeng·pee·kos

on *sobre* so·bre

once *uma vez* oo·maa vez
one-way (ticket) *ida* ① ee·daa
onion *cebola* ① se·bo·laa
only *somente* so·meng·te
open *aberto/aberta* ⓜ/① aa·berr·to/aa·berr·taa
open *abrir* aa·breerr
opening hours *horário* ⓜ *de funcionamento* o·raa·ryo de foon·syo·naa·meng·to
opera *ópera* ① o·pe·raa
opera house *casa* ① *de ópera* kaa·zaa de o·pe·raa
operation *operação* ① o·pe·raa·sowng
operator *operador/operadora* ⓜ/① o·pe·raa·dorr/o·pe·raa·do·raa
opinion *opinião* ① o·pee·nee·owng
opposite *oposto/oposta* ⓜ/① o·pos·to/o·pos·taa
optometrist *optometrista* ⓜ&① o·pee·to·me·trees·taa
or *ou* o
orange (fruit) *laranja* ① laa·rang·zhaa
orange (colour) *laranja* laa·rang·zhaa
orange juice *suco* ⓜ *de laranja* soo·ko de laa·rang·zhaa
orchestra *orquestra* ① orr·kes·traa
order (command) *pedido* ⓜ pe·dee·do
order *pedir* pe·deerr
ordinary *ordinário/ordinária* ⓜ/① orr·dee·naa·ryo/orr·dee·naa·ryaa
orgasm *orgasmo* ⓜ orr·gaas·mo
original *original* o·ree·zhee·now
other *outro/outra* ⓜ/① o·tro/o·traa
our *nosso/nossa* ⓜ/① no·so/no·saa
outside *fora* fo·raa
ovarian cyst *cisto* ⓜ *no ovário* sees·to no o·vaa·ryo
ovary *ovário* ⓜ o·vaa·ryo
oven *forno* ⓜ forr·no
overcoat *sobretudo* ⓜ so·bre·too·do
overdose *overdose* ① o·verr·do·ze
owe *dever* de·verr
owner *dono/dona* ⓜ/① do·no/do·naa
oxygen *oxigênio* ⓜ ok·see·zhe·nyo
oyster *ostra* ① os·traa
ozone layer *camada* ① *de ozônio* kaa·maa·daa de o·zo·nyo

P

pacemaker *marca* ⓜ *passo* mar·kaa pa·so
pacifier *chupeta* ① shoo·pe·taa
package *embrulho* ⓜ eng·broo·lyo
packet *pacote* ① pa·ko·te
padlock *cadeado* ⓜ kaa·de·aa·do
page *página* ① paa·zhee·naa
pain *dor* ① dorr
painful *doloroso/dolorosa* ⓜ/① do·lo·ro·zo/do·lo·ro·zaa
painkiller *analgésico* aa·now·ge·zee·ko
painter *pintor/pintora* ⓜ/① peeng·torr/peeng·to·raa
painting *pintura* ① peeng·too·raa
pair (couple) *par* ⓜ paarr
Pakistan *Paquistão* ⓜ paa·kees·towng
palace *palácio* ⓜ paa·laa·syo
pan *panela* ① paa·ne·laa
pants (trousers) *calças* ① pl kow·saas
panty liner *absorvente* ⓜ *higiênico* aab·sorr·veng·te ee·zhee·e·nee·ko
pantyhose *meia* ① *calça* may·aa kow·saa
pap smear *exame* ⓜ *papa nicolau* e·za·me paa·paa nee·ko·low
paper *papel* ⓜ paa·pel
paperwork *papelada* ① paa·pe·laa·daa
paraplegic *paraplégico/paraplégica* ⓜ/① paa·raa·ple·zhee·ko/paa·raa·ple·zhee·kaa
parcel *encomenda* ① eng·ko·meng·daa
parents *pais* ⓜ pl paa·ees
park *parque* ⓜ paarr·ke
park (vehicle) *estacionar* es·taa·syo·naarr
parliament *parlamento* ⓜ paarr·laa·meng·to
part (component) *parte* ① paarr·te
part-time *meio expediente* may·o es·pe·dee·eng·te
party (social gathering) *festa* ① fes·taa
party (politics) *partido* ⓜ paarr·tee·do
pass *passar* paa·saarr
passenger *passageiro/passageira* ⓜ/① paa·saa·zhay·ro/paa·saa·zhay·raa
passionfruit *maracujá* ⓜ maa·raa·koo·zhaa
passport *passaporte* ⓜ paa·saa·porr·te

passport number *número* ⓜ *do passaporte* noo·me·ro do paa·sa·*porr*·te
past *passado* ⓜ paa·*saa*·do
pasta *massas* ⓕ pl *maa*·saas
pastry *massa* ⓕ *maa*·saa
path *caminho* ⓜ kaa·*mee*·nyo
pay *pagar* paa·*gaarr*
payment *pagamento* ⓜ paa·gaa·*meng*·to
pea *ervilha* ⓕ err·vee·lyaa
peace *paz* ⓕ pas
peach *pêssego* ⓜ *pe*·se·go
peanut *amendoim* ⓜ aa·meng·do·*eeng*
pear *pêra* ⓕ *pe*·raa
pedal *pedal* ⓜ pe·*dow*
pedestrian *pedestre* ⓜ pe·*des*·tre
pen (ballpoint) *caneta* ⓕ ka·*ne*·taa
pencil *lápis* ⓜ *laa*·pees
penis *pênis* ⓜ *pe*·nees
penknife *canivete* ⓜ kaa·nee·*ve*·te
pensioner *pensionista* ⓜ&ⓕ peng·syo·*nees*·taa
people *pessoas* ⓕ pl pe·*so*·aas
pepper *pimenta* ⓕ pee·*meng*·taa
pepper (bell) *pimentão* ⓜ pee·meng·*towng*
per *por* porr
per cent *porcentagem* ⓕ porr·seng·*taa*·zheng
perfect *perfeito/perfeita* ⓜ/ⓕ perr·*fay*·to/perr·*fay*·taa
performance *performance* ⓕ perr·*forr*·mang·se
perfume *perfume* ⓜ perr·*foo*·me
period pain *cólica* ⓕ *menstrual* *ko*·lee·kaa mengs·troo·*ow*
permission *permissão* ⓕ perr·mee·*sowng*
permit *permissão* ⓕ per·mee·*sowng*
person *pessoa* ⓕ pe·*so*·aa
petition *petição* ⓕ pe·tee·*sowng*
petrol *petróleo* ⓜ pe·*tro*·lyo
pharmacy *farmácia* ⓕ faar·*maa*·syaa
phone book *lista* ⓕ *telefônica* *lees*·taa te·le·*fo*·nee·kaa
phone box *telefone* ⓜ *público* te·le·*fo*·ne *poo*·blee·ko
phonecard *cartão* ⓜ *telefônico* kaarr·*towng* te·le·*fo*·nee·ko
photograph *fotografia* ⓕ fo·to·graa·*fee*·aa

photographer *fotógrafo/fotógrafa* ⓜ/ⓕ fo·*to*·graa·fo/fo·*to*·gra·faa
photography *fotografia* ⓕ fo·to·graa·*fee*·aa
phrasebook *livro* ⓜ *de frases* *lee*·vro de *fraa*·zes
pickaxe *picareta* ⓕ pee·kaa·*re*·taa
pickles *pikles* ⓜ pl *pee*·kles
picnic *piquenique* ⓜ pee·ke·*nee*·ke
pie *torta* ⓕ *torr*·taa
piece *pedaço* ⓜ pe·*da*·so
pig *porco/porca* ⓜ/ⓕ *porr*·ko/*porr*·kaa
pill *pílula* ⓕ *pee*·loo·laa
Pill (the) *pílula* ⓕ *pee*·loo·laa
pillow *travesseiro* ⓜ traa·ve·*say*·ro
pillowcase *fronha* ⓕ *fro*·nyaa
pineapple *abacaxi* ⓜ aa·baa·kaa·*shee*
pink *rosa* ho·za
pistachio *pistácio* ⓜ pees·*taa*·shyo
place *lugar* ⓜ loo·*gaarr*
place of birth *local* ⓜ *de nascimento* lo·*kow* de naas·see·*meng*·to
planet *planeta* ⓜ pla·*ne*·taa
plant *planta* ⓕ *plang*·taa
plastic *plástico/plástica* ⓜ/ⓕ *plas*·tee·ko/*plas*·tee·kaa
plate *prato* ⓜ *praa*·to
plateau *planalto* ⓜ pla·*now*·to
platform *plataforma* ⓕ plaa·taa·*forr*·maa
play (theatre) *peça* ⓕ *pe*·saa
play *jogar* zho·*gaarr*
play (guitar) *tocar* to·*kaarr*
plug (bath) *tampa* ⓕ *tang*·paa
plug (electricity) *tomada* ⓕ to·*maa*·daa
plum *ameixa* ⓕ aa·*may*·shaa
poached *poché* po·she
pocket *bolso* ⓜ *bol*·so
pocket knife *canivete* ⓜ kaa·nee·*ve*·te
poetry *poesia* ⓕ po·e·*zee*·aa
point *ponto* ⓜ *pong*·to
point *apontar* aa·pong·*taarr*
poisonous *venenoso/venenosa* ⓜ/ⓕ ve·ne·*no*·zo/ve·ne·*no*·zaa
police *polícia* ⓕ po·*lee*·syaa
police station *delegacia* ⓕ *de polícia* de·le·gaa·*see*·aa de po·*lee*·sya
policy *regras* ⓕ pl *he*·graas
politician *político/política* ⓜ/ⓕ po·*lee*·tee·ko/po·*lee*·tee·kaa

politics *política* ① po-*lee*-tee-kaa
pollen *pólen* ⓜ po-leng
pollution *poluição* ① po-loo-ee-*sowng*
pool (game) *sinuca* ① see-*noo*-kaa
pool (swimming) *piscina* ① pee-*see*-naa
poor *pobre* po-bre
popular *popular* po-poo-*laarr*
pork *porco/porca* ⓜ/① porr-ko/porr-kaa
pork sausage *linguiça* ① *de porco*
leen-*gwee*-saa de porr-ko
port (sea) *porto* ⓜ porr-to
Portugal *Portugal* ⓜ porr-too-*gow*
positive *positivo/positiva* ⓜ/①
po-zee-*tee*-vo/po-zee-*tee*-vaa
possible *possível* po-*see*-vel
post office *correio* ⓜ ko-*hay*-ro
postage *postagem* ① pos-*taa*-zheng
postcard *cartão* ⓜ *postal*
kaarr-*towng* pos-*tow*
postcode *código* ⓜ *postal*
ko-dee-go pos-*tow*
poster *cartaz* ⓜ kaarr-*taz*
pot (ceramics) *louça* ① pl *de barro*
lo-saa de baa-ho
pot (dope) *bagulho* ⓜ baa-*goo*-lyo
potato *batata* ① baa-*taa*-taa
pottery *cerâmica* ① se-*ra*-mee-kaa
pound (money) *libra* ① lee-braa
poverty *pobreza* ① po-*bre*-zaa
powder *pó* ⓜ po
power *poder* ⓜ po-*derr*
prawn *camarão* ⓜ kaa-maa-*rowng*
prayer *reza* ① *he*-zaa
prefer *preferir* pre-fe-*reerr*
pregnancy test kit *teste* ⓜ *de gravidez*
tes-te de graa-vee-*dez*
pregnant *grávida* ① *graa*-vee-daa
premenstrual tension *tensão* ①
pré-menstrual teng-*sowng*
pre-mengs-troo-ow
prepare *preparar* pre-paa-*raarr*
present (gift) *presente* ⓜ pre-*zeng*-te
present (time) *presente* ⓜ pre-*zeng*-te
president *presidente* ⓜ&①
pre-zee-*deng*-te
pressure *pressão* ① pre-*sowng*
pretty *bonito/bonita* ⓜ/①
bo-*nee*-to/bo-*nee*-taa
price *preço* ⓜ *pre*-so

priest *padre* ⓜ *paa*-dre
prime minister *primeiro ministro* ⓜ •
primeira ministra ① pree-*may*-ro
mee-*nees*-tro • pree-*may*-raa
mee-*nees*-traa
prison *prisão* ① pree-*zowng*
prisoner *prisioneiro/prisioneira* ⓜ/①
pree-zyo-*nay*-ro/pree-zyo-*nay*-raa
private *privado/privada* ⓜ/①
pree-*vaa*-do/pree-*vaa*-daa
produce *produzir* pro-doo-*zeerr*
profit *lucro* ⓜ *loo*-kro
program *programa* ⓜ pro-*gra*-maa
projector *projetor* ⓜ pro-zhe-*torr*
promise *prometer* pro-me-*terr*
protect *proteger* pro-te-*zherr*
protected *protegido/protegida* ①
pro-te-*zhee*-do/pro-te-*zhee*-daa
protest *protesto* ⓜ pro-*tes*-to
protest *protestar* pro-tes-*taarr*
provisions *provisões* ① pl pro-vee-*zoyngs*
prune *ameixa* ① *seca*
aa-*may*-shaa se-kaa
pub *bar* ⓜ baarr
public gardens *jardins* ⓜ pl *públicos*
zhaarr-*deengs* poo-blee-kos
public relations *relações* ① pl *públicas*
he-la-*soyngs* poo-blee-kaas
public telephone *telefone* ⓜ *público*
te-le-*fo*-ne poo-blee-ko
public toilet *banheiro* ⓜ *público*
ba-*nyay*-ro poo-blee-ko
publishing *editoração* ①
e-dee-to-raa-*sowng*
pull *puxar* poo-*shaarr*
pump *bomba* ① *bong*-baa
pumpkin *abóbora* ① aa-*bo*-bo-raa
puncture *furo* ⓜ foo-ro
pure *puro/pura* ⓜ/① *poo*-ro/*poo*-raa
purple *roxo/roxa* ⓜ/① *ho*-sho/*ho*-shaa
push *empurrar* eng-poo-*haarr*
put *colocar* ko-lo-*kaarr*

Q

quadriplegic *quadraplégico/*
quadraplégica ⓜ/①
kwaa-draa-*ple*-zhee-ko/
kwaa-draa-*ple*-zhee-kaa

214

qualifications *qualificações* ① pl
kwaa·lee·fee·kaa·*soyngs*

quality *qualidade* ① kwaa·lee·*daa*·de

quarantine *quarentena* ①
kwaa·reng·*te*·naa

quarter *quarto* ⓜ kwaarr·to

queen *rainha* ① haa·*ee*·nyaa

question *pergunta* ① · *questão* ⓜ
perr·*goong*·ta · kes·*towng*

queue *fila* ① fee·laa

quick *rápido/rápida* ⓜ/①
haa·pee·do/haa·pee·daa

quiet *quieto/quieta* ⓜ/①
kee·e·to/kee·e·taa

quit *desistir* de·zees·*teerr*

R

rabbit *coelho* ⓜ ko·e·lyo

race (sport) *corrida* ① ko·hee·daa

racetrack *pista* ① *de corrida*
pees·taa de ko·hee·daa

racing bike *bicicleta* ① *de corrida*
bee·see·*kle*·taa de ko·hee·daa

racism *racismo* ⓜ haa·sees·mo

racquet *raquete* ① haa·ke·te

radiator *radiador* ⓜ haa·dee·aa·*dorr*

radish *rabanete* ⓜ haa·baa·ne·te

railway station *estação* ① *de trem*
es·taa·*sowng* de treng

rain *chuva* ① shoo·vaa

raincoat *casaco* ⓜ *de chuva*
kaa·*zaa*·ko de shoo·vaa

raisin *passas* ① pl paa·saas

rally *comício* ⓜ ko·mee·syo

rape *estrupo* ⓜ es·troo·po

rape *estrupar* es·troo·*paarr*

rare (food) *mal passado/passada* ⓜ/①
mow paa·*saa*·do/paa·*saa*·daa

rare (uncommon) *raro/rara* ⓜ/①
haa·ro/haa·raa

rash *irritação* ① *na pele*
ee·hee·taa·*sowng* naa pe·le

raspberry *framboesa* ① fraang·bo·e·zaa

rat *rato/ratazana* ⓜ/①
haa·to/haa·taa·*za*·naa

raw *cru/crua* ⓜ/① kroo/kroo·aa

razor *raspador* ⓜ haas·paa·*dorr*

razor blade *gilete* ① zhee·*le*·te

read *ler* lerr

ready *pronto/pronta* ⓜ/①
prong·to/prong·taa

real estate agent *agente* ⓜ&①
imobiliário aa·*zheng*·te
ee·mo·bee·lee·aa·ryo

realistic *realista* he·aa·lees·taa

reason *razão* ① haa·*zowng*

recently *recentemente* he·seng·te·*meng*·te

recommend *recomendar*
he·ko·meng·*daarr*

record *gravar* graa·*vaarr*

recording *gravação* ① graa·vaa·*sowng*

recyclable *reciclável* he·see·*klaa*·vel

recycle *reciclar* he·see·*klaar*

red *vermelho/vermelha* ⓜ/①
verr·me·lyo/verr·me·lyaa

referee *juiz/juiza* ⓜ/①
zhoo·*ees*/zhoo·ee·zaa

reference *referência* ① he·fe·*reng*·syaa

reflexology *reflexologia* ①
he·flek·so·lo·zhee·aa

refrigerator *geladeira* ① zhe·laa·*day*·raa

refugee *refugiado/refugiada* ⓜ/①
he·foo·zhee·*aa*·do/he·foo·zhee·*aa*·daa

refund *reembolso* ⓜ he·eng·*bol*·so

refuse *recusar* he·koo·*zaarr*

regional *regional* he·zhyo·*now*

registered mail *correio* ⓜ *registrado*
ko·*hay*·o he·zhees·*traa*·do

rehydration salts *sais* ⓜ pl *de hidratação*
sais de ee·draa·taa·*sowng*

reiki *reiki* ⓜ *hay*·kee

relationship *relacionamento* ⓜ
he·laa·syo·na·*meng*·to

relax *relaxar* he·la·*shaarr*

relic *rélica* ① he·*le*·kaa

religion *religião* ① he·lee·zhee·*owng*

religious *religioso/religiosa* ⓜ/①
he·lee·zhee·o·zo/he·lee·zhee·o·zaa

remote *remoto/remota* ⓜ/①
he·mo·to/he·mo·taa

remote control *controle* ⓜ *remoto*
kong·*tro*·le he·mo·to

rent *alugar* aa·loo·*gaarr*

repair *consertar* kong·serr·*taarr*

republic *república* ① he·poo·blee·kaa

reservation (booking) *reserva* ①
he-*zerr*-vaa

rest *descansar* des-*kang*-*saarr*

restaurant *restaurante* ⑩ hes-tow-*rang*-te

resume (CV) *currículum* ⑩
koo-*hee*-koo-loom

retired *aposentado/aposentada* ⑩/①
aa-po-seng-*taa*-do/aa-po-seng-*taa*-daa

return *retornar* he-torr-*naarr*

return (ticket) *ida e volta*
ee-daa e *vol*-taa

review *revisão* ① he-vee-*zowng*

rhythm *ritmo* ⑩ *hee*-tee-mo

rib *costela* ① kos-*te*-laa

rice *arroz* ⑩ aa-*hos*

rich (wealthy) *rico/rica* ⑩/①
hee-ko/*hee*-kaa

ride (car) *volta* ① *vol*-taa

ride (horse) *andar à cavalo*
ang-*daarr* aa kaa-*vaa*-lo

right (direction) *(à) direita* ①
(aa) dee-*ray*-taa

right (correct) *correto/correta* ⑩/①
ko-*he*-to/ko-*he*-taa

right-wing *direitista* dee-ray-*tees*-taa

ring (on finger) *anel* ⑩ aa-*nel*

ring (phone) *tocar* to-*kaarr*

rip-off *roubo* ⑩ *ho*-bo

risk *risco* ⑩ *hees*-ko

river *rio* ⑩ *hee*-o

road *estrada* ① es-*traa*-daa

road map *mapa* ① *da estrada*
maa-paa daa es-*traa*-daa

rob *roubar* ho-*baarr*

rock *pedra* ① *pe*-draa

rock (music) *rock* ⑩ *ho*-kee

rock climbing *alpinismo* ⑩
ow-pee-*nees*-mo

rock group *banda* ① *de rock*
bang-daa de *ho*-kee

rockmelon *melão* ⑩ me-*lowng*

roll (bread) *pão* ⑩ *powng*

rollerblading *patinação*
paa-tee-naa-*sowng*

romantic *romântico/romântica* ⑩/①
ho-*mang*-tee-ko/ho-*mang*-tee-kaa

room *quarto* ⑩ *kwaarr*-to

room number *número* ⑩ *do quarto*
noo-me-ro do *kwaarr*-to

rope *corda* ① *korr*-daa

round *redondo/redonda* ⑩/①
he-*dong*-do/he-*dong*-daa

route *rota* ① *ho*-taa

rowing *remo* ⑩ *he*-mo

rubbish *lixo* ⑩ *lee*-sho

rubella *rubéola* ① hoo-be-o-laa

rug *tapete* ⑩ taa-*pe*-te

rugby *rugby* ⑩ *hoo*-gee-bee

ruins *ruínas* ① pl hoo-ee-naas

rule *regra* ① *he*-graa

rum *rum* ⑩ hoom

run *correr* ko-*herr*

running *corrida* ① ko-*hee*-daa

runny nose *coriza* ① ko-*ree*-zaa

S

sad *triste* *trees*-te

saddle *sela* ① *se*-laa

safe *seguro/segura* ⑩/①
se-*goo*-ro/se-*goo*-raa

safe *cofre* ⑩ *ko*-fre

safe sex *sexo* ⑩ *com proteção*
sek-so kong pro-te-*sowng*

saint *santo/santa* ⑩/①
sang-to/*sang*-taa

salad *salada* ① saa-*laa*-daa

salami *salaminho* ⑩ saa-laa-*mee*-nyo

salary *salário* ⑩ saa-*laa*-ryo

sale *liquidação* ① lee-kee-daa-*sowng*

sales tax *imposto* ⑩ *sobre venda*
eeng-*pos*-to *so*-bre *veng*-daa

salmon *salmão* ⑩ sow-*mowng*

salt *sal* ⑩ sow

same *mesmo/mesma* ⑩/①
mes-mo/*mes*-maa

sand *areia* ① aa-*re*-yaa

sandal *sandália* ① sang-*daa*-lyaa

sanitary napkin *toalha* ⑩ *higiênica*
to-*aa*-lyaa ee-zhee-e-nee-kaa

sardine *sardinha* ① saarr-*dee*-nyaa

Saturday *sábado* ⑩ *saa*-baa-do

sauce *molho* ⑩ *mo*-lyo

sauna *sauna* ① *sow*-naa

sausage *salsicha* ① sow-*see*-shaa

say *dizer* dee-*zerr*

scalp *couro* ⑩ *cabeludo*
ko-ro kaa-be-*loo*-do

scarf *lenço* ⓜ *leng*·so
school *escola* ⓕ es·ko·laa
science *ciências* ⓕ pl see·*eng*·syaas
scientist *cientista* ⓜ&ⓕ see·eng·*tees*·ta
scissors *tesoura* ⓕ te·zo·raa
score *contar os pontos*
   kong·*taarr* os *pong*·tos
scoreboard *painel* ⓜ *de marcação*
   pai·*nel* de maarr·kaa·*sowng*
Scotland *Escócia* ⓕ es·*ko*·syaa
scrambled *mexido/mexida* ⓜ/ⓕ
   me·*shee*·do/me·*shee*·daa
sculptor *escultor/escultora* ⓜ/ⓕ
   es·kool·*toorr*/es·kool·*too*·ra
sculpture *escultura* ⓕ es·kool·*too*·raa
sea *mar* ⓜ maarr
seasick *enjoado/enjoada* ⓜ/ⓕ
   en·zho·*aa*·do/en·zho·*aa*·daa
seaside *beira mar* ⓕ *bay*·raa maarr
season *estação* ⓕ es·taa·*sowng*
seat *assento* ⓜ aa·*seng*·to
seatbelt *cinto* ⓜ *de segurança*
   seeng·to de se·goo·*rang*·saa
second (time) *segundo* ⓜ se·*goong*·do
second *segundo/segunda* ⓜ/ⓕ
   se·*goong*·do/se·*goong*·daa
second-hand *de segunda mão*
   de se·*goong*·daa mowng
second-hand shop *loja* ⓕ *de segunda*
   mão lo·zhaa de se·*goon*·daa mowng
secretary *secretário/secretária* ⓜ/ⓕ
   se·kre·*taa*·ryo/se·kre·*taa*·ryaa
see *ver* verr
self-employed *autônomo/*
   autônoma ⓜ/ⓕ ow·to·no·mo/
   ow·to·no·maa
selfish *egoísta* e·go·*ees*·taa
self-service *auto-serviço* ⓜ
   ow·to·serr·*vee*·so
sell *vender* veng·*derr*
send *enviar* eng·vee·*aarr*
sensible *sensível* seng·*see*·vel
sensual *sensual* seng·soo·ow
separate *separado/separada* ⓜ/ⓕ
   se·paa·*raa*·do/se·paa·*raa*·daa
September *setembro* se·*teng*·bro
serious *sério/séria* ⓜ/ⓕ se·ryo/se·ryaa
service charge *taxa* ⓕ *de serviço*
   taa·shaa de serr·*vee*·so

service station *posto* ⓜ *de gasolina*
   pos·to de gaa·zo·lee·naa
serviette *guardanapo* ⓜ
   gwaarr·daa·*naa*·po
several *diversos/diversas* ⓜ/ⓕ pl
   dee·*verr*·sos/dee·*verr*·saas
sew *costurar* kos·too·*raarr*
sex *sexo* ⓜ *sek*·so
sexism *machismo* ⓜ maa·*shees*·mo
sexy *sexy* sek·see
shadow *sombra* ⓕ *song*·braa
shampoo *xampu* ⓜ shang·*poo*
shape *forma* ⓕ *forr*·maa
share (with) *dividir* dee·vee·*deerr*
shave *fazer a barba* faa·zerr aa *baarr*·baa
shaving cream *crème* ⓜ *de barbear*
   kre·me de baarr·be·*aarr*
she *ela* e·laa
sheep *ovelha* ⓕ o·ve·lyaa
sheet (bed) *lençol* ⓜ leng·*sow*
shelf *prateleira* ⓕ praa·te·*lay*·raa
shiatsu *shiatsu* ⓜ shee·*aa*·tee·zoo
shingles (illness) *cobreiro* ⓜ ko·*bray*·ro
ship *navio* ⓜ naa·*vee*·o
shirt *camisa* ⓕ kaa·*mee*·zaa
shoe *sapato* ⓜ saa·*paa*·to
shoe shop *sapataria* ⓕ saa·paa·taa·*ree*·aa
shoot *atirar* aa·tee·*raarr*
shop *loja* ⓕ lo·zhaa
shopping centre *shopping centre* ⓜ
   sho·peeng *seng*·terr
short *curto/curta* ⓜ/ⓕ *koor*·to/*koor*·taa
shortage *escassez* ⓕ es·kaa·*ses*
shorts *bermuda* ⓕ berr·*moo*·daa
shoulder *ombro* ⓜ pl *ong*·bro
shout *gritar* gree·*taarr*
show *mostrar* mos·*traarr*
shower *chuveiro* ⓜ shoo·*vay*·ro
shrine *relicário* ⓜ he·lee·*kaa*·ryo
shut *fechado/fechada* ⓜ/ⓕ
   fe·*shaa*·do/fe·*shaa*·daa
shy *tímido/tímida* ⓜ/ⓕ
   tee·mee·do/*tee*·mee·daa
sick *doente* do·eng·te
side *lado* ⓜ *laa*·do
sign *aviso* ⓜ aa·*vee*·zo
signature *assinatura* ⓕ aa·see·naa·*too*·raa
silk *seda* ⓕ *se*·daa
silver *prata* ⓕ *praa*·taa

similar *parecido/parecida* ⓜ/ⓕ
paa·re·*see*·do/paa·re·*see*·daa
simple *simples* *seeng*·ples
since *desde* des·de
sing *cantar* kang·*taarr*
Singapore *Cingapura* seen·gaa·*poo*·raa
singer *cantor/cantora* ⓜ/ⓕ
kang·*torr*/kang·*to*·raa
single *solteiro/solteira* ⓜ/ⓕ
sol·*tay*·ro/sol·*tay*·raa
singlet *camiseta* ⓕ kaa·mee·*ze*·taa
sister *irmã* ⓕ eer·*ma*
sit *sentar* seng·*taarr*
size *tamanho* ⓜ ta·*ma*·nyo
skate *andar de skate*
ang·*daarr* de es·*kay*·te
skateboarding *skate* ⓜ ees·*kay*·te
ski *esquiar* es·kee·*aarr*
skiing *esqui* ⓜ es·*kee*
skim milk *leite* ⓜ *desnatado*
lay·te des·naa·*taa*·do
skin *pele* ⓕ *pe*·le
skirt *saia* ⓕ *saa*·yaa
skull *crânio* ⓜ *kra*·nyo
sky *céu* ⓜ *se*·oo
sleep *dormir* dorr·*meerr*
sleeping bag *saco* ⓜ *de dormir*
saa·ko de dorr·*meerr*
sleeping berth *leito* ⓜ *lay*·to
sleeping car *vagão* ⓜ *de dormir*
va·*gowng* de dorr·*meerr*
sleeping pills *pílula* ⓕ *para dormir*
pee·loo·laa *paa*·raa dorr·*meerr*
sleepy *sonolento/sonolenta* ⓜ/ⓕ
so·no·*leng*·to/so·no·*leng*·taa
slide (film) *slide* ⓜ ees·*lai*·de
slow *devagar* de·va·*gaarr*
slowly *vagarosamente*
vaa·gaa·ro·zaa·*meng*·te
small *pequeno/pequena* ⓜ/ⓕ
pe·*ke*·no/pe·*ke*·na
smell *cheiro* ⓜ *shay*·ro
smile *sorrir* so·*heerr*
smoke *fumar* foo·*maarr*
snack *lanche* ⓜ *lang*·she
snail *lesma* ⓕ *les*·maa
snake *cobra* ⓕ *ko*·braa
snorkelling *snorkel* ⓜ ees·*norr*·kel
snow *neve* ⓕ *ne*·ve

snow pea *vagem* ⓕ *chinesa* vaa·zheng
shee·*ne*·zaa
snowboarding *snowboarding* ⓜ
snow·*borr*·deeng
soap *sabonete* ⓜ saa·bo·*ne*·te
soap opera *novela* ⓕ no·*ve*·laa
soccer *futebol* ⓜ foo·te·*bol*
social welfare *seguro* ⓜ *social*
se·*goo*·ro so·see·*ow*
socialist *socialista* so·see·aa·*lees*·taa
sock *meia* ⓕ *may*·aa
soft drink *refrigerante* ⓜ
he·free·zhe·*rang*·te
soft-boiled *mole* *mo*·le
soldier *soldado* ⓜ&ⓕ sol·*daa*·do
some *alguns/algumas* ⓜ/ⓕ
ow·*goons*/ow·*goo*·maas
someone *alguém* ow·*geng*
something *alguma coisa*
ow·*goo*·maa *koy*·zaa
sometimes *às vezes* aas *ve*·zes
son *filho* ⓜ *fee*·lyo
song *canção* ⓕ kang·*sowng*
soon *em breve* eng *bre*·ve
sore *dolorido/dolorida* ⓜ/ⓕ
do·lo·*ree*·do/do·lo·*ree*·daa
soup *sopa* ⓕ *so*·paa
sour cream *creme* ⓜ *azedo*
kre·me aa·*ze*·do
south *sul* ⓜ sool
souvenir *souvenir* ⓜ soo·ve·*neerr*
souvenir shop *loja* ⓕ *de souvenir*
lo·zhaa de soo·ve·*neerr*
soy milk *leite* ⓜ *de soja* *lay*·te de so·zhaa
soy sauce *molho* ⓜ *de soja*
mo·lyo de so·*zhaa*
space *espaço* ⓜ es·*pa*·so
Spain *Espanha* ⓕ es·*pa*·nyaa
sparkling wine *vinho* ⓜ *espumante*
vee·nyo es·poo·*mang*·te
speak *falar* faa·*laarr*
special *especial* es·pe·see·*ow*
specialist *especialista* ⓜ&ⓕ
es·pe·see·aa·*lees*·taa
speed *velocidade* ⓕ ve·lo·see·*daa*·de
speed limit *limite* ⓜ *de velocidade*
lee·*mee*·te de ve·lo·see·*daa*·de
speedometer *mostrador* ⓜ *de velocidade*
mos·traa·*dorr* de ve·lo·see·*daa*·de

spider *aranha* ① aa·ra·nyaa

spinach *espinafre* ⓜ es·pee·naa·fre

spoiled *mimado/mimada* ⓜ/①
mee·*maa*·do/mee·*maa*·daa

spoke (wheel) *trave* ① *de roda*
traa·ve de *ho*·daa

spoon *colher* ① ko·*lyerr*

sport *esporte* ⓜ es·*porr*·te

sports store *loja* ① *de esportes*
lo·zhaa de es·*porr*·tes

sportsperson *esportista* ⓜ&①
es·porr·*tees*·taa

sprain *torcimento* ⓜ • *deslocamento* ⓜ
torr·see·*meng*·to • des·lo·kaa·*meng*·to

spring (coil) *molas* ① pl *mo*·laas

spring (season) *primavera* ①
pree·maa·ve·raa

square (town) *praça* ① *praa*·saa

stadium *estádio* ⓜ es·*taa*·dyo

stairway *escadaria* ① es·kaa·daa·*ree*·aa

stale *velho/velha* ⓜ/① *ve*·lyo/*ve*·lyaa

stamp *selo* ⓜ *se*·lo

standby ticket *bilhete* ⓜ *de stand by*
bee·*lye*·te de ees·*tang*·dee bai

(four-)star *(quatro) estrelas* ① pl *(kwaa·tro)*
es·*tre*·laas

star *estrela* ① es·*tre*·laa

start *começo* ⓜ ko·*me*·so

start *começar* ko·me·*saarr*

station *estação* ① es·taa·*sowng*

stationery shop *papelaria* ①
paa·pe·laa·*ree*·aa

statue *estátua* ① es·*taa*·twaa

stay (at a hotel) *ficar* fee·*kaarr*

stay (in one place) *ficar* fee·*kaarr*

steak (beef) *bife* ⓜ *bee*·fe

steal *roubar* ho·*baarr*

steep *íngreme* *eeng*·gre·me

step *passo* ⓜ *paa*·so

stereo *estéreo* ⓜ es·*te*·ryo

still water *água* ① *sem gás*
aa·gwaa seng gaas

stock (food) *caldo* ⓜ *kow*·do

stockings *meias* ① pl *finas*
may·aas *fee*·naas

stomach *estômago* ⓜ es·*to*·maa·go

stomachache *dor* ⓜ *de estômago*
dorr de es·*to*·maa·go

stone *pedra* ① *pe*·draa

stoned (drugged) *fumado/fumada* ⓜ/①
foo·*maa*·do/foo·*maa*·daa

stop (bus) *ponto* ⓜ *de ônibus*
pong·to de o·nee·boos

stop (cease) *parar* paa·*raarr*

stop (prevent) *evitar* e·vee·*taarr*

Stop! *Pare!* paa·re

storm *tempestade* ① teng·pes·*taa*·de

story *estória* ① es·*to*·ryaa

stove *fogão* ⓜ fo·*gowng*

straight *direto/direta* ⓜ/①
dee·*re*·to/dee·*re*·taa

strange *estranho/estranha* ⓜ/①
es·*tra*·nyo/es·*tra*·nyaa

stranger *estranho/estranha* ⓜ/①
es·*tra*·nyo/es·*tra*·nyaa

strawberry *morango* ⓜ mo·*rang*·go

stream *vapor* ⓜ vaa·*porr*

street *rua* ① *hoo*·aa

strike *ataque* ⓜ aa·*taa*·ke

string *barbante* ① baarr·*bang*·te

stroke (health) *derrame* ⓜ de·*ha*·me

strong *forte* *forr*·te

stubborn *teimoso/teimosa* ⓜ/①
tay·mo·zo/tay·mo·zaa

student *estudante* ⓜ&① es·too·*dang*·te

studio *estúdio* ⓜ es·*too*·dyo

stupid *burro/burra* ⓜ/①
boo·ho/*boo*·haa

style *estilo* ⓜ es·*tee*·lo

subtitles *sub-títulos* ⓜ pl
soo·bee·*tee*·too·los

suburb *bairro* ⓜ *bai*·ho

sugar *açúcar* ⓜ aa·*soo*·kaarr

suitcase *mala* ① *maa*·laa

sultana *passas* ① pl *pa*·saas

summer *verão* ⓜ ve·*rowng*

sun *sol* ⓜ sol

Sunday *domingo* ⓜ do·*meeng*·go

sunblock *proteção* ① *contra sol*
pro·te·*sowng* kong·traa sol

sunburnt *queimado/queimada* ⓜ/①
de sol kay·*maa*·do/kay·*maa*·daa de sol

sunglasses *óculos* ⓜ pl *de sol*
o·koo·los de sol

sunny *ensolarado/ensolarada* ⓜ/①
eng·so·laa·*raa*·do/eng·so·laa·*raa*·daa

sunrise *nascer* ⓜ *do sol* naa·*serr* do sol

sunset *pôr* ⓜ *do sol* porr do sol

sunstroke *insolação* ① eeng-so-laa-sowng

supermarket *supermercado* ⑩ soo-perr-merr-kaa-do

superstition *superstição* ① soo-pers-tee-sowng

supporter (sport) *torcedor/ torcedora* ⑩/① torr-se-dorr/ torr-se-do-raa

supporter (politics) *apoio* ⑩ *ao partido* aa-po-yo ow paarr-tee-do

surf *surfar* soorr-faarr

surface mail *correspondência* ① *via terrestre* ko-hes-pong-deng-syaa vee-aa te-hes-tre

surfboard *prancha* ① *de surfe* prang-shaa de soorr-fee

surfing *surfe* ⑩ soorr-fee

surname *sobrenome* ⑩ so-bre-no-me

surprise *surpresa* ① soorr-pre-zaa

sweater *suéter* ① soo-e-terr

Sweden *Suécia* ① soo-e-syaa

sweet *doce* do-se

sweets *doces* ⑩ pl do-ses

swelling *inchaço* ⑩ eeng-shaa-so

swim *nadar* naa-daarr

swimming pool *piscina* ① pee-see-naa

swimsuit *roupa* ① *de banho* ho-paa de ba-nyo

Switzerland *Suíça* ① soo-ee-saa

synagogue *sinagoga* ① see-naa-go-gaa

synthetic *sintético/sintética* ⑩/① seeng-te-tee-ko/seeng-te-tee-kaa

syringe *seringa* ① se-reeng-gaa

T

table *mesa* ① me-zaa

table tennis *tênis* ⑩ *de mesa* te-nees de me-zaa

tablecloth *toalha* ① *de mesa* to-aa-lyaa de me-zaa

tail *rabo* ⑩ haa-bo

tailor *alfaiate* ① ow-faa-yaa-te

take *levar* le-vaarr

take (photo) *tirar* tee-raarr

talk *falar* faa-laarr

tall *alto/alta* ⑩/① ow-to/ow-taa

tampon *tampão* ⑩ tang-powng

tanning lotion *loção* ① *de bronzear* lo-sowng de brong-ze-aarr

tap *torneira* ① torr-nay-raa

tap water *água* ① *da torneira* aa-gwaa daa torr-nay-raa

tasty *gostoso/gostosa* ⑩/① gos-to-zo/gos-to-zaa

tax *imposto* ⑩ eeng-pos-to

taxi *táxi* ⑩ taak-see

taxi stand *fila* ① *de táxi* fee-laa de taak-see

tea *chá* ⑩ shaa

teacher *professor/professora* ⑩/① pro-fe-sorr/pro-fe-so-raa

team *time* ⑩ tee-me

teaspoon *colher* ① *de chá* ko-lyerr de shaa

technique *técnica* ① te-kee-nee-kaa

teeth *dentes* ⑩ pl deng-tes

telegram *telegrama* ① te-le-gra-maa

telephone *telefone* ⑩ te-le-fo-ne

telephone *telefonar* te-le-fo-naarr

telephone centre *central* ① *telefônica* seng-trow te-le-fo-nee-kaa

telescope *telescópio* ① te-les-ko-pyo

television *televisão* ① te-le-vee-sowng

tell *dizer* dee-zerr

temperature *temperatura* ① teng-pe-raa-too-raa

temple *têmpora* ① teng-po-raa

tennis *tênis* ⑩ te-nees

tennis court *quadra* ① *de tênis* kwaa-draa de te-nees

tent *barraca* ① baa-haa-kaa

tent peg *estaca* ① es-taa-kaa

terrible *terrível* te-hee-vel

test *teste* ⑩ tes-te

thank *agradecer* aa-graa-de-serr

theatre *teatro* ① te-aa-tro

their *deles* de-les

they *eles* e-les

thick *grosso/grossa* ⑩/① gro-so/gro-saa

thief *ladrão/ladra* ⑩/① laa-drowng/laa-dra

thin *fino/fina* ⑩/① fee-no/fee-naa

think *pensar* peng-saarr

third *terceiro/terceira* ⑩/① terr-say-ro/terr-say-raa

thirsty *sedento/sedenta* ⓜ/ⓕ
se-*deng*-to/se-*deng*-taa

this *este/esta* ⓜ/ⓕ *es*-te/*es*-taa

throat *garganta* ⓕ gaarr-*gang*-taa

thrush (health) *cândida* ⓕ · *corrimento* ⓜ
kang-dee-daa · ko-hee-*meng*-to

Thursday *quinta-feira* ⓕ *kween*-ta-*fay*-raa

ticket *bilhete* ⓜ bee-*lye*-te

ticket machine *máquina* ⓕ *de vender
passagem* maa-kee-naa de *veng*-derr
paa-*saa*-zheng

ticket office *bilheteria* ⓕ bee-lye-te-*ree*-aa

tide *maré* ⓕ maa-*re*

tight *apertado/apertada* ⓜ/ⓕ
aa-perr-*taa*-do/aa-perr-*taa*-daa

time *tempo* ⓜ *teng*-po

time difference *diferença* ⓕ *de horário*
dee-fe-*reng*-saa de o-*raa*-ryo

timetable *horário* ⓕ o-*raa*-rio

tin (can) *lata* ⓕ *laa*-taa

tin opener *abridor* ⓜ *de lata*
aa-bree-dorr de *laa*-taa

tiny *mínimo/mínima* ⓜ/ⓕ
mee-nee-mo/mee-nee-maa

tip (gratuity) *gorgeta* ⓕ gorr-*zhe*-taa

tired *cansado/cansada* ⓜ/ⓕ
kang-*saa*-do/kang-*saa*-daa

tissue *lencinho* ⓜ *de papel*
leng-see-nyo de paa-*pel*

toast *torrada* ⓕ to-*haa*-daa

toaster *torradeira* ⓕ to-haa-*day*-raa

tobacco *tabaco* ⓜ taa-*baa*-ko

tobacconist *tabaconista* ⓜ
taa-baa-ko-*nees*-taa

tobogganing *tobogã* ⓜ to-bo-*gang*

today *hoje* o-*zhe*

toe *dedos* ⓜ pl *do pé de*-dos do pe

tofu *tofu* ⓜ to-*foo*

together *junto/junta* ⓜ/ⓕ
zhoong-to/*zhoong*-taa

toilet *banheiro* ⓜ ba-*nyay*-ro

toilet paper *papel* ⓜ *higiênico*
paa-*pel* ee-gee-*e*-nee-ko

tomato *tomate* ⓜ to-*maa*-te

tomato sauce *molho* ⓜ *de tomate*
mo-lyo de to-*maa*-te

tomorrow *amanhã* aa-ma-*nyang*

tomorrow afternoon *amanhã à tarde*
aa-ma-*nyang* aa *taarr*-de

tomorrow evening *amanhã à noite*
aa-ma-*nyang* aa noy-te

tomorrow morning *amanhã de manhã*
aa-ma-*nyang* de ma-*nyang*

tonight *hoje à noite* o-zhee aa noy-te

too (also) *também* tang-*beng*

too (much) *demais* de-*mais*

tooth *dente* ⓜ *deng*-te

toothache *dor* ⓕ *de dente*
dorr de *deng*-te

toothbrush *escova* ⓕ *de dentes*
es-ko-vaa de *deng*-tes

toothpaste *pasta* ⓕ *de dentes*
pas-taa de *deng*-tes

toothpick *palito* ⓜ *de dentes*
paa-*lee*-to de *deng*-tes

torch (flashlight) *lanterna* ⓕ lang-*terr*-naa

touch *tocar* to-*kaarr*

tour *excursão* ⓕ es-koorr-*sowng*

tourist *turista* ⓜ&ⓕ too-*rees*-taa

tourist office *escritório* ⓜ *de turismo*
es-kree-*to*-ryo de too-*rees*-mo

towards *em direção à*
eng dee-re-*sowng* aa

towel *toalha* ⓕ to-*aa*-lyaa

tower *torre* ⓕ *to*-he

toxic waste *resíduo* ⓜ *tóxico*
he-zee-dwo tok-see-ko

toy shop *loja* ⓕ *de brinquedos*
lo-zhaa de breeng-ke-dos

track (path) *caminho* ⓜ *kaa*-mee-nyo

track (sport) *pista* ⓕ *pees*-taa

trade *comércio* ⓜ ko-*merr*-syo

traffic *tráfico* ⓜ *traa*-fee-ko

traffic light *sinal* ⓜ *de trânsito*
see-now de *trang*-zee-to

trail *vestígio* ⓜ ves-*tee*-zhyo

train *trem* ⓜ treng

train station *estação* ⓕ *de trem*
es-*taa*-sowng de treng

tram *bonde* ⓜ *bong*-de

transit lounge *sala* ⓕ *de trânsito*
saa-laa de *trang*-zee-to

translate *traduzir* traa-doo-*zeerr*

transport *transporte* ⓜ trans-*porr*-te

travel *viajar* vee-aa-*zhaarr*

travel agency *agência* ⓕ *de viagens*
aa-*zheng*-syaa de vee-*aa*-zhengs

U

travel sickness *enjôo* ⓜ *de viagem*
eng·jo·o de vee·aa·zheng

travellers cheques *travellers*
cheques ⓜ pl traa·ve·ler she·kes

tree *árvore* ⓕ aarr·vo·re

trip (journey) *viagem* ⓕ vee·aa·zheng

trousers *calças* ⓕ pl kow·saas

truck *caminhão* ⓜ kaa·mee·nyowng

trust *crer* krerr

try (attempt) *tentar* teng·taarr

T-shirt *camiseta* ⓕ kaa·mee·ze·taa

tube (tyre) *câmara* ⓕ ka·maa·raa

Tuesday *terça-feira* ⓕ terr·saa·fay·raa

tumour *tumor* ⓜ too·morr

tuna *atum* ⓜ aa·toong

tune *tom* ⓜ tong

turkey *perú* ⓜ pe·roo

turn *virar* vee·raarr

TV *tevê* ⓕ te·ve

tweezers *pinça* ⓕ peeng·saa

twice *duas vezes* doo·aas ve·zes

twin beds *camas* ⓕ pl gêmeas
ka·maas zhe·me·aas

twins *gêmeos/gêmeas* ⓜ/ⓕ
zhe·me·os/zhe·me·aas

type *tipo* ⓜ tee·po

typical *típico/típica* ⓜ/ⓕ
tee·pee·ko/tee·pee·kaa

tyre *pneu* ⓜ pee·ne·oo

U

ultrasound *ultrasom* ⓜ ool·traa·song

umbrella *guarda-chuva* ⓜ
gwaarr·daa·shoo·vaa

uncomfortable *desconfortável*
des·kong·forr·taa·vel

understand *compreender*
kong·pre·eng·derr

underwear *roupa* ⓜ *de baixo*
ho·paa de bai·sho

unemployed *desempregado/*
desempregada ⓜ/ⓕ
de·zeng·pre·gaa·do/
de·zeng·pre·gaa·daa

unfair *injusto/injusta* ⓜ/ⓕ
eeng·zhoos·to/eeng·zhoos·taa

uniform *uniforme* ⓜ oo·nee·forr·me

universe *universo* ⓜ oo·nee·verr·so

university *universidade* ⓕ
oo·nee·verr·see·daa·de

unleaded *sem chumbo* seng shoong·bo

unsafe *inseguro/insegura* ⓜ/ⓕ
eeng·se·goo·ro/eeng·se·goo·raa

until *até* aa·te

unusual *atípico/atípica* ⓜ/ⓕ
aa·tee·pee·ko/aa·tee·pee·kaa

up *em cima* eng see·maa

uphill *para cima* paa·raa see·maa

urgent *urgente* oorr·zheng·te

urinary infection *infecção* ⓕ *urinária*
een·fek·sowng oo·ree·naa·ryaa

the USA *os EUA* ⓜ pl os e·waa

useful *útil* oo·til

V

vacant *vago/vaga* ⓜ/ⓕ
vaa·go/vaa·gaa

vacation *férias* ⓕ pl fe·ryaas

vaccination *vacina* ⓕ vaa·see·naa

vagina *vagina* ⓕ vaa·zhee·naa

validate *validar* vaa·lee·daarr

valley *vale* ⓜ vaa·le

valuable *valioso/valiosa* ⓜ/ⓕ
vaa·lee·o·zo/vaa·lee·o·zaa

value (price) *valor* vaa·lorr

van *van* ⓜ van

veal *bezerro/bezerra* ⓜ/ⓕ
be·ze·ho/be·ze·haa

vegetable *legumes* ⓜ pl le·goo·mes

vegetarian *vegetariano/*
vegetariana ⓜ/ⓕ ve·zhe·taa·ree·a·no/
ve·zhe·taa·ree·a·naa

vein *veia* ⓕ ve·aa

venereal disease *doença* ⓕ *venérea*
do·eng·saa ve·ne·ryaa

venue *local* ⓜ lo·kow

very *muito/muita* ⓜ/ⓕ
mweeng·to/mweeng·taa

video tape *fita* ⓕ *de vídeo*
fee·taa de vee·de·o

view *vista* ⓕ vees·taa

village *vilarejo* ⓜ vee·laa·re·zho

vine *vinho* ⓜ vee·nyo

vinegar *vinagre* ⓜ vee·naa·gre

vineyard *vinha* ⓕ vee·nyaa

virus *vírus* ⓜ vee·roos

visa *visto* ⓜ vees·to
visit *visitar* vee·zee·taarr
vitamin *vitamina* ⓕ vee·taa·mee·naa
vodka *vodka* ⓕ vo·dee·kaa
voice *voz* ⓕ voz
volleyball (sport) *vólei* ⓜ vo·lay
volume *volume* ⓜ vo·loo·me
vote *votar* vo·taarr

W

wage *salário* ⓜ saa·laa·ryo
wait *esperar* es·pe·raarr
waiter *garçon/garçonete* ⓜ/ⓕ gaarr·song/
 gaarr·so·ne·te
waiting room *sala* ⓕ *de espera*
 saa·laa de es·pe·raa
walk *andar* ang·daarr
wall (outer) *parede* ⓕ paa·re·de
want *querer* ke·rerr
war *guerra* ⓕ ge·haa
wardrobe *armário* ⓜ aarr·maa·ryo
warm *morno/morna* ⓜ/ⓕ
 morr·no/morr·naa
warn *avisar* aa·vee·zaarr
wash *lavar* laa·vaarr
wash cloth (flannel) *pano* ⓜ *de limpeza*
 pa·no de leeng·pe·zaa
washing machine *máquina* ⓕ *de lavar*
 roupa maa·kee·naa de laa·vaarr ho·paa
watch *relógio* ⓜ he·lo·zhyo
watch *cuidar · vigiar*
 kooy·daarr · vee·zhee·aarr
water *água* ⓕ aa·gwaa
water bottle *garrafa* ⓕ *d'água*
 gaa·haa·faa daa·gwaa
waterfall *cachoeira* ⓕ kaa·sho·ay·raa
watermelon *melancia* ⓕ me·lang·see·aa
waterproof *a prova d'água*
 aa pro·vaa daa·gwaa
waterskiing *eski* ⓜ *aquático*
 es·kee aa·kwaa·tee·ko
wave *onda* ⓕ ong·daa
way *caminho* ⓜ kaa·mee·nyo
we *nós* nos
weak *fraco/fraca* ⓜ/ⓕ fraa·ko/fraa·kaa
wealthy *rico/rica* ⓜ/ⓕ hee·ko/hee·kaa
wear *vestir* ves·teerr
weather *tempo* ⓜ teng·po

wedding *casamento* ⓜ kaa·zaa·meng·to
wedding cake *bolo* ⓜ *de casamento*
 bo·lo de kaa·zaa·meng·to
wedding present *presente* ⓜ
 de casamento pre·zeng·te de
 kaa·zaa·meng·to
Wednesday *quarta-feira* ⓕ
 kwaarr·taa·fay·raa
week *semana* ⓕ se·ma·naa
weekend *final* ⓜ *de semana*
 fee·now de se·ma·naa
weigh *pesar* pe·zaarr
weight *peso* ⓜ pe·zo
weights *pesos* ⓜ pl pe·zos
welcome *receber* he·se·berr
welfare *bem* ⓜ *social* beng sò·see·ow
well *bem* ⓜ beng
west *oeste* ⓜ o·es·te
wet *molhado/molhada* ⓜ/ⓕ
 mo·lyaa·do/mo·lyaa·daa
what *que* ke
wheel *roda* ⓕ ho·daa
wheelchair *cadeira* ⓕ *de rodas* kaa·day·raa
 de ho·daas
when *quando* kwang·do
where *onde* ong·de
whisky *whisky* ⓜ oo·ees·kee
white *branco/branca* ⓜ/ⓕ
 brang·ko/brang·kaa
who *quem* keng
wholemeal bread *pão* ⓜ *integral*
 powng eeng·te·grow
why *por que* porr ke
wide *largo/larga* ⓜ/ⓕ
 laarr·go/laarr·gaa
wife *esposa* ⓕ es·po·zaa
win *ganhar* ga·nyaarr
wind *vento* ⓜ veng·to
window *janela* ⓕ zhaa·ne·laa
windscreen *parabrisa* ⓜ paa·raa·bree·zaa
windsurfing *windsurfe* ⓜ wind·soorr·fee
wine *vinho* ⓜ vee·nyo
wings *asas* ⓕ pl aa·zaas
winner *ganhador/ganhadora* ⓜ/ⓕ
 ga·nyaa·dorr/ga·nyaa·do·raa
winter *inverno* ⓜ eeng·verr·no
wire *arame* ⓜ aa·ra·me
wish *desejar* de·ze·zhaarr
with *com* kong

within (an hour) *dentro de (uma hora)* deng·tro de (oo·maa aw·raa)
without *sem* seng
woman *mulher* ① moo·lyerr
wonderful *maravilhoso/maravilhosa* ⑩/① maa·raa·vee·lyo·zo/maa·raa·vee·lyo·zaa
wood *madeira* ① maa·day·raa
wool *lã* ① lang
word *palavra* ① paa·laa·vraa
work *trabalho* ⑩ traa·baa·lyo
work *trabalhar* traa·baa·lyaarr
work experience *experiência* ① de trabalho es·pe·ree·eng·syaa de traa·baa·lyo
work permit *permissão* ① para trabalhar perr·mee·sowng paa·raa traa·baa·lyaarr
workout *resolução* ① he·zo·loo·sowng
workshop *oficina* ① o·fee·see·naa
world *mundo* ⑩ moong·do
World Cup *Copa do Mundo* ① ko·paa do moong·do
worms *minhocas* ① pl mee·nyo·kaas
worried *preocupado/preocupada* ⑩/① pre·o·koo·paa·do/pre·o·koo·paa·daa
worship *reverenciar* he·ve·reng·see·aarr
wrist *punho* ⑩ poo·nyo
write *escrever* es·kre·verr

writer *escritor/escritora* ⑩/① es·kree·torr/es·kree·to·raa
wrong *errado/errada* ⑩/① e·haa·do/e·haa·daa

Y

year *ano* ⑩ a·no
yellow *amarelo/amarela* ⑩/① aa·maa·re·lo/aa·maa·re·laa
yes *sim* seeng
yesterday *ontem* ong·teng
(not) yet *ainda (não)* aa·eeng·daa (nowng)
yoga *ioga* ① ee·o·gaa
yogurt *iogurte* ⑩ ee·o·goorr·te
you *você/vocês* sg/pl vo·se/vo·ses
young *jovem* zho·veng
your *seu/sua* ⑩/① se·oo/soo·aa
youth hostel *albergue* ⑩ *da juventude* ow·berr·ge daa zhoo·veng·too·de

Z

zodiac *zodíaco* ⑩ zo·dee·aa·ko
zoo *zoológico* ⑩ zo·o·lo·zhee·ko
zucchini *abobrinha* ① aa·bo·bree·nyaa

brazilian portuguese–english

Nouns in the dictionary have their gender indicated by ⓜ or ⓕ. If it's a plural noun, you'll also see pl. Where a word that could be either a noun or a verb has no gender indicated, it's the verb. For all words relating to local food, see the **culinary reader**, page 159.

A

a bordo aa borr-do *aboard*
à direita ⓕ aa dee-ray-taa *right (direction)*
à esquerda ⓕ aã es-kerr-daa *left (direction)*
a prova d'água aa pro-vaa daa-gwaa *waterproof*
abacate ⓜ aa-baa-kaa-te *avocado*
abacaxi ⓜ aa-baa-kaa-shee *pineapple*
abaixo aa-*bai*-sho *below*
abelha ⓕ aa-*be*-lyaa *bee*
aberto/aberta ⓜ/ⓕ aa-*berr*-to/aa-*berr*-taa *open*
abóbora ⓕ aa-*bo*-bo-raa *pumpkin*
abobrinha ⓕ aa-bo-*bree*-nyaa *courgette • zucchini*
aborto ⓜ aa-*borr*-to *abortion*
— espontâneo es-pong-*ta*-ne-o *miscarriage*
abraçar aa-braa-*saarr hug*
abridor ⓜ **de garrafas** aa-bree-*dorr* de gaa-*haa*-faas *bottle opener*
abridor ⓜ **de lata** aa-bree-*dorr* de *laa*-taa *can opener • tin opener*
abril aa-*breel April*
abrir aa-*breerr open*
absorvente ⓜ **higiênico** aab-sorr-*veng*-te ee-zhee-e-ne-ko *panty liner*
academia aa-kaa-de-*mee*-aa *college*
acampamento ⓜ aa-kang-paa-*meng*-to *camping ground*
acampar aa-kang-*paarr camp*
achados e perdidos ⓜ pl aa-*shaa*-dos e perr-*dee*-dos *left luggage*
acidente ⓜ aa-see-*deng*-te *accident*
açougue ⓜ aa-*so*-ge *butcher's shop*
açougueiro/açougueira ⓜ/ⓕ aa-so-*gay*-ro/aa-so-*gay*-raa *butcher*

açúcar ⓜ aa-*soo*-kaarr *sugar*
acupuntura ⓕ aa-koo-poom-*too*-raa *acupuncture*
adaptador ⓜ aa-daa-pee-taa-*dorr adaptor*
adentro aa-*deng*-tro *indoors*
adivinhar aa-dee-vee-*nyaarr guess*
administração ⓕ aa-dee-mee-nees-traa-*sowng administration*
admitir aa-dee-mee-*teerr admit (acknowledge)*
adulto/adulta ⓜ/ⓕ aa-*dool*-to/aa-*dool*-taa *adult*
advogado/advogada ⓜ/ⓕ aa-dee-vo-*gaa*-do/aa-dee-vo-*gaa*-daa *lawyer*
aeróbica ⓕ aa-e-ro-bee-kaa *aerobics*
aeroplano ⓜ aa-e-ro-*pla*-no *aeroplane*
aeroporto ⓜ aa-e-ro-*porr*-to *airport*
África ⓕ *aa*-free-kaa *Africa*
agência ⓕ **de viagens** aa-*zheng*-syaa de vee-*aa*-zhengs *travel agency*
agente ⓜ&ⓕ **imobiliário** aa-*zheng*-te ee-mo-bee-lee-*aa*-ryo *real estate agent*
agora aa-*go*-raa *now*
agosto aa-*gos*-to *August*
agradecer aa-graa-de-*serr thank*
agricultura ⓕ aa-gree-kool-*too*-raa *agriculture*
água ⓕ *aa*-gwaa *water*
— da torneira daa torr-*nay*-raa *tap water*
— mineral mee-ne-*row mineral water*
— quente *keng*-te *hot water*
— sem gás seng gaas *still water*
agulha ⓕ aa-*goo*-lyaa *needle (sewing/syringe)*
Aids ⓕ *ai*-dees *AIDS*

ainda (não) aa-*eeng*-daa (nowng) *(not) yet*

ajuda ① aa-*zhoo*-daa *help*

ajudar aa-zhoo-*daarr* *help*

albergue ⑩ **da juventude** ow-*berr*-ge daa zhoo-veng-*too*-de *youth hostel*

álcool ⑩ *ow*-kol *alcohol*

Alemanha ① aa-le-*ma*-nyaa *Germany*

alergia ① aa-lerr-*zhee*-aa *allergy*

alface ⑩ ow-*faa*-se *lettuce*

alfaiate ow-faa-*yaa*-te *tailor*

alfândega ① aal-*fang*-de-gaa *customs*

algodão ⑩ ow-go-*downg* *cotton*

alguém ow-*geng* *someone*

alguma coisa ow-*goo*-maa *koy*-zaa *something*

alguns/algumas ⑩/① ow-*goons*/ow-goo-maas *few • some*

alho ⑩ *aa*-lyo *garlic*

alimentar aa-lee-meng-*taarr* *feed*

almoço ⑩ ow-*mo*-so *lunch*

alpinismo ⑩ ow-pee-*nees*-mo *rock climbing*

altar ⑩ ow-*taarr* *altar*

altitude ① ow-tee-*too*-de *altitude*

alto/alta ⑩/① *ow*-to/*ow*-taa *high • loud • tall*

alucinação ① aa-loo-see-naa-*sowng* *hallucination*

alugar aa-loo-*gaarr* *hire • rent*

aluguel ⑩ **de carro** aa-loo-*gel* de *kaa*-ho *car hire*

amanhã aa-ma-*nyang* *tomorrow*
— **à noite** aa *noy*-te *tomorrow evening*
— **à tarde** aa *taarr*-de *tomorrow afternoon*
— **de manhã** de ma-*nyang* *tomorrow morning*

amante ⑩&① aa-*mang*-te *lover*

amar aa-*maarr* *love*

amarelo/amarela ⑩/① aa-maa-*re*-lo/aa-maa-*re*-laa *yellow*

ambos/ambas ⑩/① *ang*-bos/*ang*-baas *both*

ameixa ① aa-*may*-shaa *plum*
— **seca** *se*-kaa *prune*

amêndoa ① aa-*meng*-dwaa *almond*

amendoim ⑩ aa-meng-do-*eeng* *groundnut • peanut*

amigo/amiga ⑩/① aa-*mee*-go/aa-*mee*-gaa *friend*

amor ⑩ aa-*morr* *love*

analgésico ⑩ aa-now-*ge*-zee-ko *painkiller*

anarquista ⑩&① aa-naarr-*kees*-taa *anarchist*

ancião/anciã ⑩/① ang-see-*owng*/ang-*see*-ang *ancient*

andar ⑩ ang-*daarr* *floor (storey)*

andar ang-*daarr* *walk*
— **a cavalo** aa kaa-*vaa*-lo *ride (horse)*
— **de bicicleta** de bee-see-*kle*-taa *cycle*
— **de skate** de ees-*kay*-te *skate*

anel ⑩ aa-*nel* *ring (on finger)*

anemia ① aa-ne-*mee*-aa *anaemia*

animal ⑩&① aa-nee-*mow* *animal*

aniversário ⑩ aa-nee-verr-*saa*-ryo *birthday*

ano ⑩ *a*-no *year*

antes *ang*-tes *before*

antes de ontem *ang*-tes de *ong*-teng *day before yesterday*

antibióticos ⑩ pl ang-tee-bee-*o*-tee-kos *antibiotics*

anticoncepcional ⑩ ang-tee-kong-sep-syo-*now* *contraceptives*

antigo/antiga ⑩/① ang-*tee*-go/ang-*tee*-gaa *antique*

antinuclear ang-tee-noo-kle-*aarr* *antinuclear*

anti-séptico ⑩ ang-tee-*sep*-tee-ko *antiseptic*

anúncio ⑩ aa-*noom*-see-o *advertisement*

ao lado de ow *laa*-do de *next to*

aparelho ⑩ **de surdez** aa-paa-*re*-lyo de soorr-*des* *hearing aid*

apartamento ⑩ aa-paarr-taa-*meng*-to *apartment • flat*

apelido ⑩ aa-pe-*lee*-do *nickname*

apêndice ⑩ aa-*peng*-dee-se *appendix (body)*

apertado/apertada ⑩/① aa-perr-*taa*-do/aa-perr-*taa*-daa *tight*

apoio ⑩ **ao partido** aa-*po*-yo ow paarr-*tee*-do *supporter (politics)*

apontar aa·pong·*taarr* point
aposentado/aposentada ⓜ/ⓕ
  aa·po·seng·*taa*·do/aa·po·seng·*taa*·daa
  retired
aposta ⓕ aa·*pos*·taa bet
aprender aa·preng·*derr* learn
apresentação ⓕ aa·pre·seng·taa·*sowng*
  gig
aproveitar aa·pro·vay·*taarr* enjoy (oneself)
aquecimento ⓜ aa·ke·see·*meng*·to
  heating
aqui aa·*kee* here
ar ⓜ aarr air
ar condicionado ⓜ aarr
  kong·dee·syo·*naa*·do air-conditioning
arame ⓜ aa·*ra*·me wire
aranha ⓕ aa·*ra*·nyaa spider
área ⓕ **de serviço** *aa*·re·aa de serr·*vee*·so
  laundry (room)
areia ⓕ aa·*re*·yaa sand
arenque ⓜ aa·*reng*·ke herring
arma ⓕ *aarr*·maa gun
armário ⓜ aarr·*maa*·ryo
  cupboard · wardrobe
aromaterapia ⓕ
  aa·ro·maa·te·raa·*pee*·aa aromatherapy
arqueológico/arqueológica ⓜ/ⓕ
  aarr·ke·o·lo·*zhe*·ko/
  aarr·ke·o·lo·*zhe*·kaa archaeological
arquiteto/arquiteta ⓜ/ⓕ
  aarr·*kee*·te·to/aarr·*kee*·te·taa architect
arquitetura ⓕ aar·kee·te·*too*·raa
  architecture
arroz ⓜ aa·*hos* rice
arte ⓕ *aarr*·te art
artes ⓕ pl **marciais** *aarr*·tes maar·see·*ais*
  martial arts
artesanato ⓜ aarr·te·zaa·*naa*·to crafts ·
  handicrafts
artista ⓜ&ⓕ aar·*tees*·taa artist
  — **de rua** de *hoo*·aa busker
árvore ⓕ *aarr*·vo·re tree
às vezes aas *ve*·zes sometimes
Ásia ⓕ *aa*·zyaa Asia
asma ⓕ *aas*·maa asthma
asparago ⓜ aas·*paarr*·go asparagus
aspirina ⓕ aas·pee·*ree*·naa aspirin

assassinar aa·saa·see·*naarr* murder
assassinato ⓜ aa·saa·see·*naa*·to murder
assento ⓜ aa·*seng*·to seat
assinatura ⓕ aa·see·naa·*too*·raa signature
assuntos ⓜ pl **atuais** aa·*soong*·tos
  aa·too·*ais* current affairs
ataque ⓜ aa·*taa*·ke strike
  — **de coração** de ko·ra·*sowng*
  heart attack
até aa·*te* until
atípico/atípica ⓜ/ⓕ
  aa·*tee*·pee·ko/aa·*tee*·pee·kaa unusual
atirar aa·tee·*raarr* shoot
ativista ⓜ&ⓕ aa·te·*vees*·taa activist
atletismo ⓜ aat·le·*tees*·mo athletiçs
atmosfera ⓕ aa·tee·mos·*fe*·raa
  atmosphere
atrás aa·*traas* behind
atrasado/atrasada ⓜ/ⓕ
  aa·traa·*zaa*·do/aa·traa·*zaa*·daa late
atraso ⓜ aa·*traa*·zo delay
através aa·traa·*ves* across
atum ⓜ aa·*toong* tuna
austrália ⓕ ows·*traa*·lya Australia
auto estrada ⓕ ow·to es·*traa*·daa
  motorway (tollway)
autônomo/autônoma ⓜ/ⓕ
  ow·to·no·mo/ow·to·no·maa
  self-employed
auto-serviço ⓜ ow·to·serr·*vee*·so
  self-service
aveia ⓕ aa·*ve*·aa oats
avelã ⓕ aa·ve·*lang* hazelnut
avenida ⓕ aa·ve·*nee*·daa avenue
avião ⓜ aa·vee·*owng* airplane
avisar aa·vee·*zaarr* warn
aviso ⓜ aa·*vee*·zo sign
avó ⓕ aa·*vaw* grandmother
avô ⓜ aa·*vo* grandfather
azeite ⓜ aa·*zay*·te olive oil
azeitona ⓕ aa·*zay*·to·naa olive
azul aa·*zool* blue

B

babá ⓕ baa·*baa* babysitter
bacana baa·*ka*·naa nice
bacon ⓜ *bay*·kong bacon

bagagem ① baa-*gaa*-zheng
  baggage • luggage
bagulho ⓜ baa-*goo*-lyo *dope (drugs)*
baía ① baa-*ee*-aa *harbour*
bairro ⓜ *bai*-ho *suburb*
baixo *bai*-sho *down*
baixo/baixa ⓜ/① *bai*-sho/*bai*-shaa *low*
bala ① *baa*-laa *candy*
balanço ⓜ baa-*lang*-so *balance (account)*
balas ① pl *baa*-laas *lollies*
balcão ⓜ bow-*kowng* *balcony •*
  counter (at bar)
balde ⓜ *bow*-de *bucket*
balé ⓜ ba-*le* *ballet*
bálsamo ⓜ **para lábios** bow-sa-mo
  paa-raa *laa*-byos *lip balm*
banana ① baa-*na*-naa *banana*
banco ⓜ *bang*-ko *bank*
banda ① **(de música)** *bang*-daa (de
  moo-zee-kaa) *band (music)*
band-aid ⓜ bang-*day*-dee *Band-Aid*
bandeira ① bang-*day*-raa *flag*
banheira ① ba-*nyay*-raa *bath*
banheiro ⓜ ba-*nyay*-ro *bathroom • toilet*
  — **público** ba-*nyay*-ro *poo*-blee-ko
  public toilet
bar ⓜ baarr *bar • pub*
barata ① baa-*raa*-taa *cockroach*
barato/barata ⓜ/①
  baa-*raa*-to/baa-*raa*-taa *cheap*
barbante ⓜ baarr-*bang*-te *string*
barbeiro ⓜ baarr-*bay*-ro *barber*
barco ⓜ *baar*-ko *boat*
barco ⓜ **à motor** *baar*-ko aa mo-*torr*
  motorboat
barraca ① baa-*haa*-kaa *tent*
barulhento/barulhenta ⓜ/①
  baa-roo-*lyeng*-to/baa-roo-*lyeng*-taa *noisy*
baseball ⓜ *bay*-ze-bol *baseball*
basquete ⓜ baas-*ke*-te *basketball*
batata ① baa-*taa*-taa *potato*
bateria ① baa-te-*ree*-aa *drum*
batida ① baa-*tee*-daa *crash*
batismo ⓜ baa-*tees*-mo *baptism*
batom ⓜ ba-*tong* *lipstick*
bêbado/bêbada ⓜ/①
  be-baa-do/be-*baa*-daa *drunk*
bebê ⓜ&① be-*be* *baby*

bebida ① be-*bee*-daa *drink*
beijar bay-*zhaarr* *kiss*
beijo ⓜ *bay*-zho *kiss*
beira mar ① *bay*-raa maarr *seaside*
bem beng *well*
bem ⓜ **social** beng so-see-*ow* *welfare*
beringela ① be-reeng-*zhe*-la
  aubergine • eggplant
bermuda ① berr-*moo*-daa *shorts*
beterraba ① be-te-*haa*-baa *beetroot*
bexiga ① be-*shee*-gaa *bladder*
bezerro/bezerra ⓜ/①
  be-ze-ho/be-ze-haa *veal*
bíblia ① *bee*-blyaa *bible*
biblioteca ① bee-blee-o-*te*-kaa *library*
bicho ⓜ *bee*-sho *bug*
bicicleta ① bee-see-*kle*-taa *bicycle • bike*
  — **de corrida** de ko-*hee*-daa *racing bike*
bife ⓜ *bee*-fe *beef • steak*
bilhete ⓜ bee-*lye*-te *ticket*
  — **de stand by** de ees-*tang*-dee bai
  standby ticket
bilheteria ① bee-lye-te-*ree*-aa *ticket office*
binóculos ⓜ pl bee-*no*-koo-los *binoculars*
biquíni ⓜ **fio dental** bee-*kee*-nee fyo
  deng-*tow* g-*string*
biscoito ⓜ bees-*koy*-to *biscuit • cookie*
  — **d'água** *daa*-gwaa *cracker*
bloqueado/bloqueada ⓜ/①
  blo-ke-*aa*-do/blo-ke-*aa*-daa *blocked*
boarding pass ⓜ borr-deeng paas
  boarding pass
boca ① *bo*-kaa *mouth*
bode ⓜ *bo*-de *goat*
bola ① *bo*-laa *ball*
  — **de golfe** de *gol*-fee *golf ball*
bolas ① pl **de algodão**
  bo-laas de ow-go-*downg* *cotton balls*
bolha ① *bo*-lyaa *blister*
bolo ⓜ *bo*-lo *cake*
  — **de casamento** de kaa-zaa-*meng*-to
  wedding cake
bolsa ① **de mão** *bol*-saa de mowng
  handbag
bolso ⓜ *bol*-so *pocket*
bom/boa ⓜ/① bong/*bo*-aa
  fine • good • kind
bomba ① *bong*-baa *pump*

bonde ⓜ *bong*-de *cable car • tram*

boneco/boneca ⓜ/ⓕ
bo-*ne*-ko/bo-*ne*-kaa *doll*

bonito/bonita ⓜ/ⓕ bo-*nee*-to/bo-*nee*-taa
handsome • beautiful

borboleta ⓕ borr-bo-*le*-taa *butterfly*

borda ⓕ *borr*-daa *border*

borracha ⓕ bo-*haa*-shaa *gum*

bota ⓕ *bo*-taa *boot (footwear)*

botânico/botânica ⓜ/ⓕ
bo-*ta*-nee-ko/bo-*ta*-nee-kaa *herbalist*

botas ⓕ pl *bo*-taas *boots (footwear)*

botões ⓜ pl bo-*toyngs* *buttons*

boxe ⓜ *bo*-kee-see *boxing*

braço ⓜ *braa*-so *arm*

branco/branca ⓜ/ⓕ
brang-ko/*brang*-kaa *white*

brandy ⓜ *brang*-dee *brandy*

brilhante bree-*lyang*-te *brilliant*

brincos ⓜ pl *breeng*-kos *earrings*

brochura ⓕ bro-*shoo*-raa *brochure*

brócolis ⓜ pl bro-ko-lees *broccoli*

bronquite ⓕ brong-*kee*-te *bronchitis*

broto ⓜ **de feijão** *bro*-to de fay-*zhowng*
beansprout

Budista boo-*dees*-taa *Buddhist*

buffet ⓜ boo-*fe* *buffet*

burro/burra ⓜ/ⓕ *boo*-ho/*boo*-haa *stupid*

business class ⓕ bee-zee-*nes* klaas
business class

C

cabeça ⓕ kaa-*be*-saa *head*

cabeleireiro/cabeleireira ⓜ/ⓕ
kaa-be-lay-*ray*-ro/kaa-be-lay-*ray*-raa
hairdresser

cabelo ⓜ kaa-*be*-lo *hair*

caça ⓕ *kaa*-saa *hunting*

cacau ⓜ ka-*kow* *cocoa*

cachoeira ⓕ kaa-sho-*ay*-raa *waterfall*

cachorro ⓜ/ⓕ kaa-*sho*-ho *dog*

cada *kaa*-daa *each*

cadeado ⓜ kaa-de-*aa*-do *padlock*

cadeira ⓕ kaa-*day*-raa *chair*
— **de criança** de kree-*ang*-saa *child seat*
— **de rodas** de ho-daas *wheelchair*
— **para refeição** paa-raa he-fay-*sowng*
highchair

caderno ⓜ kaa-*derr*-no *notebook*

café ⓜ kaa-*fe* *cafe • coffee*
— **da manhã** da ma-*nyang* *breakfast*

caixa ⓕ *kai*-shaa *box • cashier*
— **automático** ow-to-*maa*-tee-ko
automatic teller machine (ATM)
— **registradora** he-gees-traa-*do*-raa
cash register
— **de correio** de ko-*hay*-o *mailbox*
— **de papelão** de paa-pe-*lowng* *carton*

calçada ⓕ kow-*saa*-daa *footpath*

calças ⓕ pl *kow*-saas *pants • trousers*

calculadora ⓕ kow-koo-laa-*do*-raa
calculator

caldo ⓜ *kow*-do *stock (food)*

calendário ⓜ kaa-leng-*daa*-ryo *calendar*

cama ⓕ *ka*-maa *bed*
— **de casal** de kaa-*zow* *double bed*

camada ⓕ **de ozônio** kaa-*maa*-daa de
o-*zo*-nyo *ozone layer*

câmara ⓕ ka-maa-raa *tube (tyre)*
— **de ar** de aarr *inner tube*

camarão ⓜ kaa-maa-*rowng* *prawn*

camas ⓕ pl **gêmeas** *ka*-maas *zhe*-me-aas
twin beds

câmbio ⓜ **de marcha** *kang*-byo de
maarr-shaa *derailleur*

câmbio ⓜ **de valores** *kang*-byo de
vaa-*lo*-res *currency exchange*

câmera ⓕ *ka*-me-raa *camera*

caminhada ⓕ kaa-mee-*nyaa*-daa *hiking*

caminhão ⓜ kaa-mee-*nyowng* *truck*

caminhar kaa-mee-*nyaarr* *hike*

caminho ⓜ kaa-*mee*-nyo
path • track • way

camisa ⓕ kaa-*mee*-zaa *shirt*

camiseta ⓕ kaa-mee-*ze*-taa
singlet • T-shirt

camisinha ⓕ kaa-mee-*zee*-nyaa *condom*

campeonatos ⓜ pl kang-pe-o-*naa*-tos
championships

campo ⓕ **de golfe** *kang*-po de *gol*-fee
golf course

camundongo ⓜ ka-moong-*dong*-go
  mouse
Canadá ⓜ kaa-naa-*daa* Canada
canção ⓕ kang-*sowng* song
cancelar kang-se-*laarr* cancel
câncer ⓜ *kang*-serr cancer
cândida ⓕ *kang*-dee-daa thrush (health)
caneta ⓕ ka-*ne*-taa pen (ballpoint)
canivete ⓜ kaa-nee-*ve*-te
  penknife • pocket knife
cansado/cansada ⓜ/ⓕ
  kang-*saa*-do/kang-*saa*-daa tired
cantar kang-*taarr* sing
cantor/cantora ⓜ/ⓕ
  kang-*torr*/kang-*to*-raa singer
cão-guia ⓜ kowng-*gee*-aa guide dog
capacete ⓜ kaa-paa-*se*-te helmet
capacho ⓜ kaa-*paa*-sho mat
caravana ⓕ kaa-raa-*vang* caravan
cardápio ⓜ kaarr-*daa*-pyo menu
caril ⓜ kaa-*reel* curry
carne ⓕ *kaar*-ne meat
  — moída mo-ee-daa mince
caro/cara ⓜ/ⓕ kaa-ro/kaa-raa expensive
carpinteiro ⓜ karr-peeng-*tay*-ro carpenter
carregar kaa-he-*gaarr* carry
carro ⓜ *kaa*-ho car
carta ⓕ *kaarr*-taa letter (mail)
cartão ⓜ kaarr-*towng* credit card
  — de crédito de *kre*-dee-to credit card
  — postal kaarr-*towng* pos-*tow* postcard
  — telefônico kaarr-*towng*
  te-le-fo-nee-ko phonecard
cartas ⓕ pl *kaarr*-tas cards (playing)
cartaz ⓜ kaarr-*taz* poster
carteira ⓕ **de identidade** kaar-*tay*-raa de
  ee-deng-tee-*daa*-de identification card
carteira ⓕ **de motorista** kaar-*tay*-raa de
  mo-to-*rees*-taa drivers licence
cartucho ⓜ **de gás** kaarr-*too*-sho de gaas
  gas cartridge
casa ⓕ *kaa*-zaa home • house
  — de cômodos de *ko*-mo-dos
  boarding house
  — de ópera de *o*-pe-raa opera house
casaco ⓜ kaa-*zaa*-ko coat
  — de chuva de *shoo*-vaa raincoat

casamento ⓜ kaa-zaa-*meng*-to
  marriage • wedding
casar kaa-*zaarr* marry
casino ⓜ kaa-*see*-no casino
castanha ⓕ **de cajú** kas-*ta*-nyaa de
  kaa-*zhoo* cashew
castanha ⓕ **portuguesa** kaas-*ta*-nyaa
  porr-too-ge-*zaa* chestnut
castelo ⓜ kaas-*te*-lo castle
catapora ⓕ kaa-taa-po-raa chicken pox
catedral ⓕ kaa-te-*drow* cathedral
Católico/Católica ⓜ/ⓕ
  kaa-to-lee-ko/kaa-to-lee-kaa Catholic
cavalgada ⓕ kaa-vaal-*gaa*-daa
  horse riding
cavalo ⓜ kaa-*vaa*-lo horse
caverna ⓕ kaa-*verr*-naa cave
caxumba ⓕ kaa-*shoong*-baa mumps
CD ⓜ se-*de* CD
cebola ⓕ se-*bo*-laa onion
cedo ⓜ *se*-do early
cego/cega ⓜ/ⓕ *se*-go/*se*-gaa blind
celular ⓜ se-loo-*laarr* mobile phone
cem seng hundred
cenoura ⓕ se-*no*-raa carrot
centavos ⓜ pl seng-*taa*-vos cent
centímetro ⓜ seng-*tee*-me-tro centimetre
central ⓕ **telefônica** seng-*trow*
  te-le-fo-nee-kaa telephone centre
centro ⓜ *seng*-tro centre
  — da cidade daa see-*daa*-de city centre
cerâmica ⓕ se-*ra*-mee-kaa
  ceramics • pottery
cerca ⓕ *serr*-kaa fence
cereal ⓜ se-re-*ow* cereal
cereja ⓕ se-re-*zhaa* cherry
certidão ⓕ **de nascimento**
  serr-tee-*downg* de naa-see-*meng*-to birth
  certificate
certificado ⓜ serr-tee-fee-*kaa*-do
  certificate
cerveja ⓕ serr-*ve*-zhaa beer
cesta ⓕ *ses*-taa basket
céu ⓜ *se*-oo sky
chá ⓜ shaa tea
chão ⓜ *showng* floor
chapéu ⓜ shaa-*pe*-oo hat

charmoso/charmosa ⓜ/ⓕ
shaarr·mo·zo/shaarr·mo·zaa charming

charuto ⓜ shaa·roo·to cigar

chave ⓕ shaa·ve key

checar she·kaarr check

check in ⓜ she·keeng check-in (desk)

chefe ⓜ&ⓕ de cozinha she·fe de
ko·zee·nyaa chef

chegada(s) ⓕ sg/pl she·gaa·daa(s) arrival

chegar she·gaarr arrive

cheio/cheia ⓜ/ⓕ shay·o/shay·aa full

cheiro ⓜ shay·ro smell

cheque ⓜ she·ke cheque (banking)

chocolate ⓜ sho·ko·laa·te chocolate

chupeta ⓕ shoo·pe·taa dummy · pacifier

chutar shoo·taarr kick (a ball)

chuva ⓕ shoo·vaa rain

chuveiro ⓜ shoo·vay·ro shower

ciclismo ⓜ see·klees·mo cycling

ciclista ⓜ&ⓕ see·klees·taa cyclist

cidadania ⓕ see·daa·da·nee·aa citizenship

cidade ⓕ see·daa·de city

cidra ⓕ see·draa cider

ciências ⓕ pl see·eng·syaas science

cientista ⓜ&ⓕ see·eng·tees·taa scientist

cigarro ⓜ see·gaa·ho cigarette

cinema ⓜ see·ne·maa cinema · movie

Cingapura seen·gaa·poo·raa Singapore

cinto ⓜ de segurança seeng·to de
se·goo·rang·saa seatbelt

cinza seeng·zaa gray

cinzeiro ⓜ seen·zay·ro ashtray

circo ⓜ seerr·ko circus

ciroula ⓕ se·ro·laa boxer shorts

cistite ⓕ sees·tee·te cystitis

cisto ⓜ no ovário sees·to no o·vaa·ryo
ovarian cyst

ciumento/ciumenta ⓜ/ⓕ
see·oo·meng·to/see·oo·meng·taa jealous

classe ⓕ klaa·se class (category)
— econômica e·ko·no·mee·kaa
economy class

clássico/clássica ⓜ/ⓕ
klaa·see·ko/klaa·see·kaa classical

cliente ⓜ&ⓕ klee·eng·te client

cobertor ⓜ ko·berr·torr blanket

cobra ⓕ ko·braa snake

cobreiro ⓜ ko·bray·ro shingles (illness)

cocaína ⓕ ko·kaa·ee·naa cocaine

coceira ⓕ ko·say·raa itch

côco ⓜ ko·ko coconut

código ⓜ postal ko·dee·go pos·tow
postcode

coelho ⓜ ko·e·lyo rabbit

cofre ⓜ ko·fre safe

cogumelo ⓜ ko·goo·me·lo mushroom

coisa ⓕ koy·zaa it

cola ⓕ ko·laa glue

colar ko·laarr necklace

colchão ⓜ kol·showng mattress

colega ⓜ&ⓕ ko·le·gaa colleague

colete salva-vidas ⓜ ko·le·te
sow·vaa·vee·daas life jacket

colheita ⓕ de frutas ko·lyay·taa de
froo·taas fruit picking

colher ⓕ ko·lyerr spoon
— de chá de shaa teaspoon

cólica ⓕ menstrual ko·lee·kaa
mengs·troo·ow period pain

colírio ⓜ ko·lee·ryo eye drops

colocar ko·lo·kaarr put

com kong with

com pressa kong pre·saa in a hurry

começar ko·me·saarr start

começo ⓜ ko·me·so start

comédia ⓕ ko·me·dyaa comedy

comemoração ⓕ ko·me·mo·raa·sowng
celebration

comer ko·merr eat

comércio ⓜ ko·merr·syo trade

comício ⓜ ko·mee·syo rally

comida ⓕ ko·mee·daa food
— de bebê de be·be baby food

como ⓜ ko·mo how

companheiro/companheira ⓜ/ⓕ
kong·pa·nyay·ro/kong·pa·nyay·raa
companion

companhia ⓕ kong·paa·nhaa company

compasso ⓜ kong·paa·so compass

comprar kong·praarr buy

compreender kong·pre·eng·derr
understand

computador ⓜ kong·poo·taa·dorr
computer

comunhão ⓕ ko·moo·nyowng
communion

comunicação ① ko·moo·nee·kaa·*sowng*
communication • communications
(profession)

comunista ⓜ&① ko·moo·*nees*·taa
communist

concordar kong·korr·*daarr* *agree*

condicionador ⓜ kong·dee·syo·naa·*dorr*
conditioner

conecção ① ko·ne·kee·*sowng*
connection (phone)

confeitaria ① kong·fay·taa·*ree*·aa
cake shop

confirmar kong·feerr·*maarr*
confirm (a booking)

confissão ① kong·fee·*sowng* *confession*

confortável kong·forr·*taa*·vel *comfortable*

congelar kong·zhe·*laarr* *freeze*

conjuntivite ① kong·zhoong·tee·*vee*·te
conjunctivitis

conselho ⓜ kong·*se*·lyo *advice*

consertar kong·serr·*taarr* *repair*

conservador/conservadora ⓜ/①
kong·serr·vaa·*dorr*/kong·serr·vaa·*do*·raa
conservative

constipação ① kongs·tee·paa·*sowng*
constipation

construir kongs·troo·*eerr* *build*

construtor ⓜ kongs·troo·*tor* *builder*

consulado ⓜ kong·soo·*laa*·do *consulate*

consulta ① kong·*sool*·taa *appointment*

conta ① kong·taa *bill • cheque*
— **bancária** bang·*kaa*·rya *bank account*

contar kong·*taarr* *count*

contar os pontos kong·*taarr* os *pong*·tos
score

contrato ⓜ kong·*traa*·to *contract*

controle ⓜ **remoto** kong·*tro*·le he·*mo*·to
remote control

convento ⓜ kong·*veng*·to *convent*

conversar kong·verr·*saarr* *chat*

convidar kong·vee·*daar* *invite*

Copa do Mundo ① ko·paa do *moong*·do
World Cup

cor ① korr *colour*

coração ⓜ ko·ra·*sowng* *heart*

corajoso/corajosa ⓜ/①
ko·raa·*zho*·zo/ko·raa·*zho*·zaa *brave*

corda ① korr·daa *rope*
— **de roupa** de ho·paa *clothesline*

cordilheira ① korr·dee·*lyay*·raa
mountain range

coriza ① ko·*ree*·zaa *runny nose*

corpo ⓜ korr·po *body*

corredor ⓜ ko·he·*dorr* *aisle*

correia ① ko·*hay*·aa *fanbelt*

correio ⓜ ko·*hay*·o *post office*
— **registrado** he·zhees·*traa*·do
registered mail

corrente ① ko·*heng*·te
chain • current (electricity)
— **de bicicleta** de bee·see·*kle*·taa
bike chain

correr ko·*herr* *run*

correspondência ①
ko·hes·pong·*deng*·syaa *mail*
— **via aéreo/aérea** ⓜ/①
vee·aa aa·e·re·o/aa·e·re·aa *airmail*
— **via terrestre** *vee*·aa te·*hes*·tre
surface mail

correto/correta ⓜ/① ko·*he*·to/
ko·*he*·taa *right (correct)*

corrida ① ko·*hee*·daa
jogging • race • running

corrimão ⓜ ko·hee·*mowng*
handlebars

corrimento ⓜ ko·hee·*meng*·to
thrush (health)

corrupto/corrupta ⓜ/① koo·*hoo*·pee·to/
koo·*hoo*·pee·taa *corrupt*

cortador ⓜ **de unhas** korr·taa·*dorr* de
oo·nyaas *nail clippers*

cortar korr·*taarr* *cut*

corte ① korr·te *court (legal)*

costa ① kos·taa *coast*

costas ① kos·taas *back (body)*

costela ① kos·te·laa *rib*

costurar kos·too·*raarr* *sew*

cotonete ⓜ ko·to·ne·te *cotton buds*

couro ⓜ ko·ro *leather*
— **cabeludo** kaa·be·*loo*·do *scalp*

couve ① **flor** ko·ve florr *cauliflower*

couvert ⓜ **artístico** koo·*verr*
aarr·*tees*·tee·ko *cover charge*

cozido/cozida ⓜ/①
ko·*zee*·do/ko·*zee*·daa *hard-boiled*

cozinha ① ko-*zee*-nyaa *kitchen*
cozinhar ko-zee-*nyaarr* *cook*
cozinheiro/cozinheira ⓜ/①
  ko-zee-*nyay*-ro/ko-zee-*nyay*-raa *cook*
crânio ⓜ *kra*-nyo *skull*
creche ① *kre*-she *creche*
creme ⓜ *kre*-me *cream*
  — azedo aa-*ze*-do *sour cream*
  — de barbear de baarr-be-*aarr*
  shaving cream
crer krerr *trust*
crescer kres-*serr* *grow*
criança kree-*ang*-saa *child*
crianças pl kree-*ang*-saas *children*
cricket ⓜ *kree*-ke-tee *cricket (sport)*
Cristão/Cristã ⓜ/①
  krees-*towng*/krees-*tayng* *Christian*
cru/crua ⓜ/① kroo/*kroo*-aa *raw*
cruz ① kroos *cross (religious)*
cuidado ⓜ **da criança** kooy-*daa*-do de
  kree-*ang*-saa *childminding*
cuidar kooy-*daarr* *look after • watch*
culpa ① *kool*-paa *(someone's) fault*
culpado/culpada ⓜ/① kool-*paa*-do/
  kool-*paa*-daa *guilty*
cupom ⓜ koo-*pong* *coupon*
curativo ⓜ koo-raa-*tee*-vo *bandage*
currículum ⓜ koo-*hee*-koo-loom
  resume (CV)
curto/curta ⓜ/① *koor*-to/*koor*-taa *short*
cuscuz ⓜ **marroquino** koos-*koos*
  maa-ho-*kee*-no *couscous*
custar koos-*taarr* *cost*
CV ⓜ se-*ve* *CV*

D

dados ⓜ pl *daa*-dos *dice*
damasco ⓜ daa-*maas*-ko *apricot*
dança ① *dang*-saa *dancing*
dançar dang-*saarr* *dance*
dar daarr *give • deal (cards)*
data ① *daa*-taa *date (day)*
  — de nascimento de naa-see-*meng*-to
  date of birth
de costas de *kos*-taas *back (position)*
de segunda mão de se-*goong*-daa
  mowng *second-hand*

decidir de-see-*deer* *decide*
dedo ⓜ *de*-do *finger*
  — do pé do pe *toe*
defeituoso/defeituosa ⓜ/①
  de-fay-too-o-zo/de-fay-too-o-zaa *faulty*
deficiente de-fee-see-*eng*-te *disabled*
deitar day-*taarr* *lie (not stand)*
dela de-*laa* *her*
dele de-*le* *his*
delegacia ① **de polícia** de-le-gaa-*see*-aa
  de po-*lee*-sya *police station*
deles de-*les* *their*
delicatessen ① de-lee-kaa-*te*-seng
  delicatessen
demais de-*mais* *too (much)*
democracia ① de-mo-kraa-*see*-aa
  democracy
demonstração ① de-mongs-traa-*sowng*
  demonstration
dente(s) ⓜ *deng*-te(s) *tooth (teeth)*
dentista ⓜ&① deng-*tees*-taa *dentist*
dentro *deng*-tro *inside*
  — de (uma hora) de (oo-maa *aw*-raa)
  within (an hour)
depois de-*poys* *after*
  — de amanhã de aa-maa-*nyang*
  day after tomorrow
depósito ⓜ de-po-zee-to *deposit*
derrame ⓜ de-*ha*-me *stroke (health)*
desabrigado/desabrigada ⓜ/①
  de-zaa-bree-*gaa*-do/de-zaa-bree-*gaa*-daa
  homeless
descansar des-kang-*saarr* *rest*
descendente ⓜ&① de-seng-*deng*-te
  descendent
desconfortável des-kong-forr-*taa*-vel
  uncomfortable
descontar (um cheque) des-kong-*taarr*
  (oom *she*-ke) *cash (a cheque)*
desconto ⓜ des-*kong*-to *discount*
desde *des*-de *since*
desejar de-ze-*zhaarr* *wish*
deserto ⓜ de-*zerr*-to *desert*
desflorestamento ⓜ
  des-flo-res-taa-*meng*-to *deforestation*
design ⓜ *design* *design*
desistir de-zees-*teerr* *quit*

deslocamento ⓜ des·lo·kaa·*meng*·to *sprain*

desodorante ⓜ de·zo·do·*rang*·te *deodorant*

despertador ⓜ des·perr·taa·*dorr* *alarm clock*

destino ⓜ des·*tee*·no *destination*

detalhes ⓜ pl de·*taa*·lyes *details*

deus ⓜ *de*·oos *god*

devagar de·vaa·*gaarr* *slow*

dever de·*verr* *owe*

dezembro de·*zeng*·bro *December*

dia ⓕ *dee*·aa *day*

Dia ⓜ **de Ano Novo** *dee*·aa de a·no *no*·vo *New Year's Day*

Dia ⓜ **de Natal** *dee*·aa de naa·*tow* *Christmas Day*

diabetes ⓕ dee·aa·*be*·tes *diabetes*

diafragma ⓜ dee·aa·*fraa*·gee·maa *diaphragm*

diário ⓜ dee·*aa*·ryo *diary*

diarréia ⓕ dee·aa·*hay*·aa *diarrhoea*

dicionário ⓜ dee·syo·*naa*·ryo *dictionary*

dieta ⓕ dee·e·*taa diet*

diferença ⓕ **de horário** dee·fe·*reng*·saa de o·*raa*·ryo *time difference*

diferente dee·fe·*reng*·te *different*

difícil dee·*fee*·seel *difficult*

Dinamarca ⓕ dee·naa·*maarr*·kaa *Denmark*

dinheiro ⓜ dee·*nyay*·ro *money*

(à) direita ⓕ (aa) dee·*ray*·taa *right (direction)*

direitista dee·ray·*tees*·taa *right-wing*

direto/direta ⓜ/ⓕ dee·*re*·to/dee·*re*·taa *direct • straight*

diretor/diretora ⓜ/ⓕ dee·*re*·torr/ dee·*re*·to·raa *director*

direitos ⓜ pl **civis** dee·*ray*·tos see·*vees* *civil rights*

direitos ⓜ pl **humanos** dee·*ray*·tos oo·*ma*·nos *human rights*

dirigir dee·ree·*zheerr* *drive*

disco ⓜ *dees*·ko *disco*

discriminação ⓕ dees·kree·mee·naa·*sowng* *discrimination*

discutir dees·koo·*teerr* *argue*

disk ⓜ deesk *disk (computer)*

DIU ⓜ *dee*·oo *IUD*

diversos/diversas ⓜ/ⓕ pl dee·*verr*·sos/dee·*verr*·saas *several*

divertido/divertida ⓜ/ⓕ dee·verr·*tee*·do/dee·verr·*tee*·daa *fun*

divertir-se dee·verr·*teerr*·se *have fun*

dividir dee·vee·*deerr* *share (with)*

dizer dee·*zerr say • tell*

doce *do*·se *sweet*

documentário ⓜ do·koo·meng·*taa*·ryo *documentary*

doença ⓕ do·*eng*·saa *disease*

— venérea ve·ne·ryaa *venereal disease*

doente do·*eng*·te *sick*

dólar ⓜ *do*·laarr *dollar*

dolorido/dolorida ⓜ/ⓕ do·lo·*ree*·do/do·lo·*ree*·daa *sore*

doloroso/dolorosa ⓜ/ⓕ do·lo·*ro*·zo/do·lo·*ro*·zaa *painful*

domingo ⓜ do·*meeng*·go *Sunday*

dona ⓕ **de casa** do·naa de *kaa*·zaa *homemaker*

dono/dona ⓜ/ⓕ *do*·no/*do*·naa *owner*

dor ⓕ dorr *pain*

— de cabeça de kaa·*be*·saa *headache*

— de dente de *deng*·te *toothache*

— de estômago de es·*to*·maa·go *stomachache*

dormir dorr·*meerr* *sleep*

drama ⓜ *dra*·maa *drama*

droga ⓕ *dro*·gaa *drug*

duas vezes *doo*·aas *ve*·zes *twice*

duplo/dupla ⓜ/ⓕ *doo*·plo/*doo*·plaa *double*

duro/dura ⓜ/ⓕ *doo*·ro/*doo*·raa *hard*

dúzia ⓕ *doo*·zyaa *dozen*

DVD ⓜ de·ve·*de DVD*

E

e e *and*

eczema ⓜ e·kee·ze·maa *eczema*

editor/editora ⓜ/ⓕ e·dee·*torr*/e·dee·to·raa *editor*

editoração ⓕ e·dee·to·raa·*sowng* *publishing*

educação ⓕ e·doo·ka·*sowng* *education*

egoísta e·go·*ees*·taa *selfish*

ela e·laa *she*

ele e·le *he*

eleição ① e·lay·*sowng* *election*

eles e·les *they*

eletricidade ① e·le·tree·see·*daa*·de *electricity*

elevador ⓜ e·le·vaa·*dorr* *elevator · lift (elevator)*

em eng *in*
— **em breve** *bre*·ve *soon*
— **cima** *see*·maa *up*
— **direção à** dee·re·*sowng* aa *towards*
— **espécie** es·*pe*·sye *cash*
— **frente** *freng*·te *ahead*

embaixada ① eng·bai·*shaa*·daa *embassy*

embaixador/embaixadora ⓜ/①
eng·bai·shaa·*dorr*/eng·bai·shaa·do·raa
ambassador

embreagem ① eng·bre·*aa*·zheng *clutch (car)*

embrulho ⓜ eng·*broo*·lyo *package*

emergência ① e·merr·*zheng*·syaa *emergency*

empregado/empregada ⓜ/①
eng·pre·*gaa*·do/eng·pre·*gaa*·daa
employee

empregador/empregadora ⓜ/①
eng·pre·gaa·*dorr*/eng·pre·gaa·do·raa
employer

emprego ⓜ eng·*pre*·go *job*

emprestar eng·pres·*taarr* *borrow*

empurrar eng·poo·*haarr* *push*

enchente ① eng·*sheng*·te *flood*

encher eng·*sherr* *fill*

encomenda ① eng·ko·*meng*·daa *parcel*

encontrar eng·kong·*traarr* *find · meet*

endereço ⓜ eng·de·*re*·so *address*

energia ① e·nerr·*zhee*·aa *energy*
— **nuclear** noo·kle·*aarr* *nuclear energy*

enfermeira ① eng·ferr·*may*·raa *nurse*

engenharia ① eng·zhe·nya·*ree*·aa *engineering*

engenheiro/engenheira ⓜ/①
eng·zhe·*nyay*·ro/eng·zhe·*nyay*·raa
engineer

engraçado/engraçada ⓜ/①
eng·graa·*saa*·do/eng·graa·*saa*·daa
funny

enguiçar eng·gee·*saarr* *break down*

enjoado/enjoada ⓜ/①
en·zho·*aa*·do/en·zho·*aa*·daa *seasick*

enjôo ⓜ en·*zho*·o *morning sickness*
— **de viagem** de vee·*aa*·zheng *travel sickness*

enorme e·*norr*·me *huge*

ensolarado/ensolarada ⓜ/①
eng·so·laa·*raa*·do/eng·so·laa·*raa*·daa
sunny

entediado/entediada ⓜ/①
eng·te·dee·*aa*·do/eng·te·dee·*aa*·daa
bored

entediante eng·te·dee·*ang*·te *boring*

enterro ⓜ eng·*te*·ho *funeral*

entrar eng·*traarr* *enter*

entre *eng*·tre *between*

entregar eng·tre·*gaarr* *deliver*

entrevista ① eeng·tre·*vees*·taa *interview*

envelope ⓜ eng·ve·*lo*·pe *envelope*

envergonhado/envergonhada ⓜ/①
en·verr·go·*nyaa*·do/en·verr·go·*nyaa*·daa
embarrassed

enviar eng·vee·*aarr* *send*

enxaqueca ① en·shaa·*ke*·kaa *migraine*

epilepsia ① e·pee·le·*psee*·aa *epilepsy*

equipamento ⓜ e·kee·paa·*meng*·to *equipment*
— **de mergulho** de merr·*goo*·lyo *diving equipment*

errado/errada ⓜ/① e·*haa*·do/e·*haa*·daa
wrong

erro ⓜ e·*ho* *mistake*

ervilha ① err·*vee*·lyaa *pea*

escada ① **rolante** es·*kaa*·daa ho·*lang*·te
escalator

escadaria ① es·kaa·daa·*ree*·aa *stairway*

escassez ① es·kaa·*ses* *shortage*

Escócia ① es·*ko*·syaa *Scotland*

escola ① es·*ko*·laa *school*

escolher es·ko·*lyerr* *choose*

escova ① es·*ko*·vaa *brush (hair)*
— **de dentes** de *deng*·tes *toothbrush*

escrever es·kre·*verr* *write*

escritor/escritora ⓜ/ⓕ
es·kree·torr/es·kree·to·raa *writer*

escritório ⓜ es·kree·to·ryo *office*
— **de achados e perdidos** de
aa·*shaa*·dos e perr·*dee*·dos
lost-property office
— **de turismo** de too·*rees*·mo
tourist office

escriturário/escriturária ⓜ/ⓕ
es·kree·too·*raa*·ryo/es·kree·too·*raa*·ryaa
office worker

escultor/escultor ⓜ/ⓕ
es·kool·*toorr*/es·kool·*too*·ra *sculptor*

escultura ⓕ es·kool·*too*·raa *sculpture*

escuro/escura ⓜ/ⓕ es·*koo*·ro/es·*koo*·raa
dark

escutar es·koo·*taarr* *hear · listen*

esempregado/desempregada ⓜ/ⓕ
de·zeng·pre·*gaa*·do/
de·zeng·pre·*gaa*·daa *unemployed*

esgotado/esgotada ⓜ/ⓕ es·go·*taa*·do/
es·go·*taa*·daa *booked out*

esgrima ⓕ es·*gree*·maa *fencing (sport)*

eski ⓜ **aquático** es·*kee* aa·*kwaa*·tee·ko
waterskiing

espaço ⓜ es·*pa*·so *space*

Espanha ⓕ es·*pa*·nyaa *Spain*

especial es·pe·see·*ow* *special*

especialista ⓜ&ⓕ es·pe·see·aa·*lees*·taa
specialist

espécies ⓕ pl **ameaçadas de extinção**
es·*pe*·syes aa·me·aa·*saa*·daas de
es·teeng·*sowng* *endangered species*

espelho ⓜ es·*pe*·lyo *mirror*

esperar es·pe·*raarr* *hope · wait*

espinafre ⓜ es·pee·*naa*·fre *spinach*

esporte ⓜ es·*porr*·te *sport*

esportista ⓜ&ⓕ es·porr·*tees*·taa
sportsperson

esposa ⓕ es·*po*·zaa *wife*

esquecer es·ke·*serr* *forget*

(à) esquerda ⓕ (aa) es·*kerr*·daa *left
(direction)*

esquerdista es·kerr·*dees*·taa *left-wing*

esqui ⓜ es·*kee* *skiing*

esquiar es·kee·*aarr* *ski*

esquina ⓕ es·*kee*·naa *corner*

esta ⓕ es·*taa* *this*

estaca ⓕ es·*taa*·kaa *tent peg*

estação ⓕ es·taa·*sowng* *season · station*
— **de trem** de treng *railway station*

estacionamento ⓜ
es·taa·syo·naa·*meng*·to *car park*

estacionar es·taa·syo·*naarr* *park (vehicle)*

estádio ⓜ es·*taa*·dyo *stadium*

estado ⓜ **civil** es·*taa*·do see·*veel*
marital status

estar es·*taarr* *be (temporary)*
— **resfriado** hes·free·*aa*·do *have a cold*

estátua ⓕ es·*taa*·twaa *statue*

este ⓜ *es·*te *this*

estéreo ⓜ es·*te*·ryo *stereo*

estilo ⓜ es·*tee*·lo *style*

estômago ⓜ es·*to*·maa·go *stomach*

estória ⓕ es·*to*·ryaa *story*

estrada ⓕ es·*traa*·daa *road*

estragado/estragada ⓜ/ⓕ
es·traa·*gaa*·do/es·traa·*gaa*·daa *off (food)*

estrangeiro/estrangeira ⓜ/ⓕ
es·trang·*zhay*·ro/es·trang·*zhay*·raa
foreign

estranho/estranha ⓜ/ⓕ es·*tra*·nyo/
es·*tra*·nyaa *strange · stranger*

estrela ⓕ es·*tre*·laa *star*

estrupar es·troo·*paarr* *rape*

estrupo ⓜ es·*troo*·po *rape*

estudante es·too·*dang*·te *student*

estúdio ⓜ es·*too*·dyo *studio*

estufa ⓕ es·*too*·faa *heater*

etiqueta ⓕ **de bagagem** e·tee·*ke*·taa de
baa·gaa·*zheng* *luggage tag*

eu e·oo *I*

EUA ⓜ pl e·*waa* *USA*

euro ⓜ e·oo·ro *euro*

Europa ⓕ e·oo·ro·paa *Europe*

eutanásia ⓕ e·oo·taa·*naa*·zyaa
euthanasia

evitar e·vee·*taarr* *stop (prevent)*

exame ⓜ **de sangue** e·*za*·me de *sang*·ge
blood test

exame ⓜ **papa nicolau** e·*za*·me *paa*·paa
nee·ko·*low* *pap smear*

exaustor ⓜ e·zows·*torr* *exhaust (car)*

excelente e·se·*leng*·te *excellent*

excluído/excluída ⓜ/ⓕ es·kloo·*ee*·do/
es·kloo·*ee*·daa *excluded*

excursão ① es·koorr·*sowng* tour
— **guiada** ① gee·*aa*·daa *guided tour*
exemplo ⓜ e·*zeng*·plo *example*
experiência ① es·pe·ree·*eng*·syaa
experience
exploração ① es·plo·raa·*sowng*
exploitation
exposição ① es·po·zee·*sowng* *exhibition*
expresso/expressa ⓜ/①
es·*pre*·so/es·*pre*·saa *express*
êxtase ⓜ *es·*taa·ze *ecstasy (drug)*
extensão ① es·teng·*sowng*
extension
exterior es·te·ree·*orr abroad*

F

fã ⓜ&① fang *fan (sport, etc)*
fábrica ① *faa·*bree·kaa *factory*
faca ① *faa·*kaa *knife*
fácil *faa·*seel *easy*
falar faa·*laarr* *speak · talk*
falta ① *fow·*taa *foul*
família ① faa·*mee·*lyaa *family*
faminto/faminta ⓜ/① faa·*meeng*·to/
faa·*meeng*·taa *hungry*
famoso/famosa ⓜ/① faa·*mo*·zo/
faa·*mo*·zaa *famous*
farinha ① faa·*ree*·nyaa *flour*
farmácia ① faar·*maa*·syaa *pharmacy*
faróis ⓜ pl faa·*roys* *headlight*
fazenda ① faa·*zeng*·daa *farm*
fazendeiro/fazendeira ⓜ/①
faa·zeng·*day*·ro/faa·zeng·*day*·raa *farmer*
fazer faa·*zerr* *do · make*
febre ① *fe·*bre *fever*
— **do feno** do *fe·*no *hay fever*
— **glandular** glang·doo·*laar*
glandular fever
fechado/fechada ⓜ/① fe·*shaa*·do/
fe·*shaa*·daa *closed · shut*
fechar fe·*shaarr close*
feijão ⓜ fay·*zhowng* *bean*
feito/feita ⓜ/① à mão *fay*·to/*fay*·taa aa
mowng *handmade*
feliz fe·*lees* *happy*
férias ① pl *fe*·ryaas *holiday · vacation*
ferimento ⓜ fe·ree·*meng*·to *injury*

ferro ⓜ **de passa roupas** *fe*·ho de
paa·*saarr* ho·paas *iron (clothes)*
festa ① *fes*·taa *party (social gathering)*
festival ⓜ fes·tee·*vow* *festival*
fevereiro fe·ve·*ray*·ro *February*
ficar fee·*kaarr stay*
ficção ① feek·*sowng* *fiction*
fígado ⓜ *fee*·gaa·do *liver*
figo ⓜ *fee*·go *fig*
fila ① *fee*·laa *queue*
— **de táxi** de *taak*·see *taxi stand*
filé ⓜ fee·*le* *fillet*
filha ① *fee*·lyaa *daughter*
filho ⓜ *fee*·lyo *son*
filme ⓜ *feel*·me *film (cinema)*
— **fotográfico** fo·to·*graa*·fee·ko
film (photography)
filtrado/filtrada ⓜ/① feel·*traa*·do/
feel·*traa*·daa *filtered*
fim ⓜ feeng *end*
final ⓜ **de semana** fee·*now* de se·*ma*·naa
weekend
fino/fina ⓜ/① *fee*·no/*fee*·naa *thin*
fio ⓜ **dental** *fee*·o deng·*tow* *dental floss*
fita ① **cassete** *fee*·taa kaa·*se*·te *cassette*
fita ① **de vídeo** *fee*·taa de *vee*·de·o
video tape
flanela ① fla·*ne*·laa *flannel*
flash ⓜ **luminoso** flash loo·mee·*no*·zo
flashlight
flor ① florr *flower*
floresta ① flo·*res*·taa *forest*
floricultura ① flo·ree·kool·*too*·raa
florist (shop)
florista ⓜ&① flo·*rees*·taa *florist (person)*
fogão ⓜ fo·*gowng* *stove*
fogo ⓜ *fo*·go *fire*
folha ① *fo*·lyaa *leaf*
fora fo·*raa outside*
forma ① *forr*·maa *shape*
formiga ① forr·*mee*·gaa *ant*
forno ⓜ *forr*·no *oven*
forte *forr*·te *strong*
fósforos ⓜ pl *fos*·fo·ros *matches*
fotografia ① fo·to·graa·*fee*·aa *photograph ·
photography*
fotógrafo/fotógrafa ⓜ/① fo·*to*·graa·fo/
fo·*to*·gra·faa *photographer*

fotômetro ⓜ fo·to·me·tro *light meter*
fraco/fraca ⓜ/ⓕ fraa·ko/fraa·kaa *weak*
frágil fraa·zheel *fragile*
fralda ⓕ frow·daa *diaper • nappy*
framboesa ⓕ frang·bo·e·zaa *raspberry*
freio ⓜ fray·o *brake*
freira ⓕ fray·raa *nun*
frequentemente fre·kweng·te·*meng*·te *often*
frigideira ⓕ free·zhee·*day*·raa *frying pan*
frio ⓜ free·o *cold*
frio/fria ⓜ/ⓕ free·o/free·aa *cold*
fritar free·*taarr* *fry*
frito/frita ⓜ/ⓕ free·to/free·taa *fried*
fronha ⓕ fro·nyaa *pillowcase*
fruta ⓕ froo·taa *fruit*
frutas ⓕ pl **secas** froo·taas se·kaas *dried fruit*
fumado/fumada ⓜ/ⓕ foo·*maa*·do/foo·*maa*·daa *stoned (drugged)*
fumar foo·*maarr* *smoke*
furo ⓜ foo·ro *puncture*
futebol ⓜ **americano** foo·te·bol aa·me·ree·*ka*·no *American football*
futebol ⓜ foo·te·bol *football • soccer*
futuro ⓜ foo·too·ro *future*

G

galeria ⓕ **de arte** gaa·le·*ree*·aa de *aarr*·te *art gallery*
galinha ⓕ gaa·lee·nyaa *chicken*
ganhador/ganhadora ⓜ/ⓕ ga·nyaa·*dorr*/ga·nyaa·do·raa *winner*
ganhar ga·*nyaarr* *earn • win*
garçon/garçonete ⓜ/ⓕ gaarr·song/gaarr·so·ne·te *waiter*
garfo ⓜ *gaarr*·fo *fork*
garganta ⓕ gaarr·*gang*·taa *throat*
garrafa ⓕ gaa·*haa*·faa *bottle*
— **d'água** daa·gwaa *water bottle*
gás ⓜ gas *gas (for cooking)*
gasolina ⓕ gaa·zo·lee·na *gas (petrol)*
gastrenterite ⓕ gaas·treng·te·*ree*·te *gastroenteritis*
gato/gata ⓜ/ⓕ *gaa*·to/*gaa*·taa *cat*
gay gay *gay*
gaze ⓕ gaa·ze *gauze*

geada ⓕ zhe·*aa*·daa *frost*
geladeira ⓕ zhe·laa·*day*·raa *refrigerator*
geléia ⓕ zhe·*le*·yaa *jam*
gelo ⓜ zhe·lo *ice*
gêmeos/gêmeas ⓜ/ⓕ zhe·me·os/zhe·me·aas *twins*
gengiva ⓕ zheng·zhee·vaa *gum (part of mouth)*
gerente ⓜ&ⓕ zhe·*reng*·te *manager*
gilete ⓕ zhee·le·te *razor blade*
gin ⓜ zheen *gin*
ginástica ⓕ zhee·*naas*·tee·kaa *gym*
— **olímpica** o·*leeng*·pee·kaa *gymnastics*
ginecologista ⓜ&ⓕ zhee·ne·ko·lo·*zhees*·taa *gynaecologist*
gol ⓜ gol *goal (sport)*
goleiro/goleira ⓜ/ⓕ go·lay·ro/go·lay·raa *goalkeeper*
goma ⓕ **de mascar** go·maa de maas·*kaarr* *chewing gum*
gordo/gorda ⓜ/ⓕ *gorr*·do/*gorr*·daa *fat*
gorgeta ⓕ gorr·*zhe*·taa *tip (gratuity)*
gostar gos·*taarr* *like*
gostar (de alguém) gos·*taarr* (de ow·*geng*) *care (for someone)*
gostoso/gostosa ⓜ/ⓕ gos·to·zo/gos·to·zaa *tasty*
governo ⓜ go·*verr*·no *government*
grama ⓕ *graa*·maa *gram • grass*
grande *grang*·de *large • big*
grão ⓜ **de bico** growng de *bee*·ko *chickpea*
gratuito/gratuita graa·too·ee·to/graa·too·ee·taa *free (gratis)*
graus ⓜ pl grows *degrees (temperature)*
gravação ⓕ graa·vaa·*sowng* *recording*
gravar graa·*vaarr* *record*
grávida ⓕ graa·vee·daa *pregnant*
gripe ⓕ gree·pe *influenza*
gritar gree·*taarr* *shout*
grosso/grossa ⓜ/ⓕ gro·so/gro·saa *thick*
grupo ⓜ **sanguíneo** groo·po sang·*gwee*·ne·o *blood group*
guarda ⓜ **volumes** gwaarr·daa vo·loo·mes *cloakroom • luggage locker*
guarda-chuva ⓕ gwaarr·daa·shoo·vaa *umbrella*

guardanapo ⓜ gwaar·daa·*naa*·po
napkin • serviette
guerra ⓕ *ge*·haa war
guia ⓜ/ⓕ *gee*·aa guide (person)
guia ⓜ *gee*·aa guidebook
— **auditivo** ⓜ ow·dee·*tee*·vo
guide (audio)
— **de entretenimento** de
eng·tre·te·nee·*meng*·to
entertainment guide
guitarra ⓕ gee·*taa*·haa guitar

H

há (três dias) aa (tres *dee*·aas)
(three days) ago
halal aa·*low* halal
handebol ⓜ *heng*·de·bol handball
hematoma ⓜ e·maa·to·maa bruise
hepatite ⓕ e·paa·*tee*·te hepatitis
heroína ⓕ e·ro·*ee*·naa heroin
hidratante ⓜ ee·draa·*tang*·te moisturiser
Hindu eeng·*doo* Hindu
história ⓕ ees·to·rya history
histórico/histórica ⓜ/ⓕ ees·to·*ree*·ko/
ees·to·*ree*·kaa historical
HIV ⓜ aa·*gaa* ee ve HIV
hockey ⓜ *ho*·kay hockey
hoje o·zhe today
hoje à noite o·zhe aa *noy*·te tonight
homem ⓜ o·meng man
— **de negócios** de ne·*go*·syos
businessman
homeopatia ⓕ o·me·o·paa·*tee*·aa
homeopathy
homosexual o·mo·sek·soo·*ow*
homosexual
hora ⓕ **marcada** *aw*·raa maarr·*kaa*·daa
date (appointment)
horário ⓜ o·*raa*·rio timetable
horário ⓜ **de funcionamento** o·*raa*·ryo
de foon·syo·naa·*meng*·to opening hours
horóscopo ⓜ o·*ros*·ko·po horoscope
horrível o·*hee*·vel awful
hospedagem ⓕ os·pe·*daa*·zheng
accommodation
hospital ⓜ os·pee·*tow* hospital
hospitalidade ⓕ os·pee·taa·lee·*daa*·de
hospitality
hotel ⓜ o·*tel* hotel
humanidades ⓕ pl oo·ma·nee·*daa*·des
humanities

I

ida ⓕ *ee*·daa one-way (ticket)
ida e volta *ee*·daa e *vol*·taa return (ticket)
idade ⓕ ee·*daa*·de age
identificação ⓕ ee·deng·tee·fee·kaa·*sowng*
identification
idiota ⓜ&ⓕ ee·dee·o·taa idiot
igreja ⓕ ee·*gre*·zhaa church
igualdade ⓕ ee·gwow·*daa*·de equality
ilha ⓕ *ee*·lyaa island
imigração ⓕ ee·mee·graa·*sowng*
immigration
importante eeng·porr·*tang*·te important
imposto ⓜ eeng·*pos*·to tax
— **de renda** de *heng*·daa income tax
— **sobre venda** so·bre *veng*·daa
sales tax
inchaço ⓜ eeng·*shaa*·so swelling
incluso/inclusa ⓜ/ⓕ eeng·*kloo*·zo/
eeng·*kloo*·zaa included
Índia ⓕ *eeng*·dyaa India
indicador ⓜ eeng·dee·kaa·*dorr* indicator
indigestão ⓕ eeng·dee·zhes·*towng*
indigestion
indústria ⓕ eeng·*doos*·tryaa industry
infecção ⓕ eeng·fek·*sowng* infection
— **urinária** oo·ree·*naa*·ryaa
urinary infection
inflamação ⓕ eeng·fla·maa·*sowng*
inflammation
Inglaterra ⓕ eeng·glaa·*te*·haa England
Inglês ⓜ eeng·*gles* English (language)
ingrediente ⓜ eeng·gre·dee·*eng*·te
ingredient
íngreme *eeng*·gre·me steep
injeção ⓕ eeng·zhe·*sowng* injection
injetar eeng·zhe·*taarr* inject
injusto/injusta ⓜ/ⓕ eeng·*zhoos*·to/
eeng·*zhoos*·taa unfair
inocente ee·no·*seng*·te innocent

inseguro/insegura ⓜ/ⓕ eeng-se-goo-ro/
eeng-se-goo-raa *unsafe*
insolação ⓕ eeng-so-laa-*sowng sunstroke*
instrutor/instrutora ⓜ/ⓕ
eengs-troo-*torr*/eengs-troo-*to*-raa
instructor
interessante eeng-te-re-*sang*-te *interesting*
interior ⓜ eeng-te-ree-*orr countryside*
internacional eeng-*terr*-naa-syo-now
international
Internet ⓕ eeng-*terr*-ne-te *Internet*
intérprete ⓜ&ⓕ eeng-*terr*-pre-te
interpreter
intervalo ⓜ eeng-*terr*-vaa-lo *intermission*
inverno ⓜ eeng-*verr*-no *winter*
ioga ⓕ ee-o-gaa *yoga*
iogurte ⓕ ee-o-*goorr*-te *yogurt*
ir eerr *go*
Irlanda ⓕ eerr-*lang*-daa *Ireland*
irmã ⓕ eer-*ma sister*
irmão ⓜ eerr-*mowng brother*
irritação ⓕ ee-hee-ta-*sowng irritation*
 — **à fralda** aa *frow*-daa *nappy rash*
 — **na pele** naa *pe*-le *rash*
isqueiro ⓜ ees-*kay*-ro *cigarette lighter*
Israel ⓜ ees-haa-*el Israel*
IT ⓜ ai-*tee* IT *(information technology)*
itinerário ⓜ ee-tee-ne-*raa*-ryo *itinerary*

J

já zhaa *already*
janeiro ⓜ zhaa-*nay*-ro *January*
janela ⓕ zhaa-*ne*-laa *window*
jantar ⓜ zhang-*taarr dinner*
Japão ⓜ zhaa-*powng Japan*
jaqueta ⓕ zhaa-*ke*-taa *jacket*
jardim ⓜ zhaarr-*deeng garden*
 — **botânico** bo-*ta*-nee-ko
 botanic garden
 — **de infância** de eeng-*fang*-syaa
 kindergarten
jardineiro/jardineira ⓜ/ⓕ
zhaarr-dee-*nay*-ro/zhaarr-dee-*nay*-raa
gardener
jardins ⓜ pl *públicos* zhaarr-*deengs*
poo-blee-kos *public gardens*
jeans ⓜ zheens *jeans*

jeep ⓜ *zhee*-pe *jeep*
joalheria ⓕ zho-a-lye-*ree*-aa *jewellery*
joelho ⓜ zho-*e*-lyo *knee*
jogar zho-*gaarr play*
jogo ⓜ *zho*-go *game (sport)*
 — **de computador** de
 kong-poo-taa-*dorr computer game*
Jogos Olímpidos ⓜ pl *zho*-gos
o-*leeng*-pee-kos *Olympic Games*
jornal ⓜ zhorr-*now newspaper*
jornaleiro ⓜ zhorr-na-*lay*-ro
news stand • newsagency
jornalista ⓜ&ⓕ zhorr-naa-*lees*-taa
journalist
jovem *zho*-veng *young*
Judeu/Judia ⓜ/ⓕ zhoo-*de*-oo/
zhoo-*dee*-aa *Jewish*
juiz/juiza ⓜ/ⓕ zhoo-*ees*/zhoo-*ee*-zaa
judge • referee
julho ⓜ *zhoo*-lyo *July*
junho ⓜ *zhoo*-nyoo *June*
junto/junta ⓜ/ⓕ *zhoong*-to/*zhoong*-taa
together

K

ketchup ⓜ ke-tee-*shoo*-pee *ketchup*
kilograma ⓜ/ⓕ kee-lo-*gra*-maa *kilogram*
kilômetro ⓜ kee-*lo*-me-tro *kilometre*
kit ⓜ **de primeiros socorros** *kee*-tee de
pree-*may*-ros so-*ko*-hos *first-aid kit*
kiwi ⓜ kee-*wee kiwifruit*
kosher ko-*sherr kosher*

L

lã ⓕ lang *wool*
lábios ⓜ pl *laa*-byos *lips*
lado ⓜ *laa*-do *side*
ladrão/ladra ⓜ/ⓕ laa-*drowng*/*laa*-dra
thief
lagarto ⓜ laa-*gaarr*-to *lizard*
lago ⓜ *laa*-go *lake*
lama ⓕ *la*-maa *mud*
lâmpada ⓕ *lang*-paa-daa *light bulb*
lanche ⓜ *lang*-she *snack*
lanterna ⓕ lang-*terr*-naa *torch (flashlight)*
lápis ⓜ *laa*-pees *pencil*

laptop ⓜ le·pee·to·*pee* laptop
laranja ⓕ laa·*rang*·zhaa orange
laranja laa·*rang*·zhaa orange
largo/larga ⓜ/ⓕ laarr·go/*laarr*·gaa wide
lata ⓕ *laa*·taa can • tin
lavanderia ⓕ laa·vang·de·*ree*·aa
  laundrette
lavar laa·*vaarr* wash
laxante ⓜ la·*shang*·te laxative
legal le·*gow* legal
legislação ⓕ le·zhees·la·*sowng* legislation
legumes ⓜ pl le·*goo*·mes
  legumes • vegetables
lei ⓕ lay law
leite ⓜ *lay*·te milk
  — de soja de so·zhaa *soy milk*
  — desnatado des·naa·*taa*·do *skim milk*
leito ⓜ *lay*·to *sleeping berth*
lencinho ⓜ **de papel** leng·*see*·nyo de
  paa·*pel* *tissue*
lenço ⓜ *leng*·so scarf
lençol ⓜ leng·*sow* sheet (bed)
lenha ⓕ *le*·nyaa firewood
lentes ⓕ pl *leng*·tes lenses
  — de contato de kong·*taa*·to *contact
  lenses*
lentilha ⓕ leng·*tee*·lyaa lentil
ler lerr read
lésbica ⓕ *les*·bee·kaa lesbian
lesma ⓕ *les*·maa snail
leste ⓜ *les*·te *east*
levar le·*vaarr* take
leve *le*·ve light (not heavy)
libra ⓕ *lee*·braa pound (money)
licença ⓕ lee·*seng*·saa licence
líder ⓜ&ⓕ *lee*·derr *leader*
ligação ⓕ **à cobrar** lee·gaa·*sowng* aa
  ko·*braarr* collect call
ligação ⓕ **direta** lee·gaa·*sowng* dee·*re*·taa
  direct-dial call
limão ⓜ lee·*mowng* lemon • lime
limite ⓜ **de peso** lee·*mee*·te de *pe*·zo
  baggage allowance
limite ⓜ **de velocidade** lee·*mee*·te de
  ve·lo·see·*daa*·de *speed limit*
limonada ⓕ lee·mo·*naa*·daa lemonade
limpo/limpa ⓜ/ⓕ *leeng*·po/*leeng*·paa
  clean

língua ⓕ *leeng*·gwaa language • tongue
linguiça ⓕ **de porco** leen·*gwee*·saa de
  porr·ko *pork sausage*
linha ⓕ *lee*·nyaa dial tone
linha aérea ⓕ pl *lee*·nyaa aa·e·re·aa *airline*
liquidação ⓕ lee·kee·daa·*sowng* sale
lista ⓕ **telefônica** lees·taa te·le·*fo*·nee·kaa
  phone book
listado/listada ⓜ/ⓕ lees·*taa*·do/
  lees·*taa*·daa *itemised*
livraria ⓕ lee·vraa·*ree*·aa book shop
livre *lee*·vre free (not bound)
livro ⓜ *lee*·vro book
  — de frases de fraa·zes *phrasebook*
lixo ⓜ *lee*·sho garbage • rubbish
local lo·*kow* local
local ⓜ lo·*kow* venue
  — de nascimento de naas·see·*meng*·to
  place of birth
  — para acampar paa·raa aa·kang·*paarr*
  camp site
loção ⓕ **de bronzear** lo·*sowng* de
  brong·ze·*aarr* tanning lotion
loja ⓕ *lo*·zhaa shop
  — de aparelhos elétricos
  de aa·paa·re·lyos e·*le*·tree·kos
  electrical store
  — de bebidas de be·*bee*·daas
  bottle shop • liquor store
  — de bicicleta de bee·see·*kle*·taa
  bike shop
  — de brinquedos de breeng·*ke*·dos
  toy shop
  — de departamentos de
  de·paarr·taa·*meng*·tos *department store*
  — de equipamentos fotográficos
  de e·kee·pa·*meng*·tos fo·to·*graa*·fee·kos
  camera shop
  — de esportes de es·*porr*·tes
  sports store
  — de ferramentas de fe·haa·*meng*·taas
  hardware store
  — de música de moo·zee·kaa
  music shop

— **de roupas** de ho-*paas* clothing store

— **de segunda mão** de se-*goon*-daa mowng *second-hand shop*

— **de souvenir** de soo-ve-*neerr* *souvenir shop*

— **de acampamento** de aa-kam-paa-*meng*-to *camping store*

longe *long*-zhe *far*

longo/longa ⓜ/ⓕ *long*-go/*long*-gaa *long*

lotado/lotada ⓜ/ⓕ lo-*taa*-do/lo-*taa*-daa *crowded*

louça ⓕ **de barro** lo-*saa* de *baa*-ho *pot (ceramics)*

louco/louca ⓜ/ⓕ *lo*-ko/*lo*-kaa *crazy*

lua ⓕ *loo*-aa *moon*

— **de mel** de mel *honeymoon*

lubrificante ⓜ loo-bree-fee-*kang*-te *lubricant*

lucro ⓜ *loo*-kro *profit*

lugar ⓜ loo-*gaarr* *place*

luta ⓕ *loo*-ta *fight*

luvas ⓕ pl *loo*-vaas *gloves*

luxo ⓜ *loo*-sho *luxury*

luz ⓕ *looz* *light*

M

maçã ⓕ maa-*sang* *apple*

macarrão ⓜ **chinês** maa-kaa-*howng* shee-*nes* *noodles*

machismo ⓜ maa-*shees*-mo *sexism*

machucar maa-shoo-*kaarr* *hurt*

maconha ⓕ maa-*ko*-nyaa *marijuana*

madeira ⓕ maa-*day*-raa *wood*

madrugada ⓕ maa-droo-*gaa*-daa *dawn*

mãe ⓕ *mayng* *mum*

maio *maa*-yo *May*

maionese ⓕ maa-yo-*ne*-ze *mayonnaise*

mais *maas* *more*

— **perto/perta** ⓜ/ⓕ *perr*-to/*perr*-taa *nearest*

mal mal *ill*

mal passado/passada ⓜ/ⓕ mow paa-*saa*-do/paa-*saa*-daa *rare (food)*

mala ⓕ *maa*-laa *suitcase*

mamãe ⓕ ma-*mayng* *mother*

mamograma ⓜ maa-mo-*gra*-maa *mammogram*

mandíbula ⓕ mang-*dee*-boo-laa *jaw*

manga ⓕ *mang*-gaa *mango*

manhã ⓕ ma-*nyang* *morning*

manteiga ⓕ man-*tay*-gaa *butter*

mantimentos ⓜ pl mang-tee-*meng*-tos *groceries*

mão ⓕ *mowng* *hand*

mapa ⓕ *maa*-paa *map*

— **da estrada** daa es-*traa*-daa *road map*

maquiagem ⓕ maa-kee-*aa*-zheng *make-up*

máquina ⓕ *maa*-kee-naa *machine*

— **de lavar roupa** de laa-*vaarr* ho-paa *washing machine*

— **de vender passagem** de *veng*-derr paa-*saa*-zheng *ticket machine*

mar ⓜ *maarr* *sea*

maracujá ⓜ maa-raa-koo-*zhaa* *passionfruit*

maravilhoso/maravilhosa ⓜ/ⓕ maa-raa-vee-*lyo*-zo/maa-raa-vee-*lyo*-zaa *wonderful*

marca ⓕ **passo** mar-kaa *pa*-so *pacemaker*

março *maar*-so *March*

maré ⓕ maa-*re* *tide*

margarina ⓕ maarr-gaa-*ree*-naa *margarine*

marido ⓜ maa-*ree*-do *husband*

marmelada ⓕ maarr-me-*laa*-daa *marmalade*

marron maa-*hong* *brown*

martelo ⓜ maarr-*te*-lo *hammer*

mas maas *but*

massa ⓕ *maa*-saa *pastry*

massagem ⓕ maa-*saa*-zheng *massage*

massagista ⓜ&ⓕ maa-saa-*zhees*-taa *masseur*

massas ⓕ pl *maa*-saas *pasta*

matar maa-*taarr* *kill*

mecânico/mecânica ⓜ/ⓕ me-*ka*-nee-ko/me-*ka*-nee-kaa *mechanic*

medicina ⓕ me-dee-*see*-naa *medicine*

médico/médica ⓜ/ⓕ *me*-dee-ko/*me*-dee-kaa *doctor*

meditação ⓕ me-dee-taa-*sowng* *meditation*

meia ⓕ *may*-aa *sock*

— **calça** kow-*saa* *pantyhose*

meia-noite ① *may·aa·noy·te* midnight

meio ⑩ ambiente *may·o ang·bee·eng·te* environment

meio expediente *may·o es·pe·dee·eng·te* part-time

meio-dia ⑩ *may·o dee·aa* noon

mel ⑩ mel honey

melancia ① *me·lang·see·aa* watermelon

melão ⑩ *me·lowng* cantaloupe • melon • rockmelon

melhor *me·lyorr* best • better

membro ⑩&① *meng·bro* member

menina ① *me·nee·naa* girl

menino *me·nee·no* boy

menos *me·nos* less

mensagem ① *meng·sa·zheng* message

menstruação ① *mengs·troo·aa·sowng* menstruation

mentiroso/mentirosa ⑩/① *meng·tee·ro·zo/meng·tee·ro·zaa* liar

mercado ⑩ *merr·kaa·do* market

mercearia ① *merr·se·aa·ree·aa* convenience store

mergulho ⑩ *merr·goo·lyo* diving

mês ⑩ mes month

mesa ① *me·zaa* table

mesmo/mesma ⑩/① *mes·mo/mes·maa* same

metade ① *me·taa·de* half

metal ⑩ *me·tow* metal

metro ⑩ *me·tro* metre

meu/minha ⑩/① *me·oo/mee·nyaa* my

mexido/mexida ⑩/① *me·shee·do/ me·shee·daa* scrambled

mexilhão ⑩ *me·shee·lyowng* mussel

microondas ⑩ *mee·kro·ong·daas* microwave

mídia ① *mee·dyaa* media

milhão ⑩ *mee·lowng* million

milho ⑩ *mee·lyo* corn

milímetro ⑩ *mee·lee·me·tro* millimetre

militar *mee·lee·taarr* military

mimado/mimada ⑩/① *mee·maa·do/mee·maa·daa* spoiled

minhocas ① pl *mee·nyo·kaas* worms

mínimo/mínima ⑩/① *mee·nee·mo/mee·nee·maa* tiny

minuto ⑩ *mee·noo·to* minute

mirante ⑩ *mee·rang·te* lookout

missa ① *mee·saa* mass (Catholic)

misturar *mees·too·raar* mix

mochila ① *mo·shee·la* backpack

modem ⑩ *mo·deng* modem

moedas ① pl *mo·e·daas* coins

molas ① pl *mo·laas* spring (coil)

mole *mo·le* soft-boiled

molestamento ⑩ *mo·les·taa·meng·to* harassment

molhado/molhada ⑩/① *mo·lyaa·do/mo·lyaa·daa* wet

molho ⑩ *mo·lyo* sauce
— de pimenta de *pee·meng·taa* chilli sauce
— de soja de *so·zhaa* soy sauce
— de tomate de *to·maa·te* tomato sauce

monastério ⑩ *mo·naas·te·ryo* monastery

monge ⑩ *mong·zhe* monk

montanha ① *mong·ta·nyaa* mountain

montanhismo ⑩ *mong·ta·nyees·mo* mountaineering

monumento ⑩ *mo·noo·meng·to* monument

morango ⑩ *mo·rang·go* strawberry

morar *mo·raarr* live (somewhere)

mordida ① *morr·dee·daa* bite (dog/insect)

morno/morna ⑩/① *morr·no/morr·naa* warm

morrer *mo·herr* die

morro ⑩ *mo·ho* hill

morto/morta ⑩/① *morr·to/morr·taa* dead

mosquiteiro ⑩ *mos·kee·tay·ro* mosquito net

mosquito ⑩ *mos·kee·to* mosquito

mosteiro ⑩ *mos·tay·ro* mosque

mostrador de velocidade *mos·traa·dorr de ve·lo·see·daa·de* speedometer

mostrar *mos·traarr* show

motocicleta ① *mo·to·see·kle·taa* motorbike

motor ⑩ *mo·torr* engine

mountain bike ⑩ *maa·oong·tayng bai·kee* mountain bike

móveis ⑩ pl *mo·vays* furniture

Muçulmano/Muçulmana ⓜ/ⓕ
moo·sool·*ma*·no/moo·sool·*ma*·naa
Muslim
mudo/muda ⓜ/ⓕ *moo*·do/*moo*·daa
mute
muesli ⓜ *moos*·lee *muesli*
muito/muita ⓜ/ⓕ *mweeng*·to/
mweeng·taa *(a) lot • very*
mulher ⓕ moo·*lyerr woman*
— **de negócios** de ne·*go*·syos
business person
multa ⓕ *mool*·taa *fine (payment)*
mundo ⓜ *moong*·do *world*
músculo ⓜ *moos*·koo·lo *muscle*
museu ⓜ mo·se·oo *museum*
música ⓕ *moo*·zee·kaa *music*
músico/música ⓜ/ⓕ *moo*·zee·ko/
moo·zee·kaa *musician*
mustarda ⓕ moos·*taar*·daa *mustard*

N

na frente de naa *freng*·te de *in front of*
nacionalidade ⓕ naa·syo·naa·lee·*daa*·de
nationality
nada *naa*·daa *nothing*
nadar naa·*daarr swim*
namorada ⓕ naa·mo·*raa*·daa *girlfriend*
namorado ⓜ naa·mo·*raa*·do *boyfriend*
namorar naa·mo·*raarr date (a person)*
não nowng *no • not*
não-fumante nowng·foo·*mang*·te
non-smoking
nariz ⓜ naa·*rees nose*
nascer ⓜ **do sol** naa·serr do sol *sunrise*
natureza ⓕ naa·too·re·zaa *nature*
naturopatia ⓕ naa·too·ro·paa·*tee*·a
naturopathy
náusea ⓕ *now*·se·aa *nausea*
navio ⓜ naa·*vee*·o *ship*
nebuloso/nebulosa ⓜ/ⓕ
ne·boo·*lo*·zo/ne·boo·*lo*·zaa *foggy*
necessário/necessária ⓜ/ⓕ
ne·se·*sa*·ryo/ne·se·*sa*·ryaa *necessary*
negativo/negativa ⓜ/ⓕ ne·gaa·*tee*·vo/
ne·gaa·*tee*·vaa *negative*
negócios ⓜ pl ne·*go*·syos *business*
nenhum ne·*yoom none*

nenhum deles ne·*yoom de*·les *neither*
neto/neta ⓜ/ⓕ ne·to/ne·taa *grandchild*
neve ⓕ *ne*·ve *snow*
nódulo ⓜ no·doo·lo *lump*
noite ⓕ *noy*·te *evening • night*
Noite ⓕ **de Natal** *noy*·te de na·*tow*
Christmas Eve
noiva ⓕ *noy*·vaa *fiancee*
noivado ⓜ noy·*vaa*·do *engagement*
noivo ⓜ *noy*·vo *fiance*
nome ⓜ *no*·me *name*
— **Cristão** ⓜ krees·*towng*
Christian name
norte ⓜ *norr*·te *north*
Noruega ⓕ no·roo·e·gaa *Norway*
nós nos *we*
nosso/nossa ⓜ/ⓕ *no*·so/*no*·saa *our*
nota ⓕ *no*·taa *banknote*
notícias ⓕ pl no·*tee*·syaas *news*
Nova Zelândia ⓕ *no*·vaa ze·*lang*·dyaa
New Zealand
novamente no·vaa·*meng*·te *again*
novela ⓕ no·*ve*·laa *soap opera*
novembro no·*veng*·bro *November*
novidades ⓕ pl no·vee·*daa*·des *news*
novo/nova ⓜ/ⓕ *no*·vo/*no*·vaa *new*
noz ⓕ noz *nut*
nublado/nublada ⓜ/ⓕ
noo·*blaa*·do/noo·*blaa*·daa *cloudy*
número ⓜ *noo*·me·ro *number*
— **da placa** daa *plaa*·kaa *license plate
number • numberplate*
— **do passaporte** do paa·saa·*porr*·te
passport number
— **do quarto** do *kwaarr*·to
room number
nunca *noong*·kaa *never*
nuvem ⓕ *noo*·veng *cloud*

O

objetivo ⓜ o·bee·zhe·*tee*·vo *goal*
oceano ⓜ o·se·*a*·no *ocean*
óculos ⓜ pl o·koo·los *glasses (spectacles)*
— **de natação** de naa·taa·*sowng*
goggles (swimming)
— **de ski** de es·*kee goggles (skiing)*
— **de sol** de sol *sunglasses*

ocupado/ocupada ⓜ/ⓕ oo·koo·*paa*·do/o·koo·*paa*·daa busy

oeste ⓜ o·*es*·te west

oficina ⓕ o·fee·*see*·naa garage • workshop

óleo ⓜ o·lyo oil

olho ⓜ o·lyo eye

ombro ⓜ pl ong·bro shoulder

onda ⓕ ong·daa wave

onde ong·de where

ônibus ⓜ o·nee·boos bus

ontem ong·teng yesterday

ópera ⓕ o·pe·raa opera

operação ⓕ o·pe·raa·*sowng* operation

operador/operadora ⓜ/ⓕ o·pe·raa·*dorr*/o·pe·raa·*do*·raa operator

operário/operária ⓜ/ⓕ o·pe·*raa*·ryo/o·pe·*raa*·ryaa factory worker

opinião ⓕ o·pee·nee·*owng* opinion

oportunidade ⓕ o·porr·too·nee·*daa*·de chance

oportunidades ⓕ pl **iguais** o·porr·too·nee·*daa*·des ee·*gwaa*·ees equal opportunity

oposto/oposta ⓜ/ⓕ o·*pos*·to/o·*pos*·taa opposite

optometrista ⓜ&ⓕ o·pee·to·me·*trees*·taa optometrist

ordinário/ordinária ⓜ/ⓕ orr·dee·*naa*·ryo/orr·dee·*naa*·ryaa ordinary

orelha ⓕ o·re·lyaa ear

orgasmo ⓜ orr·*gaas*·mo orgasm

original o·ree·zhee·*now* original

orquestra ⓕ orr·kes·traa orchestra

os EUA ⓜ pl os e·waa the USA

osso ⓜ o·so bone

ostra ⓕ os·traa oyster

ótimo/ótima ⓜ/ⓕ o·tee·mo/o·tee·maa great

ou ⓜ o or

ouro ⓜ o·ro gold

outono ⓜ o·to·no autumn • fall

outro/outra ⓜ/ⓕ o·tro/o·traa other

outubro o·too·bro October

ovário ⓜ o·vaa·ryo ovary

ovelha ⓕ o·ve·lyaa lamb • sheep

ovo ⓜ o·vo egg

oxigênio ⓜ ok·see·*zhe*·nyo oxygen

P

pacote ⓜ pa·ko·te packet

padaria ⓕ paa·daa·*ree*·aa bakery

padre ⓜ paa·dre priest

pães ⓜ pl payngs bread rolls

pagamento ⓜ paa·gaa·*meng*·to payment

pagar paa·*gaarr* pay

página ⓕ paa·zhee·naa page

pai ⓜ pai father

painel ⓜ **de marcação** pai·*nel* de maarr·kaa·*sowng* scoreboard

país ⓜ paa·ees country

pais ⓜ pl paa·ees parents

Países ⓜ pl **Baixos** paa·ee·zes bai·shos Netherlands

palácio ⓜ paa·*laa*·syo palace

palavra ⓕ paa·*laa*·vraa word

palito ⓜ **de dentes** paa·*lee*·to de deng·tes toothpick

panela ⓕ paa·*ne*·laa pan

pano ⓜ **de limpeza** pa·no de leeng·pe·zaa wash cloth (flannel)

pão ⓜ powng bread
  — integral eeng·te·*grow* wholemeal bread

papel ⓜ paa·*pel* paper
  — higiênico ee·zhee·e·nee·ko toilet paper

papelada ⓕ paa·pe·*laa*·daa paperwork

papelaria ⓕ paa·pe·laa·*ree*·aa stationery shop

Paquistão ⓜ paa·kees·*towng* Pakistan

par ⓜ paarr pair (couple)

para paa·raa for
  — baixo bai·sho downhill
  — cima see·maa uphill
  — sempre seng·pre forever

parabrisa ⓜ paa·raa·*bree*·zaa windscreen

parada ⓕ **cardíaca** paa·*raa*·daa kaarr·dee·aa·kaa cardiac arrest

parapeito ⓜ paa·raa·*pay*·to ledge

paraplégico/paraplégica ⓜ/ⓕ paa·raa·*ple*·zhee·ko/paa·raa·*ple*·zhee·kaa paraplegic

parar paa·*raarr* stop (cease)

P

DICTIONARY

parecido/parecida ⓜ/ⓕ
paa·re·*see*·do/paa·re·*see*·daa *similar*
parede ⓕ paa·*re*·de *wall (outer)*
parlamento ⓜ paarr·laa·*meng*·to
parliament
parque ⓜ *paarr*·ke *park*
— **nacional** naa·syo·*now* *national park*
parte ⓕ *paarr*·te *part (component)*
partida ⓕ paarr·*tee*·daa *departure* • *match (sport)*
partido ⓜ paarr·*tee*·do *party (politics)*
partir paarr·*teerr* *depart (leave)*
Páscoa ⓕ *paas*·kwaa *Easter*
passada (semana) ⓕ paa·*saa*·daa
(se·*ma*·naa) *last (week)*
passado ⓜ paa·*saa*·do *past*
passageiro/passageira ⓜ/ⓕ
paa·saa·*zhay*·ro/paa·saa·*zhay*·raa
passenger
passaporte ⓜ paa·saa·*porr*·te *passport*
passar paa·*saarr* *pass*
pássaro ⓜ *paa*·saa·ro *bird*
passas ⓕ pl *paa*·saas *raisin* • *sultana*
passo ⓜ *paa*·so *step*
pasta ⓕ *pas*·taa *briefcase*
— **de dentes** de *deng*·tes *toothpaste*
patinaçao ⓕ paa·tee·naa·*sowng*
rollerblading
pato/pata ⓜ/ⓕ *paa*·to/*paa*·taa *duck*
paz ⓕ pas *peace*
pé ⓜ pe *foot*
peça ⓕ *pe*·saa *play (theatre)*
pedaço ⓜ pe·*da*·so *piece*
pedal ⓜ pe·*dow* *pedal*
pedestre ⓜ pe·*des*·tre *pedestrian*
pedido ⓜ pe·*dee*·do *order (command)*
pedinte ⓜ&ⓕ pe·*deeng*·te *beggar*
pedir pe·*deerr* *ask (for something)* • *order*
pedra ⓕ *pe*·draa *rock* • *stone*
pegar pe·*gaarr* *get*
— **carona** kaa·ro·naa *hitchhike*
peito ⓜ *pay*·to *chest* • *breast*
peixaria ⓕ pay·sha·*ree*·aa *fish shop*
peixe ⓜ *pay*·she *fish*
peixeiro/peixeira ⓜ/ⓕ pay·*shay*·ro/
pay·*shay*·raa *fish monger*
pele ⓕ *pe*·le *skin*
pensão ⓕ peng·*sowng* *boarding house*

penhasco ⓜ pe·*nyaas*·ko *cliff*
pênis ⓜ *pe*·nees *penis*
pensar peng·*saarr* *think*
pensionista ⓜ&ⓕ peng·syo·*nees*·taa
pensioner
pente ⓜ *peng*·te *comb*
pepino ⓜ pe·*pee*·no *cucumber*
pequeno/pequena ⓜ/ⓕ pe·*ke*·no/
pe·*ke*·naa *little* • *small*
pêra ⓕ *pe*·raa *pear*
perder perr·*derr* *lose*
perdido/perdida ⓜ/ⓕ
perr·*dee*·do/perr·*dee*·daa *lost*
perdoar perr·do·*aarr* *forgive*
perfeito/perfeita ⓜ/ⓕ
perr·*fay*·to/perr·*fay*·taa *perfect*
performance ⓕ perr·forr·*mang*·se
performance
perfume ⓜ perr·*foo*·me *perfume*
pergunta ⓕ perr·*goong*·taa *question*
perguntar perr·goong·*taarr*
ask (a question)
perigoso/perigosa ⓜ/ⓕ pe·ree·*go*·zo/
pe·ree·*go*·zaa *dangerous*
permissão ⓕ perr·mee·*sowng* *permission* • *permit*
— **para trabalhar** paa·raa
traa·baa·*lyaarr* *work permit*
perna ⓕ *perr*·naa *leg*
perto *perr*·to *near*
perú ⓜ pe·*roo* *turkey*
pesado/pesada ⓜ/ⓕ
pe·*zaa*·do/pe·*zaa*·daa *heavy*
pesar pe·*zaarr* *weigh*
pesca ⓕ *pes*·kaa *fishing*
peso ⓜ *pe*·zo *weight*
pesos ⓜ pl *pe*·zos *weights*
pêssego ⓜ *pe*·se·go *peach*
pessoa ⓕ pe·*so*·aa *person*
pessoas ⓕ pl pe·*so*·aas *people*
petição ⓕ pe·tee·*sowng* *petition*
petróleo ⓜ pe·*tro*·lyo *petrol*
pharmacista ⓜ&ⓕ faarr·maa·*sees*·taa
chemist
piada ⓕ pee·*aa*·daa *joke*
picareta ⓕ pee·kaa·re·taa *pickaxe*
pico ⓜ *pee*·ko *peak (mountain)*
pifar pee·*faarr* *break down*

pikles ⓜ pl *pee-*kles *pickles*
pilha ⓕ *pee-*lyaa *battery*
pílula ⓕ *pee-*loo-laa *pill • Pill (the)*
pimenta ⓕ pee-*meng-*taa *chilli • pepper*
pimentão ⓜ pee-meng-*towng capsicum •*
   pepper (bell)
pinça ⓕ *peeng-*saa *tweezers*
pintor/pintora ⓜ/ⓕ peeng-*torr/*
   peeng-to-raa *painter*
pintura ⓕ peeng-*too-*raa *painting*
piolho ⓜ pee-o-lyo *lice*
piquenique ⓜ pee-ke-*nee-*ke *picnic*
piscina ⓕ pee-*see-*naa *swimming pool*
pista ⓕ *pees-*taa *track (sport)*
   — de corrida de ko-*hee-*daa *racetrack*
pistáchio ⓜ pees-*taa-*shyo *pistachio*
planalto ⓜ pla-*now-*to *plateau*
planeta ⓜ pla-*ne-*taa *planet*
plano/plana ⓜ/ⓕ *pla-*no/pla-naa *flat*
planta ⓕ *plang-*taa *plant*
plástico/plástica ⓜ/ⓕ
   *plas-*tee-ko/*plas-*tee-kaa *plastic*
plataforma ⓕ plaa-taa-*forr-*maa *platform*
pneu ⓜ pee-*ne-*oo *tyre*
pó ⓜ po *powder*
pobre po-bre *poor*
pobreza ⓕ po-*bre-*zaa *poverty*
poché po-*she poached*
pochete ⓕ po-*she-*te *bumbag*
poder po-*derr can*
   (be able/have permission)
poder ⓜ po-*derr power*
poesia ⓕ po-e-*zee-*aa *poetry*
pólen ⓜ po-leng *pollen*
polícia ⓕ po-*lee-*syaa *police*
política ⓕ po-*lee-*tee-kaa *politics*
político/política ⓜ/ⓕ po-*lee-*tee-ko/
   po-*lee-*tee-kaa *politician*
poluição ⓕ po-loo-ee-*sowng pollution*
pomelo ⓜ po-*me-*lo *grapefruit*
ponte ⓕ pong-te *bridge*
ponto ⓜ pong-to *point*
   — de controle de kong-*tro-*le
   checkpoint (border)
   — de ônibus de o-nee-boos *bus stop*
popular po-poo-*laarr popular*

por porr *per*
   — perto perr-to *nearby*
   — que ke *because • why*
pôr ⓜ **do sol** porr do sol *sunset*
porcentagem ⓕ porr-seng-*taa-*zheng
   per cent
porco/porca ⓜ/ⓕ porr-ko/porr-kaa
   pig • pork
porta ⓕ porr-taa *door*
portão ⓜ porr-*towng gate (airport, etc)*
   — de partida de paarr-*tee-*daa
   departure gate
porto ⓜ porr-to *port (sea)*
pós barba ⓜ pos baarr-baa *aftershave*
positivo/positiva ⓜ/ⓕ po-zee-*tee-*vo/
   po-zee-*tee-*vaa *positive*
possível po-see-vel *possible*
postagem ⓕ pos-*taa-*zheng *postage*
posto ⓜ **de gasolina** pos-to de
   gaa-zo-*lee-*naa *service station*
pouco/pouca ⓜ/ⓕ po-ko/po-kaa
   little (not much)
praça ⓕ *praa-*saa *square (town)*
praia ⓕ *prai-*aa *beach*
prancha ⓕ **de surfe** *prang-*shaa de
   soorr-fee *surfboard*
prata ⓕ *praa-*taa *silver*
prateleira ⓕ praa-te-*lay-*raa *shelf*
prato ⓜ *praa-*to *plate*
precisar pre-see-*zaarr need*
preço ⓜ *pre-*so *price*
   — da entrada daa eng-*traa-*daa
   admission price
prédio ⓜ *pre-*dyo *building*
prefeito/prefeita ⓜ/ⓕ
   pre-*fay-*to/pre-*fay-*taa *mayor*
preferir pre-fe-*reerr prefer*
preguiçoso/preguiçosa ⓜ/ⓕ
   pre-gee-*so-*zo/pre-gee-*so-*zaa *lazy*
prender preng-*derr arrest*
preocupado/preocupada ⓜ/ⓕ
   pre-o-koo-*paa-*do/pre-o-koo-*paa-*daa
   worried
preparar pre-paa-*raarr prepare*
presente ⓜ pre-*zeng-*te
   gift • present (time)
   — de casamento de kaa-zaa-*meng-*to
   wedding present

Q

presidente ⑩&① pre-zee-*deng*-te
   president
pressão ① pre-*sowng* pressure
   — arterial aar-te-ree-ow *blood pressure*
presunto ⑩ pre-*zoong*-to *ham*
preto e branco *pre*-to e *brang*-ko
   B&W (film)
preto/preta ⑩/① *pre*-to/*pre*-taa *black*
primavera ① pree-maa-*ve*-raa
   spring (season)
primeira classe ① pree-*may*-raa *klaa*-se
   first class
primeira ministra ① pree-*may*-raa
   mee-*nees*-traa *prime minister*
primeiro/primeira ⑩/①
   pree-*may*-ro/pree-*may*-raa *first*
primeiro ministro ⑩ pree-*may*-ro
   mee-*nees*-tro *prime minister*
principal ⑩&① preeng-see-*pow* *main*
prisão ① pree-*zowng* *jail · prison*
prisioneiro/prisioneira ⑩/①
   pree-zyo-*nay*-ro/pree-zyo-*nay*-raa
   prisoner
privado/privada ⑩/①
   pree-*vaa*-do/pree-*vaa*-daa *private*
problema ① **de coração** pro-*ble*-maa de
   ko-ra-*sowng* *heart condition*
produzir pro-doo-*zeerr* *produce*
professor/professora ⑩/① pro-fe-*sorr*/
   pro-fe-*so*-raa *lecturer · teacher*
profundo/profunda ⑩/①
   pro-*foong*-do/pro-*foong*-daa *deep*
programa ⑩ pro-*gra*-maa *program*
projetor ⑩ pro-zhe-*torr* *projector*
pronto/pronta ⑩/①
   prong-to/*prong*-taa *ready*
proprietário/proprietária ⑩/①
   pro-pree-e-*taa*-ryo/pro-pree-e-*taa*-ryaa
   landlord/landlady
proteção ① **contra sol** pro-te-*sowng*
   kong-traa sol *sunblock*
proteger pro-te-*zherr* *protect*
protegido/protegida ⑩ pro-te-*zhee*-do/
   pro-te-*zhee*-daa *protected*
protestar pro-tes-*taarr* *protest*
protesto ⑩ pro-*tes*-to *protest*
provador ⑩ pro-vaa-*dorr* *changing room*
provisões ① pl pro-vee-*zoyngs* *provisions*

próximo/próxima ⑩/①
   pro-*see*-mo/pro-*see*-maa *next*
pular poo-*laarr* *jump*
pulga ① *pool*-gaa *flea*
pulmão ⑩ pool-*mowng* *lung*
punho ⑩ *poo*-nyo *wrist*
puro/pura ⑩/① *poo*-ro/*poo*-raa *pure*
puxar poo-*shaarr* *pull*

Q

quadra ① *kwaa*-draa *court (tennis)*
   — de tênis de *te*-nees *tennis court*
quadraplégico/quadraplégica ⑩/①
   kwaa-draa-*ple*-zhee-ko/
   kwaa-draa-*ple*-zhee-kaa *quadriplegic*
qualidade ① kwaa-lee-*daa*-de *quality*
qualificações ① pl
   kwaa-lee-fee-kaa-*soyngs* *qualifications*
qualquer kwow-*kerr* *any*
quando *kwang*-do *when*
quanto *kwang*-to *how much*
quarentena ① kwaa-reng-*te*-naa
   quarantine
quarta-feira ① kwaarr-*taa*-*fay*-raa
   Wednesday
quarto ⑩ *kwaarr*-to *bedroom · room ·
   quarter*
   — de casa de kaa-*zow* *double room*
quase *kwaa*-ze *almost*
que ke *what*
quebrado/quebrada ⑩/①
   ke-*braa*-do/ke-*braa*-daa *broken*
quebrador ⑩ **de gelo**
   ke-braa-*dorr* de *zhe*-lo *ice axe*
quebrar ke-*braarr* *break*
queda ① *ke*-daa *fall (down)*
queijaria ① kay-zhaa-*ree*-aa *cheese shop*
queijo ⑩ *kay*-zho *cheese*
queimado/queimada ⑩/①
   kay-*maa*-do/kay-*maa*-daa *burnt*
   — de sol de sol *sunburnt*
queimadura ① kay-maa-*doo*-raa *burn*
quem keng *who*
quente *keng*-te *hot*
querer ke-*rerr* *want*
questão ① kes-*towng* *question*

DICTIONARY

248

quieto/quieta ⓜ/ⓕ kee·e·to/kee·e·taa
quiet

quinta-feira ⓕ kween·ta·fay·raa *Thursday*

quinzena ⓕ keeng·ze·naa *fortnight*

quiroprático/quiroprática ⓜ/ⓕ
kee·ro·praa·tee·ko/kee·ro·praa·tee·kaa
chiropractor

R

rabanete ⓜ haa·baa·ne·te *radish*

rabo ⓜ haa·bo *tail*

racismo ⓜ haa·sees·mo *racism*

radiador ⓜ haa·dee·aa·dorr *radiator*

rainha ⓕ haa·ee·nyaa *queen*

rápido/rápida ⓜ/ⓕ
haa·pee·do/haa·pee·daa *fast*

raquete ⓕ haa·ke·te *racquet*

raro/rara ⓜ/ⓕ haa·ro/haa·raa
rare (uncommon)

raspador ⓜ haas·paa·dorr *razor*

ratazana ⓕ haa·taa·za·naa *rat*

rato ⓜ haa·to *rat*

razão ⓕ haa·zowng *reason*

realista ⓔ·aa·lees·taa *realistic*

recarregador ⓜ **de bateria**
he·kaa·he·gaa·dorr de baa·te·ree·aa
jumper leads

receber he·se·berr *welcome*

recentemente he·seng·te·meng·te
recently

recibo ⓜ he·see·bo *receipt*

reciclar he·see·klaar *recycle*

reciclável he·see·klaa·vel *recyclable*

reclamar he·klaa·marr *complain*

recomendar he·ko·meng·daarr
recommend

recursos ⓜ pl **humanos** he·koor·sos
oo·ma·nos *human resources*

recusar he·koo·zaarr *refuse*

rede ⓕ he·de *hammock • net*

redondo/redonda ⓜ/ⓕ
he·dong·do/he·dong·daa *round*

reembolso ⓜ he·eng·bol·so *refund*

referência ⓕ he·fe·reng·syaa *reference*

reflexologia ⓕ he·flek·so·lo·zhee·aa
reflexology

refrigerante ⓜ he·free·zhe·rang·te
soft drink

refugiado/refugiada ⓜ/ⓕ
he·foo·zhee·aa·do/he·foo·zhee·aa·daa
refugee

regional he·zhyo·now *regional*

registro ⓜ **de carro** he·zhees·tro de
kaa·ho *car registration*

regra ⓕ he·graa *rule*

regras ⓕ pl he·graas *policy*

rei ⓜ hay *king*

reiki ⓜ hay·kee *reiki*

relacionamento ⓜ he·laa·syo·na·meng·to
relationship

relações ⓕ pl **públicas** he·la·soyngs
poo·blee·kaas *public relations*

relaxar he·la·shaarr *relax*

rélica ⓕ he·lee·kaa *relic*

relicário ⓜ he·lee·kaa·ryo *shrine*

religião ⓕ he·lee·zhee·owng *religion*

religioso/religiosa ⓜ/ⓕ he·lee·zhee·o·zo/
he·lee·zhee·o·zaa *religious*

relógio ⓜ he·lo·zhyo *clock • watch*

remo ⓜ he·mo *rowing*

remoto/remota ⓜ/ⓕ
he·mo·to/he·mo·taa *remote*

renda ⓕ heng·daa *lace*

repelente ⓜ **em aspiral** he·pe·leng·te eng
aas·pee·row *mosquito coil*

repolho ⓜ he·po·lyo *cabbage*

república ⓕ he·poo·blee·kaa *republic*

requerimento ⓜ **de bagagem**
he·ke·ree·meng·to de baa·gaa·zhèng
baggage claim

reserva ⓕ he·zerr·vaa
reservation (booking)

reservar he·zerr·vaarr
book (make a booking)

resíduo ⓜ **nuclear** he·zee·doo·o
noo·kle·aarr *nuclear waste*

resíduo ⓜ **tóxico** he·zee·dwo tok·see·ko
toxic waste

resolução ⓕ he·zo·loo·sowng *workout*

respirar hes·pee·raarr *breathe*

resposta ⓕ hes·pos·taa *answer*

restaurante ⓜ hes·tow·rang·te *restaurant*

retornar he·torr·naarr *return*

reverenciar he·ve·reng·see·aarr *worship*

revisão ① he-vee-*zowng* review
revista ① he-*vees*-taa *magazine*
reza ① he-zaa *prayer*
rico/rica ⑩/① *hee*-ko/*hee*-kaa
  rich (wealthy)
rin ⑩ pl heeng *kidney*
rio ⑩ *hee*-o *river*
rir heerr *laugh*
risco ⑩ *hees*-ko *risk*
ritmo ⑩ *hee*-tee-mo *rhythm*
rock ⑩ *ho*-kee *rock (music)*
roda ① *ho*-daa *wheel*
rodoviária ① ho-do-vee-*aa*-ryaa
  bus station
romântico/romântica ⑩/①
  ho-*mang*-tee-ko/ho-*mang*-tee-kaa
  romantic
rosa *ho*-za *pink*
rosto ⑩ *hos*-to *face*
rota ① *ho*-taa *route*
  — **de bicicleta** de bee-see-*kle*-taa
    bike path
  — **de caminhada** de kaa-mee-*nyaa*-daa
    hiking route
roubar ho-*baarr* rob • *steal*
roubo ⑩ *ho*-bo *rip-off*
roupa ① pl *ho*-paa *clothes*
  — **de banho** de *ba*-nyo *bathing suit* •
    swimsuit
  — **de cama** de *ka*-maa *bedding*
  — **de baixo** de *bai*-sho *underwear*
roxo/roxa ⑩/① ho-sho/ho-shaa *purple*
rua ① *hoo*-aa *street*
  — **principal** preeng-see-*pow* *main road*
rubéola ① hoo-*be*-o-laa *rubella*
rugby ⑩ *hoo*-gee-bee *rugby*
ruim hoo-*eeng* *bad*
ruínas ① pl hoo-*ee*-naas *ruins*
rum ⑩ hoom *rum*

S

sábado ⑩ *saa*-baa-do *Saturday*
saber saa-*berr* *know*
sabonete ⑩ saa-bo-*ne*-te *soap*
saco ⑩ *saa*-ko *bag*
  — **de dormir** de dorr-*meerr*
    sleeping bag

saguão ⑩ saag-*wowng* *foyer*
saia ① *saa*-yaa *skirt*
saída ① saa-*ee*-daa *exit*
sair saa-*eerr* *go out with*
sais ⑩ pl **de hidratação** sais de
  ee-draa-taa-*sowng* *rehydration salts*
sal ⑩ sow *salt*
sala ① **de espera** *saa*-la de es-pe-*raa*
  waiting room
sala ① **de trânsito** *saa*-laa de *trang*-zee-to
  transit lounge
salada ① saa-*laa*-daa *salad*
salaminho ⑩ saa-laa-*mee*-nyo *salami*
salão ⑩ **de beleza** saa-*lowng* de be-*le*-zaa
  beauty salon
salário ⑩ saa-*laa*-ryo *salary* • *wage*
salmão ⑩ sow-*mowng* *salmon*
salsicha ① sow-*see*-shaa *sausage*
sandália ① sang-*daa*-lyaa *sandal*
sangue ⑩ *sang*-ge *blood*
santo/santa ⑩/① *sang*-to/*sang*-taa *saint*
sapataria ① saa-paa-taa-*ree*-aa *shoe shop*
sapato ⑩ saa-*paa*-to *shoe*
sarampo ⑩ saa-*rang*-po *measles*
sardinha ① saarr-*dee*-nyaa *sardine*
saúde ① sa-*oo*-de *health*
sauna ① *sow*-naa *sauna*
se se *if*
secar se-*kaarr* *dry*
seco/seca ⑩/① se-ko/se-kaa *dried* • *dry*
secretário/secretária ⑩/① se-kre-*taa*-ryo/
  se-kre-*taa*-ryaa *secretary*
seda ① se-*daa* *silk*
sedento/sedenta ⑩/①
  se-*deng*-to/se-*deng*-taa *thirsty*
seguir se-*geerr* *follow*
segunda-feira ① se-*goong*-daa-*fay*-raa
  Monday
segundo ⑩ se-*goong*-do *second (time)*
segundo grau ⑩ se-*goong*-do grow
  high school
segundo/segunda ⑩/①
  se-*goong*-do/se-*goong*-daa *second*
seguro ⑩ se-*goo*-ro *insurance*
  — **social** so-see-*ow* *social welfare* • *dole*
seguro/segura ⑩/①
  se-*goo*-ro/se-*goo*-raa *safe*
seios ⑩ pl *say*-os *breasts*

sela ① *se·laa saddle*

selo ⓜ *se·lo stamp*

sem *seng without*

   — chumbo *shoong·bo unleaded*

semana ① *se·ma·naa week*

sempre *seng·pre always*

sensível *seng·see·vel emotional • sensible*

sensual *seng·soo·ow sensual*

sentar *seng·taarr sit*

sentimentos ⓜ pl *seng·tee·meng·tos feelings*

sentir *seng·teerr feel*

   — falta *fow·taa miss (feel absence of)*

separado/separada ⓜ/① *se·paa·raa·do/ se·paa·raa·daa separate*

ser *serr be (ongoing)*

seringa ① *se·reeng·gaa syringe*

sério/séria ⓜ/① *se·ryo/se·ryaa serious*

serviço ⓜ **militar** *serr·vee·so mee·lee·taarr military service*

serviço ⓜ **postal rápido** *serr·vee·so pos·tow haa·pee·do express mail*

setembro *se·teng·bro September*

seu/sua ⓜ/① *se·oo/soo·aa your*

sexo ⓜ *sek·so sex*

   — com proteção *kong pro·te·sowng safe sex*

sexta-feira ① *ses·taa·fay·raa Friday*

sexy *sek·see sexy*

shiatsu ⓜ *shee·aa·tee·zoo shiatsu*

shopping centre ⓜ *sho·peeng seng·terr shopping centre*

show ⓜ *show concert*

sim *seeng yes*

simples *seeng·ples simple*

sinagoga ① *see·naa·go·gaa synagogue*

sinal ⓜ **de trânsito** *see·now de trang·zee·to traffic light*

sintético/sintética ⓜ/① *seeng·te·tee·ko/ seeng·te·tee·kaa synthetic*

sinuca ① *see·noo·kaa pool (game)*

sistema ⓜ **de classes** *sees·te·maa de klaa·ses class system*

skate ⓜ *ees·kay·te skateboarding*

slide ⓜ *ees·lai·de slide (film)*

snorkel ⓜ *ees·norr·kel snorkelling*

snowboarding ⓜ *snow·borr·deeng snowboarding*

sobre *so·bre about • above • on*

sobremesa ① *so·bre·me·zaa dessert*

sobrenome ⓜ *so·bre·no·me family name • surname*

socialista *so·see·aa·lees·taa socialist*

sogra ① *so·graa mother-in-law*

sogro ⓜ *so·gro father-in-law*

sol ⓜ *sol sun*

soldado ⓜ&① *sol·daa·do soldier*

solteiro/solteira ⓜ/① *sol·tay·ro/sol·tay·raa single*

solto/solta ⓜ/① *sol·to/sol·taa loose*

somente *so·meng·te only*

sonho ⓜ *so·nyo dream*

sonolento/sonolenta ⓜ/① *so·no·leng·to/ so·no·leng·taa sleepy*

sopa ① *so·paa soup*

sorte ① *sorr·te luck*

sortudo/sortuda ⓜ/① *sorr·too·do/sorr·too·daa lucky*

sorvete ⓜ *sorr·ve·te ice cream*

sorveteria ① *sorr·ve·te·ree·aa ice-cream parlour*

souvenir ⓜ *soo·ve·neerr souvenir*

sozinho/sozinha ⓜ/① *so·zee·nyo/so·zee·nyaa alone*

subir *soo·beerr climb*

suborno ⓜ *soo·bor·no bribe*

sub-títulos ⓜ pl *soo·bee·tee·too·los subtitles*

suco ⓜ *soo·ko juice*

   — de laranja *de laa·rang·zhaa orange juice*

Suécia ① *soo·e·syaa Sweden*

suéter ① *soo·e·terr jumper • sweater*

suficiente *soo·fee·see·eng·te enough*

Suíça ① *soo·ee·saa Switzerland*

sujo/suja ⓜ/① *soo·zho/soo·zhaa dirty*

sul ⓜ *sool south*

supermercado ⓜ *soo·perr·merr·kaa·do supermarket*

surdo/surda ⓜ/① *soor·do/soor·daa deaf*

surfar *soorr·faarr surf*

surfe ⓜ *soor·fee surfing*

surpresa ① *soor·pre·zaa surprise*

sutiã ⓜ *soo·tee·ang bra*

S

brazilian portuguese–english

251

T

tabaco ⓜ taa-*baa*-ko *tobacco*
tabaconista ⓜ taa-baa-ko-*nees*-taa *tobacconist*
talco ⓜ *tow*-ko *baby powder*
talheres ⓜ pl taa-*lye*-res *cutlery*
talvez tow-*ves maybe*
tamanho ⓜ ta-*ma*-nyo *size*
também tang-*beng also • too*
tampa ① *tang*-paa *plug (bath)*
tampão ⓜ tang-*powng tampon*
tampões de ouvido tang-*powng* de o-*vee*-do *earplugs*
tangerina ① tang-zhe-*ree*-naa *mandarin*
tapete ⓜ taa-*pe*-te *rug*
tarde ① *taarr*-de *afternoon*
taxa ① *taa*-shaa
  — de aeroporto *taa*-shaa de aa-e-ro-*porr*-to *airport tax*
  — de câmbio *taa*-shaa de *kang*-byo *exchange rate*
  — de serviço *taa*-shaa de serr-*veee*-so *service charge*
táxi ⓜ *taak*-see *taxi*
teatro ⓜ te-*aa*-tro *theatre*
tecido ⓜ te-*see*-do *fabric*
técnica ① te-*kee*-nee-kaa *technique*
técnico/técnica ⓜ/① te-*kee*-nee-ko/te-*kee*-nee-kaa *coach*
teimoso/teimosa ⓜ/① tay-*mo*-zo/tay-*mo*-zaa *stubborn*
teleférico ⓜ te-le-*fe*-ree-ko *chairlift (skiing)*
telefonar te-le-fo-*naarr telephone*
telefone ⓜ te-le-*fo*-ne *telephone*
  — público poo-blee-ko *public telephone*
telegrama ⓜ te-le-*gra*-maa *telegram*
telescópio ⓜ te-les-*ko*-pyo *telescope*
televisão ① te-le-vee-*sowng television*
temperatura ① teng-pe-raa-*too*-raa *temperature*
tempestade ① teng-pes-*taa*-de *storm*
tempo ⓜ *teng*-po *time • weather*
tempo integral eeng-te-*grow* full-time
têmpora ① *teng*-po-raa *temple*
tênis ⓜ *te*-nees *tennis*
  — de mesa de *me*-zaa *table tennis*

tentar teng-*taarr try (attempt)*
ter terr *have*
terça-feira ① terr-saa-*fay*-raa *Tuesday*
terceiro/terceira ⓜ/① terr-*say*-ro/terr-*say*-raa *third*
terminar terr-mee-*naarr finish*
término ⓜ *terr*-mee-no *finish*
Terra ① te-*haa Earth*
terra ① te-*haa land*
terremoto ⓜ te-he-*mo*-to *earthquake*
terrível te-*hee*-vel *terrible*
tesoura ① te-*zo*-raa *scissors*
teste ⓜ *tes*-te *test*
  — de gravidez de graa-vee-*dez* *pregnancy test kit*
tevê ① te-*ve* TV
tia ① *tee*-aa *aunt*
tigela ① tee-*zhe*-laa *bowl*
time ⓜ *tee*-me *team*
tímido/tímida ⓜ/① *tee*-mee-do/*tee*-mee-daa *shy*
típico/típica ⓜ/① *tee*-pee-ko/*tee*-pee-kaa *typical*
tipo ⓜ *tee*-po *type*
tirar tee-*raarr take (photo)*
toalha ① to-*aa*-lyaa *towel*
  — de rosto de *hos*-to *face cloth*
  — higiênica ee-zhee-e-nee-kaa *sanitary napkin*
tocar to-*kaarr touch • play (guitar) • ring (phone)*
tofu ⓜ to-*foo tofu*
tom ⓜ tong *tune*
tomada ① to-*maa*-daa *plug (electricity)*
tomate ⓜ to-*maa*-te *tomato*
tonto/tonta ⓜ/① *tong*-to/*tong*-taa *dizzy*
torcedor/torcedora ⓜ/① torr-se-*dorr*/torr-se-*do*-raa *supporter (sport)*
torcimento ⓜ torr-see-*meng*-to *sprain*
torneira ① torr-*nay*-raa *faucet • tap*
tornozelo ⓜ torr-no-*ze*-lo *ankle*
torrada ① to-*haa*-daa *toast*
torradeira ① to-haa-*day*-raa *toaster*
torre ① *to*-he *tower*
torta ① *torr*-taa *pie*
tosa ① to-*zaa crop*
tossir to-*seerr cough*

trabalhador/trabalhadora ⓜ/ⓕ **de obra**
traa·baa·lyaa·*dorr*/traa·baa·lyaa·*do*·raa
de o·braa *labourer*

trabalhador/trabalhadora ⓜ/ⓕ **manual**
traa·baa·lyaa·*dorr*/traa·baa·lyaa·*do*·raa
maa·noo·*ow* *manual worker*

trabalhar traa·baa·*lyaarr* *work*

trabalho ⓜ traa·*baa*·lyo *work*
— **de casa** de *kaa*·zaa *housework*
— **em bar** eng baarr *bar work*

traduzir traa·doo·*zeerr* *translate*

traficante ⓜ&ⓕ traa·fee·*kang*·te
drug dealer

tráfico ⓜ *traa*·fee·ko *traffic*

tranca ⓕ *trang*·kaa *lock*
— **de bicicleta** de bee·see·*kle*·taa
bike lock

trancado/trancada ⓜ/ⓕ
trang·*kaa*·do/trang·*kaa*·daa *locked*

trancar trang·*kaarr* *lock*

transporte ⓜ trans·*porr*·te *transport*

traseiro ⓜ traa·*zay*·ro *bottom (body)*

trave ⓕ **de roda** *traa*·ve de ho·daa
spoke (wheel)

travellers cheques ⓜ pl traa·ve·*ler* she·kes
travellers cheques

travesseiro ⓜ traa·ve·*say*·ro *pillow*

trem ⓜ treng *train*

trilha ⓕ *tree*·lyaa *mountain path*

triste *trees*·te *sad*

troca ⓕ *tro*·kaa *exchange*

trocado ⓜ tro·*kaa*·do *loose change*

trocar tro·*kaarr* *change* • *exchange*

troco ⓜ *tro*·ko *change (coins)*

tudo *too*·do *everything*

tudo/tuda ⓜ/ⓕ *too*·do/*too*·daa *all*

tumor ⓜ too·*morr* *tumour*

túmulo ⓜ *too*·moo·lo *grave*

turista ⓜ&ⓕ too·*rees*·taa *tourist*

U

último/última ⓕ *ool*·tee·mo/*ool*·tee·maa
last

ultrasom ⓜ ool·traa·*song* *ultrasound*

uma vez oo·maa vez *once*

uniforme ⓜ oo·nee·*forr*·me *uniform*

universidade ⓕ oo·nee·verr·see·*daa*·de
university • *college*

universo ⓜ oo·nee·*verr*·so *universe*

urgente oorr·zheng·te *urgent*

usuário/usuária ⓜ/ⓕ **de drogas**
oo·zoo·*aa*·ryo/oo·zoo·*aa*·ryaa de
dro·gaas *drug user*

útil oo·*til* *useful*

uvas ⓕ pl *oo*·vaas *grapes*

V

vaca ⓕ *vaa*·kaa *cow*

vacina ⓕ vaa·*see*·naa *vaccination*

vagão ⓜ **de dormir** va·*gowng* de
dorr·*meerr* *sleeping car*

vagão ⓜ **restaurante** vaa·*gowng*
hes·tow·*rang*·te *dining car*

vagarosamente vaa·gaa·ro·zaa·*meng*·te
slowly

vagem ⓕ **chinesa** vaa·zheng shee·*ne*·zaa
snow pea

vagina ⓕ vaa·*zhee*·naa *vagina*

vago/vaga ⓜ/ⓕ *vaa*·go/*vaa*·gaa *vacant*

vale ⓜ *vaa*·le *valley*

validar vaa·lee·*daarr* *validate*

valor vaa·*lorr* *value (price)*

van ⓕ van *van*

vapor ⓜ vaa·*porr* *stream*

varanda ⓕ vaa·*rang*·daa *balcony*

vários/várias ⓜ/ⓕ *vaa*·ryos/*vaa*·ryaas
many

vazio/vazia ⓜ/ⓕ vaa·*zee*·o/vaa·*zee*·aa
empty

vegetariano/vegetariana ⓜ/ⓕ
ve·zhe·taa·ree·*a*·no/ve·zhe·taa·ree·*a*·naa
vegetarian

veia ⓕ *ve*·aa *vein* • *candle*

velho/velha ⓜ/ⓕ *ve*·lyo/*ve*·lyaa
old • *stale*

velocidade ⓕ ve·lo·see·*daa*·de *speed*
— **do filme** do *feel*·me *film speed*

vender veng·*derr* *sell*

venenoso/venenosa ⓜ/ⓕ
ve·ne·no·zo/ve·ne·no·zaa *poisonous*

ventilador ⓜ veng·tee·laa·*dorr*
fan (machine)

vento ⓜ *veng*·to *wind*

ver verr *look · see*
verão ⓜ ve·*rowng* *summer*
verde verr·de *green*
verdureiro/verdureira ⓜ/ⓕ
  verr·doo·*ray*·ro/verr·doo·*ray*·raa
  greengrocer
vermelho/vermelha ⓜ/ⓕ
  verr·me·lyo/verr·me·lyaa *red*
Véspera ⓕ **de Ano Novo** *ves*·pe·raa de
  a·no no·vo *New Year's Eve*
vestido ⓜ ves·*tee*·do *dress*
vestígio ⓜ ves·*tee*·zhyo *trail*
vestir ves·*teerr* *wear*
via ⓕ **aérea** *vee*·aa aa·e·re·aa *airmail*
viagem ⓕ vee·*aa*·zheng *journey · trip*
  — **de negócios** de ne·*goo*·syos
  business trip
viajar vee·aa·*zhaarr* *travel*
vício ⓜ *vee*·syo *addiction*
  — **de drogas** de *dro*·gaas
  drug addiction
vida ⓕ *vee*·daa *life*
vidente ⓜ&ⓕ vee·*deng*·te *fortune teller*
vidro ⓜ *vee*·dro *glass · jar*
vigiar vee·zhee·*aarr* *watch*
vilarejo ⓜ vee·laa·*re*·zho *village*
vinagre ⓜ vee·*naa*·gre *vinegar*
vinha ⓕ *vee*·nyaa *vineyard*
vinho ⓜ *vee*·nyo *vine · wine*
  — **espumante** es·poo·*mang*·te
  sparkling wine
violão ⓜ vee·o·*lowng* *guitar*
vir veerr *come*
virar vee·*raarr* *turn*
vírus ⓜ *vee*·roos *virus*

visitar vee·zee·*taarr* *visit*
vista ⓕ *vees*·taa *view*
visto ⓜ *vees*·to *visa*
vitamina ⓕ vee·taa·*mee*·naa *vitamin*
voar vo·*aarr* *fly*
você vo·*se* *you*
vocês pl vo·*se* *you*
vodka ⓕ *vo*·dee·kaa *vodka*
vôlei ⓜ *vo*·lay *volleyball (sport)*
  — **de praia** de *praa*·yaa *beach volleyball*
volta ⓕ *vol*·taa *ride (car)*
volume ⓜ vo·*loo*·me *volume*
vôo ⓜ *vo*·o *flight*
votar vo·*taarr* *vote*
voz ⓕ voz *voice*

W

whisky ⓜ oo·*ees*·kee *whisky*
windsurfe ⓜ wind·*soorr*·fee *windsurfing*

X

xadrez ⓜ shaa·*dres* *chess*
xampú ⓜ shang·*poo* *shampoo*
xarope ⓜ shaa·*ro*·pe *cough medicine*
xícara ⓕ *shee*·kaa·raa *cup*

Z

zangado/zangada ⓜ/ⓕ
  zang·*gaa*·do/zang·*gaa*·daa *angry*
zodíaco ⓜ zo·*dee*·aa·ko *zodiac*
zoológico ⓜ zo·o·*lo*·zhee·ko *zoo*

INDEX

INDEX

D

E

F

G

What kind of traveller are you?

A. You're eating chicken for dinner *again* because it's the only word you know.

B. When no one understands what you say, you step closer and shout louder.

C. When the barman doesn't understand your order, you point frantically at the beer.

D. You're surrounded by locals, swapping jokes, email addresses and experiences – other travellers want to borrow your phrasebook or audio guide.

If you answered A, B, or C, you NEED Lonely Planet's language products ...

- **Lonely Planet Phrasebooks** – for every phrase you need in every language you want
- **Lonely Planet Language & Culture** – get behind the scenes of English as it's spoken around the world – learn and laugh
- **Lonely Planet Fast Talk & Fast Talk Audio** – essential phrases for short trips and weekends away – read, listen and talk like a local
- **Lonely Planet Small Talk** – 10 essential languages for city breaks
- **Lonely Planet Real Talk** – downloadable language audio guides from lonelyplanet.com to your MP3 player

... and this is why

- **Talk to everyone everywhere**
  Over 120 languages, more than any other publisher
- **The right words at the right time**
  Quick-reference colour sections, two-way dictionary, easy pronunciation, every possible subject – and audio to support it

Lonely Planet Offices

Australia
90 Maribyrnong St, Footscray,
Victoria 3011
☎ 03 8379 8000
fax 03 8379 8111
✉ talk2us@lonelyplanet.com.au

USA
150 Linden St, Oakland,
CA 94607
☎ 510 893 8555
fax 510 893 8572
✉ info@lonelyplanet.com

UK
2nd floor, 186 City Rd
London EC1V 2NT
☎ 020 7106 2100
fax 020 7106 2101
✉ go@lonelyplanet.co.uk

lonelyplanet.com